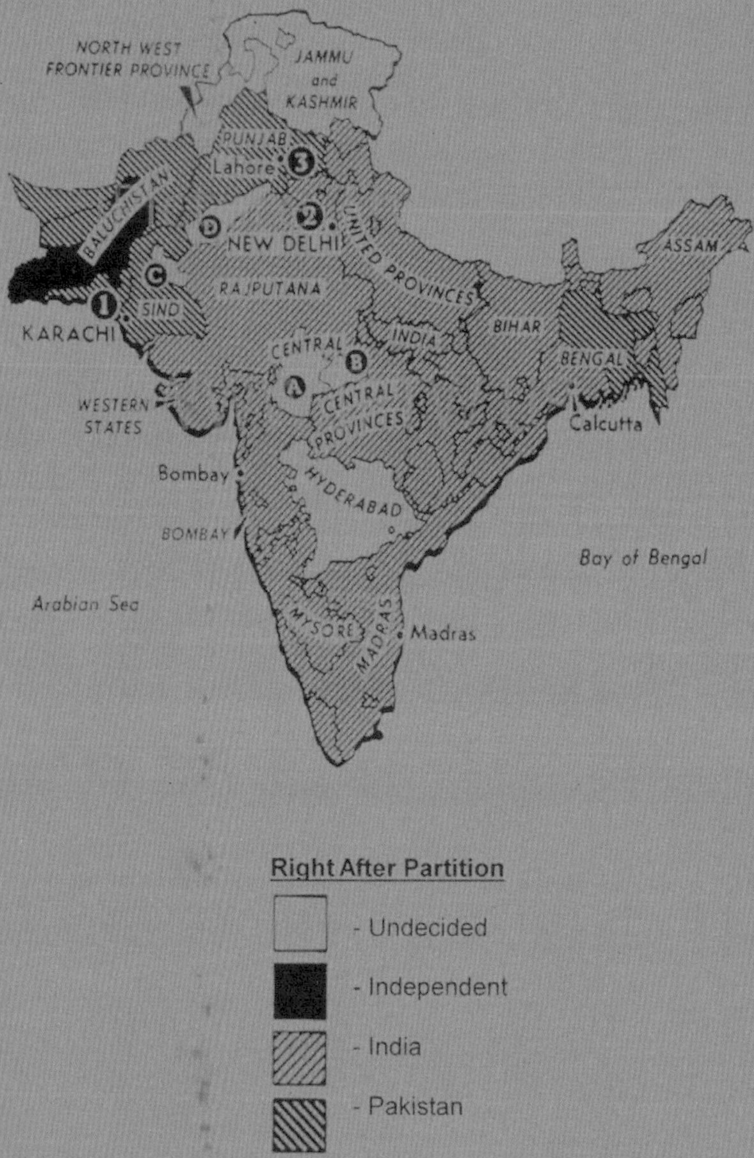
NORTH WEST FRONTIER PROVINCE
JAMMU and KASHMIR
PUNJAB
Lahore
BALUCHISTAN
NEW DELHI
UNITED PROVINCES
ASSAM
SIND
KARACHI
RAJPUTANA
CENTRAL INDIA
BIHAR
BENGAL
CENTRAL PROVINCES
WESTERN STATES
Calcutta
Bombay
HYDERABAD
BOMBAY
Bay of Bengal
Arabian Sea
MYSORE
MADRAS
Madras
Right After Partition
- Undecided
- Independent
- India
- Pakistan

INDIA

The decision of the British Government to partition Bengal came into effect in October, 1905 and separated the largely Muslim eastern areas from the largely Hindu western areas of the province. The seeds of separatism in the sub-continent were abundantly manifest with the founding of the All India Muslim League in Dacca in December, 1906. The League was destined to be, in later years, the vehicle for the demand of a separate nation-state.

Bengal, re-united in 1911, was divided, for the second time, in 1947 as part of the Partition of India. In 1955, East Bengal became East Pakistan and, in 1971, a sovereign Bangladesh, after breaking away from Pakistan.

INDIA

Shedding The Past, Embracing The Future (1906-2017)

ARUN BHATNAGAR

Konark Publishers Pvt Ltd
New Delhi · Seattle

Konark Publishers Pvt. Ltd
206, First Floor,
Peacock Lane, Shahpur Jat,
New Delhi-110 049.
Phone: +91-11-41055065, 65254972
e-mail: india@konarkpublishers.com
Website: www.konarkpublishers.com

Konark Publishers International
8615, 13th Ave SW,
Seattle, WA 98106
Phone: (415) 409-9988
e-mail: us@konarkpublishers.com

Cataloging in Publication Data--DK

Courtesy: D.K. Agencies (P) Ltd. <docinfo@dkagencies.com>

Bhatnagar, Arun, author.
India : shedding the past, embracing the future (1906-2017) / Arun Bhatnagar.
pages cm
Includes index.
ISBN 9789322008901

1. India--History--Partition, 1947. 2. Prime ministers--India--Biography. 3. Hinduism and politics--India. 4. India--Politics and government--20th century. 5. India--Politics and government--21st century. I. Title.

LCC DS480.84.B43 2018 | DDC 954.04 23

Editor: Narayan Swamy

Typeset by 3P Solutions, New Delhi

Printed and bound at Thomson Press (India) Ltd.

Dedicated to the memory of my grandfather,
Shanti Swarup Bhatnagar (1894–1955),
educationist, researcher, poet and visionary and a
founding-father of science and technology in modern India.

Contents

Acknowledgements

For long years after the Partition, it was not uncommon to hear, especially from those who had been forced to leave their homes in the western Punjab that:

Jis Lahore Nai Vekhya, O Janmya Hi Nai
[One who has not seen Lahore has not been born]

❖

THE SENTIMENT REFLECTED AN ENDURING affection, even passion, for one of the world's great cities, notwithstanding the terrible sufferings of the Hindus and Sikhs who were left with no option but to flee.

Equally, the statement, Lahore is Lahore, conveyed a sense of pride in the uniqueness of the city that was once the capital of Maharaja Ranjit Singh's dominions and was called the 'Paris of the East'. There are still people, now in their late eighties or nineties, whose nostalgia for Lahore is beyond description and knows no bounds. This trickled down to my generation, born in the last years of the British Raj, in the form of fascinating stories of the undivided Punjab, with Lahore at the centre, instilling in me a deep interest in the subject.

Lahore was home to my father's side of the family, even after their move to Calcutta and, then Delhi, in the early 1940s. They were thus unaffected by the horrors of the division, except for the loss of an elegant bungalow on the upmarket Jail Road. A number of relatives who were fortunate enough to reach India in one piece had to fend for themselves in the sprawling refugee camp established in Delhi's Purana Qila and a few ended up in places like Karnal and Panipat.

My parents took me to Lahore as an infant and the second time, I went some forty years later, in an official capacity in connection with discussions of the Indus Waters Commission. The Indian delegation visited the districts of Gujranwala and Gujrat (sites of the fiercest battles of the Anglo-Sikh Wars), Jhelum and Sialkot, as also the Mangla Multipurpose Dam in Mirpur.

I recollect deciding to forego a trip to the United States in lieu of the one to Lahore to see my late grandfather's house and visit academic institutions like the Forman Christian (FC) College and Government College.

An abiding debt of gratitude is owed by me to the immediate family, my wife, Kalpana, sons Siddharth and Harshvardhan, and daughter-in-law, Aditi for their unflinching support and encouragement; eleven year old Abhay, my grandson, often made intelligent enquiries about the progress of work.

I was lucky to have struck up a friendship, some years back, with Javed Talat, formerly of the Civil Service of Pakistan (CSP) – akin to the IAS – when he was on a visit to New Delhi. Javed was the Finance Secretary at Islamabad when Benazir Bhutto was last in power and is now settled in Canada. He gladly provided valuable insights and advice and I can hardly thank him enough.

Friends from different walks of life and erstwhile government colleagues have extended assistance in the analyses offered by me of events and developments over the previous four decades or so. Referring to only a few would seem unfair to the others. I must, however, single out Sahib Dayal (SD) Saxena to whom I have been close for a period of time. A senior and one of the ablest members of the P&T Accounts Service (as it was then called), he has helped me in more ways than I can remember. My special thanks go to him and his accomplished wife, Sadhana, who was also in the same service.

I am deeply grateful to Nair Saheb (KPR Nair, Managing Director, Konark Publishers Pvt. Ltd.) for his keen interest and guidance. His inputs and suggestions were exceptionally useful. One is at a loss for words to appreciate the patience and understanding of the Editor-in-Chief, Ms Priyanka Sarkar, whose entire team invested a good deal of time and diligence in the publication of this book.

Over the last several months, I was fortunate to have K. Sambasiva Rao (and Krishna Rao) – who hail from Visakhapatnam – by my side for secretarial assistance; their professionalism, hard work and calm temperament made it so much easier for me to complete the book. I am sincerely thankful to them.

A long-time member of the India International Centre (IIC), New Delhi, I was often at its Library and Reference Section and must record my admiration for the resourcefulness of each and every member of the staff.

August, 2017

Introduction

Many years before Congress started on the road to mass rebellion under Gandhi's leadership, the Indian Muslims were not a nation in the modern sense of the term. But a quarter of a century later, they were on the way to becoming one. Had Congress leaders been wiser, they need not have become one.

AMAURY DE RIENCOURT: THE SOUL OF INDIA (1960)
[HISTORIAN, SOUTHEAST ASIA EXPERT, TIBETOLOGIST]

❖

THIS BOOK HAS TAKEN QUITE A WHILE to come to fruition. My quest to put pen to paper began with a study of the 1947 Partition. While a few articles on the subject of enduring interest appeared in print, I did not succeed in articulating the range and scope that was envisioned by me in the 1980s in regard to the most defining event in Asia in the twentieth century, the tremors of which can be felt to this day.

At the outset, the question may legitimately arise as to whether the Indian sub-continent (present-day Pakistan, India and Bangladesh) constituted a single nation in the past, except when ruled with an iron hand by the early Mughal Emperors and, later under the British who had, perforce, to keep a Princely India alive, post 1857.

Another question begs an answer. On the premise that the Partition was a very costly mistake for the sub-continent as a whole, at that point in time, can it be said that the then colonial power was the most to blame for this? Or was it the main parties (or any group of individuals) opposing the British who were more responsible for a catastrophic turn of events?

An attempt is made to suggest answers.

Many memories of my early years centre around my late grandfather who lived in a government bungalow allotted to him at 4, York Place (now Motilal Nehru Place) in New Delhi. A trifle hazy is a recollection of seeing M.A. Jinnah and his sister, Fatima[1], when they were out for a walk, just weeks before Partition. My aunt and I were standing at the gate of our house. Jinnah stayed close by at 10, Aurangzeb Road, a magnificent property, which was sold by the founder of Pakistan to a staunch Hindu, Ramkrishna Dalmia, then a leading industrialist. Jinnah and Dalmia were good friends. It is said that Dalmia replaced the green and white banner of the Muslim League with a flag of the Anti-Cow Slaughter movement when he bought the house which, in later years, came into the ownership of the Dutch Embassy.

Early next year (January 30, 1948), Mahatma Gandhi was assassinated at Birla House on Albuquerque Road (now Tees January Marg) which again is not far from York Place through which the millions who joined the funeral procession walked. The crowds were immense. Desperate to catch a final glimpse of their beloved Mahatma, a section of the mourners could not be prevented from climbing on to the roof of our new 1947 Buick, parked inside the house and had to be sent for repairs later on!

In several ways, it is possible to view the seeds of the troubles and challenges that have confronted Independent India, as having been sown in August 1947 itself. An early casualty was the steady erosion of the British Indian scheme of administration. A majority of the Muslim members of the Indian Civil Service (ICS), the Indian Police (IP) and at other levels of the government opted for Pakistan and kept that newly-born nation going in the early days. This migration, however, weakened the bureaucratic structure on the Indian side to some extent.

Few can deny that Partition was effected in very nearly the worst possible way, the overarching presence of Mahatma Gandhi and of Mountbatten, Nehru and Patel on the scene notwithstanding; it involved the loss of millions of lives and the displacement of men, women and children on a scale never before witnessed in recorded history. The retributive killings were to total up to a figure of fatalities of anywhere between 200,000 and 20,00,000, with at least 14 million Muslims, Hindus and Sikhs being uprooted.

---

1 Fatima Jinnah (1893-1967), known as '*Maadar-e-Millat*', was a dental surgeon by training and was the Quaid-i-Azam's younger sister and lifelong confidant. She co-founded the Pakistan Women's Association and challenged Ayub Khan in the 1965 presidential election, winning two of the country's largest cities, Karachi and Dacca (now Dhaka).

Train killings on the railways were also a site of the most bestial violence.

The Punjab Boundary Force which might have been able to reduce the violent atrocities was not functional until just two weeks before Partition and was disbanded, under duress, after only a month.

The 'human cost' of the Partition was incalculable and the tragic memories have long exacerbated the severely strained relations between Pakistan and India.

My endeavour, first and foremost, is to place before readers in the sub-continent (and elsewhere), a summary account of the events, the underlying factors and considerations and of the main personalities that culminated in the end of British rule, the emergence of Pakistan and, subsequently, of Bangladesh. From this follows an analysis of some aspects of the political and socio-economic profile of the Republic of India, post-1950, extending to the current regime of Narendra Modi. A few of the contemporary issues have been examined and commented upon.

Even as the dominant theme is the 'Why and How' of the Partition of India, the continuing failure to upgrade the standards of governance and ensure the delivery of benefits to the poor, is a recurring concern. The repercussions of Partition appear and re-appear throughout the narrative. Narendra Modi has, today, to address the entire gamut of India-Pakistan animosity, no less than Lal Bahadur Shastri in 1965-66.

In the pre-1947 period, I have touched upon the lives and work of such outstanding sons of India as Lokmanya Bal Gangadhar Tilak, Deshbandhu Chittaranjan (CR) Das, Lala Lajpat Rai – the Punjab Kesari – and Mahamana Pandit Madan Mohan Malaviya who are yet to find, in my view, their well-deserved place in the history of the Indian freedom struggle.

There are many others. Barring Malaviya, they died relatively early and Das at just 56 years.

The course that political events took in the thirties and forties might have been quite different had a broader spectrum of national leaders lived longer and Subhas Bose not forced to exit the Congress in 1939. Rajarshi Purushottam Das (P.D.) Tandon, who was elected to the Congress presidency in 1950, was compelled to quit, within months, under Jawaharlal Nehru's pressure, shortly after the demise of Sardar Patel whose candidate he was for this position, trouncing Acharya Kripalani.

Not one vote was cast for Kripalani from Gujarat. Patel thought Nehru had to understand that his will was not law with the Congress, but he personally discouraged Nehru from resigning when the latter felt that the party had lost confidence in him.

In 1934, Subhas Bose wrote about C.R. Das:

> June 1925 proved to be a turning point in the history of India. The disappearance of the towering personality of the Deshbandhu from the political arena was for India a colossal misfortune. The Swaraj Party, which owed so much to him, was paralysed … The weakening of the Swaraj Party served to strengthen the forces of reaction in India and in England, while it let loose a flood of communal strife in India … as we look back on the year 1925, we cannot help feeling that if Providence had spared the Deshbandhu for a few years more, the history of India would probably have taken a different turn.

With regard to whether a free India should have been united or divided, Gandhi and the Congress lost the argument to Jinnah and his Muslim League. The hope that Partition would be a step towards resolving the Hindu-Muslim question in the longer term has been belied. At no stage or juncture have India-Pakistan relations been on an even keel, bordering on some degree of normalcy.

Until the outbreak of World War II, Jinnah did not (unlike Iqbal, to an extent) enjoy the international reputation of Gandhi, Tagore and Jawaharlal Nehru. The Session of the All India Muslim League at Lahore in 1940 in which the Pakistan Resolution was unanimously carried marks the beginning of Jinnah's appearance in the global arena.

Jinnah strove to be recognized as the sole spokesman of Indian Muslims on the national stage. From the late 1930s, after he had returned from Britain, his main concern was with the arrangements by which power at the Centre was to be shared once the British had left. His appeal to religion was ambiguous and was not characteristic of his political style before 1937. There is also evidence to suggest that his use of the communal factor was a political tactic, not an ideological commitment. For the League to play its part at the Centre, it needed a mandate from Muslims in the provinces where Jinnah's influence had started to penetrate in the early forties.

From a British perspective, a balanced view of Jinnah is provided in a letter of June 23, 1954 from an ex-Vicereine, Lady (Eugenie) Wavell to Jinnah's New Zealand-born biographer, Hector Bolitho:

> … My husband (Viceroy Wavell) thought that his (Jinnah's) judgment was often marred by personal vanity – that his intransigence and nerves

prevented his approaching large problems in a large way.

> On the other hand, Lord Wavell had great sympathy for the Muslims and their fear of being in a minority and he had immense admiration for their troops – as indeed all the Indian Army ... He was, as you know, determined to see fairplay for all as long as he was Viceroy ... I do believe that my husband felt Jinnah was honestly trying to do the best he could for the cause he had so much at heart. I was sorry for him – he looked so ill and overstrained.

In Lady Wavell's view 'Jinnah was one of the handsomest of men – he combined the clear cut, almost Grecian, features of the West with Oriental grace of movement!'[2]

A conversation took place in Calcutta (now Kolkata) in the fifties between Clement Attlee (the British Prime Minister in 1947) and Justice P.B. Chakraborty, Acting Governor of West Bengal, about the hasty withdrawal of the British. Attlee cited several reasons, the chief among them being the declining loyalty to the British Crown in the Indian Army and Navy personnel as a result of the military activities of Netaji Subhas Bose. Justice Chakraborty asked Attlee about the extent of Gandhi's influence upon the British decision to leave. Attlee's lips became twisted in a sarcastic smile as he said 'MINIMAL'.

We, in India, need to do much more to keep alive the legacies of nationalists, scholars and liberals like Gopal Krishna Gokhale, B.R. Ambedkar, Acharya Narendra Deva, Jayaprakash Narayan (J.P.) and others of the calibre of Syama Prasad Mookerjee and Deen Dayal Upadhyaya; the latter two never belonged to the Congress fold, nor did Ambedkar. The short point is that all those who sought to build a new India must be given legitimate space.

A part was played by the Hindu Mahasabha whose president during a critical phase, Veer Savarkar (1883–1966), coined the term – Hindutva.

The country should also be made better aware of the sidelining in the Congress, successively, of Subhas Bose, Bhulabhai Desai and Maulana Azad, among others, the patently unfair treatment meted out to Viceroy Wavell in the final months leading to Dominion Status for India and Pakistan and the virtual eclipse (post-Patel) of, arguably, the most outstanding civil servant of the

2 *In Quest of Jinnah, Diary, Notes and Correspondence of Hector Bolitho*: Edited by Sharif al Mujahid (Oxford University Press, 2007), p. 148-149.

time, V.P. Menon who, as Constitutional Adviser and Reforms Commissioner, had unfettered access to the last three Viceroys. On June 27, 1947, the States Department was set up, its Indian wing under Sardar Patel whose Secretary, V.P. Menon (not an ICS), virtually replaced Sir Conrad Corfield as the last Viceroy's Political Adviser.

In the Nehru government, the only recognition of Menon's contributions, which were invaluable in the processes of the Transfer of Power and the Integration of the Princely States, came by way of an acting governorship of Orissa (now Odisha) for a few months in 1951.

The price that was paid by the Congress leadership – Gandhi, Nehru and Patel – for the status of a Dominion within the British Commonwealth was the loss of the Unity of India.

The ominous shadow of Partition continues to linger over the subcontinent and has not disappeared with the flux of time.

After Dominion Status came about in August 1947 (which, itself, was contrary to the promise of Purna Swaraj made under the presidentship of a 40-year old Jawaharlal Nehru at the Lahore Congress in 1929), India has mostly remained under the sway of dynastic rule, first of one family at the Centre and then of other families in several States.

Over the years, dynastic politics has become a permanent feature of the Indian model of democracy, even more so than in Pakistan, Bangladesh and Sri Lanka.

It has been said that the formal institution of 'dynastic democracy' in India occurred on 31 October, 1984 when Rajiv Gandhi succeeded his mother as Prime Minister. I venture to argue that its roots lie as far back as in 1928 when Pandit Motilal Nehru, as President of the Calcutta Congress, virtually entreated, implored and then ensured, through the intercession of Mahatma Gandhi, that Jawaharlal succeed him (the father) at the Lahore Congress the following year. The appointment of the son to the '*gaddi*' (position) was not materially different from Indira Gandhi assuming the presidency of the Grand Old Party (GOP) in 1959, except that India was by then a sovereign Republic. Indira did eventually succeed her father as Prime Minister, with the Shastri interregnum of nineteen months coming in between.

In other words, Nehru was doing for Indira what his father had done for him, passing on to him the highest office then open to an Indian nationalist, the Congress presidency.

The veteran journalist, Kuldip Nayar, was in his early forties when Nehru passed away. He had served as the Information Officer to two successive

Home Ministers, Pant and Shastri. In the context of the succession to Nehru, he recalls Shastri, then Minister without Portfolio, saying:

> I would prefer a unanimous election … Were a contest to become inevitable, I would like to stand against Morarjibhai because I can defeat him, not Indiraji … We need a person like Jayaprakash Narayan to head the government at this stage ….

Sometime earlier, when Nayar had asked Shastri: 'Who do you think Nehru has in mind as his successor', Shastri had responded: '*Unke dil mein to unki suputri hain* [In his heart, it is his daughter] … but it won't be easy.' Nayar persisted and said: 'People think you are such a staunch devotee of Nehru that you yourself will propose Indira Gandhi's name after his death', to which Shastri replied: 'I am not that much of a sadhu as you imagine me to be. Who would not like to be India's prime minister?'[3]

Even more than her late father, Indira Gandhi had opportunities (which were frittered away) to stabilize the political conditions in the troubled State of Jammu and Kashmir which had their origins, in the first place, in the Partition and Maharaja Hari Singh's inordinately delayed Accession to the Dominion of India.

In June 1966, J.P, a lifelong friend of Sheikh Abdullah (who had been re-arrested in 1965), wrote to the Prime Minister urging that the Sheikh be released in time for the next elections due the following year. His words were prophetic:

> … if we miss the chance of using the next general election to win the consent of the people to their place within the Union, I cannot see what other device will be left to India to settle the problem. To think that we will eventually wear down the people [of Kashmir] and force them to accept … the Union is to delude ourselves. That might conceivably have happened had Kashmir not been geographically located where it is. In its present location, and with seething discontent among the people, it would never be left in peace by Pakistan ….

In the event, it was not before another eight years that Sheikh Abdullah could re-enter active politics. At no point did Indira Gandhi welcome his

3 Kuldip Nayar: *Beyond The Lines (An Autobiography)* Lotus-Roli Books, 2012 (p.131).

return and she was even more displeased when he passed on the mantle to his son, Farooq, setting in motion, thereby, another political dynasty.

Sheikh Abdullah became the Chief Minister in February 1975 and JP welcomed the move, although he was, by now, irrevocably opposed to the Prime Minister. However, at this stage, the Sheikh seemed reconciled, more or less, to paying homage to New Delhi. He was also inclined to place the interests of his own family above the steps that needed to be taken for fulfilling the aspirations of the Kashmiri people.

The question remains as to what might have been the fate of Jammu and Kashmir and its people had Indira Gandhi heeded JP's advice in June 1966, released the Sheikh, allowed him to contest a free and fair election – which he was almost certain to win – and let him run a benevolent and caring administration.

Indira Gandhi not only refused to see reason then, she went on to remove Farooq Abdullah from the chief ministership in 1984 and had him replaced by the Sheikh's son-in-law, Ghulam Mohammad (Gul) Shah who had defected from the National Conference and lasted in the job till March 1986. The ensuing elections of 1987 were rigged and manipulated and heralded the beginning of a violent turbulence and a breakdown of public order and tranquillity that has only got worse over the years.

The Kashmir problem has been called the 'unfinished agenda of Partition'.

The successful commissioning of the Chenani-Nashri tunnel connecting Udhampur to Ramban and the benefits that would accrue therefrom are unlikely – just on their own – to help defuse the current unrest and violence in the State.

It is undisputed that the Sikh community suffered terribly during the Partition riots. Many years later, when Rajiv Gandhi became the head of the Youth Congress, it was widely perceived that his mother was already grooming him for the Prime Ministership. In October-November 1984, it was his deplorable failing that, having taken over the PM's mantle through the dynastic compulsions of the Congress (even if on the night of his mother's death), Rajiv Gandhi remained oblivious of having also taken over governance responsibilities for the whole of India. His only public reference to the anti-Sikh riots at the time can only be interpreted as remorseless, even inhuman: 'When a giant tree falls, the mother earth below shakes'. During his years in power, he exercised neither his moral nor his political authority to redress the calamity of 1984. It is the greatness of the Sikh community that they still try to forgive the Congress.

The previous Prime Minister, Sardar Manmohan Singh, who lost his only Lok Sabha election in 1999 by a substantial margin, did not hesitate to try to cover himself in glory when, at the inauguration of the re-designed Vallabhbhai Patel Museum at Ahmedabad, he stated that he was proud to be of the same Party as Sardar Patel and that there were more areas of convergence between Patel and Nehru than the divergence. As the Prime Minister for a decade, he might have known that Nehru had once shot down a proposal to raise a National Memorial to Sardar Patel – a proposal which was endorsed by the Congress Working Committee (CWC).

An amount of Rs 1 crore was to be raised for the National Memorial and G.D. Birla, a leading industrialist and a close friend of Sardar Patel collected Rs.50 lakhs for the purpose. S.K. Patil, a confidant of the Sardar (and a later day Union Minister) who was the Bombay Congress supremo, raised around Rs.10 lakhs but the other Pradesh Congress Committees failed to make significant contributions.

When Patil broached the matter of a Sardar Patel Memorial, Nehru discouraged the idea, saying that Patel was essentially a farmer and that the funds raised for the Memorial ought to be utilized for the 'digging of wells and constructing approach roads'.[4]

Despite Nehru's observations, Patil was able to secure a venue on Parliament Street in New Delhi for a statue of Sardar Patel. The Circle has been known as Patel Chowk where several offices and banks are located.

The observance of Sardar Patel's Birth Centenary in October 1975 (four months after the Emergency was promulgated under Indira Gandhi) was a low-key affair, in stark contrast to the year-long celebrations organized for a similar event for Jawaharlal Nehru which culminated in November 1989, weeks before Rajiv Gandhi's defeat at the hustings.

On November 14, 2013, Russian children stood on the stage at the Indian Embassy in Moscow, dressed in different, ethnic attire; the Embassy was celebrating the birth anniversary of Jawaharlal Nehru. Three years later, things were quiet on November 14, 2016; the only celebrations the Mission held were on October 31 to commemorate another Indian icon, Sardar Vallabhbhai Patel.

Since the time the Modi government has been in power, the Missions abroad are reflecting the political shift on whom to celebrate – and who to

4 Pran Nath Chopra: *The Sardar of India, Biography of Vallabhbhai Patel* (Konark Publishers, 2015).

ignore. The Prime Minister who calls Sardar Patel a role model has designated October 31 as National Unity Day.

Nehru's foreign policy priorities continue, to some extent, to underpin India's diplomatic stance. There was no official diktat asking the Indian Missions to not celebrate November 14, just as there was no clear order of the government's keenness to honour Patel. But the celebrations on Patel's birth anniversary and the silence on Nehru suggest that the Indian Embassies and High Commissions got the government's message anyway.

In the media coverage on Sardar Patel, little note has been taken of an insult to his legacy: the abolition of the Privy Purses, first by a Presidential Order and later, by a Constitutional Amendment. Neither the Janata Party in 1977 nor any of the non-Congress governments of a later day thought it fit to even discuss the failure to redeem the Sardar's solemn pledge made in the Constituent Assembly. Perhaps, building the tallest statue in his memory, the Statue of Unity, in Gujarat will serve to highlight his incredible achievement of unifying India.

The present is a time to remind ourselves that we have to stop becoming a country only for the ultra-rich and that the political class, as a whole, who depend on the votes of the poor of India, must realize that economic and social inequalities and disparities cannot grow indefinitely and cannot be perpetuated. According to one estimate, India's 25 Richest People have a combined net worth of US $ 174.8 billion which is about as much as Ukraine's GDP.

A recent *Forbes* assessment says that India is home to the world's fourth highest number of billionaires.

At the other extreme is the plight of newborns in India who have a lesser chance of survival than babies born in Afghanistan and Somalia, according to the latest Global Burden of Disease (GBD) study published in *The Lancet,* a leading medical journal. In the GBD rankings for healthcare access and quality (HAQ), India has fallen 11 places and is now placed at 154 out of 195 countries. Further, the healthcare index of 44.8 is the lowest among the sub-continental nations. Having a strong economy or having advanced medical technology does not guarantee good health care. The need of the hour is that the people at large ought to be getting the care that should be expected for diseases with established treatments.

Our problem is that one is identified as a reformer in India if he or she is instrumental in opening up FDI, which does not represent the totality of reforms. Despite all the reforms under the NDA-I and the UPA-I and II, the poor of India not only remain very poor but largely deprived of basic amenities.

The issue at hand is not only about opening up the economy; it is also imperative to recognize that there has been a very steep fall in the quality of people manning institutions: legislative, judicial and administrative. The heart of the matter is that we need to have the best of people and we need to have institutional reforms.

It is good to remember that while we require our doctors, scientists, engineers and administrators, we also need a society based on honesty, equity and justice. It is not enough to 'Make in India'; we must also 'Make good people in India'.

Dishonesty and greed are big barriers to growth. Our education system will have to hammer home the basic truth that genuine wealth creation can happen only when resources are equitably distributed. The late J.R.D. Tata once said: 'I don't want India to be an economic superpower. I want India to be a happy country'[5].

This holds the key to our future. For some time to come, that future is expected to remain in the hands of Narendra Modi and his closest advisers. The track record of an inept and scam-ridden UPA II headed by an ineffectual Prime Minister (albeit, under the watchful supervision of 10, Janpath) makes a definite change for the better so much easier for the NDA-II to achieve during its remaining term and, possibly, beyond.

Halfway through his current innings, the time is right for Prime Minister Modi to demonstrate control over the functioning of the BJP Chief Ministers. The ones in Rajasthan, Madhya Pradesh and Chhatisgarh (Vasundhara Raje Scindia, Shivraj Singh Chouhan and Raman Singh respectively, none of whose administrations are free of blemish) commenced their terms when the UPA II was in power at the Centre. Others like Devendra Fadnavis, the comparatively young Chief Minister in Maharashtra, Manohar Lal in Haryana and Raghubar Das in Jharkhand were handpicked by Modi.

Taking a cue from Shivraj Singh Chouhan, the Andhra Pradesh Chief Minister, N. Chandrababu Naidu, an NDA ally, announced a separate Happiness Index Department. However, Chouhan trails behind Naidu in what should be a matter of great personal importance, which is that while Naidu's son, Nara Lokesh, is already a minister (one of the very rare instances of a father-son duo being in the same cabinet), Chouhan's son, Kartikey, all of 24 years, is only now being groomed by the father for onerous responsibilities. He addressed an impressively large gathering in his ancestral village near Bhopal and is

5 In the article 'The Business Ethics of J.R.D. Tata' (*The Hindu* dated July 29, 2005).

participating actively in functions in the area. Keeping alive the already well established traditions of dynastic politics, both the chief ministerial progeny can soon be expected to make their mark, at any rate in the press reports.

In Chouhan's Madhya Pradesh, one Narayan Tiwari (72 years) of Fatehpur village in Shahdol district was left with no option but to bury his wife, Kunti Bai (68 years) in the courtyard when she died in July 2016 because he could not incur the funeral expenses.

In another first, the state witnessed clashes between farmers (at least six of whom perished in the firing) and the police in June 2017 in several places like Sehore, Neemuch, Indore and Ratlam. The agitation was handled, in typical lackadaisical fashion, by Chouhan's government with the police even beating up those not participating in the protests.

The Chief Minister has chosen to run the administration through a coterie of the most corrupt bureaucrats working in the state. At long last, Chouhan appears vulnerable – the farmers' agitation has done what even the Vyapam scam, involving the gravest charges of bribery, could not do.

Chouhan, a self-proclaimed '*kisan putra*' (farmer son), had to abruptly terminate his indefinite fast at Bhopal after only 28 hours, without addressing the main demands and amid clear signs that the central BJP leadership was not behind him.

The massive extent of corruption in the Madhya Pradesh bureaucracy came to the fore when a former Municipal Commissioner of Satna was caught red-handed earlier this year by the Special Police Establishment (SPE) of the Lok Ayukta. The State Government's embarrassment become more acute upon finding that this official was awarded a Medal by the Chief Minister for efficiency in connection with the Simhastha event of 2016.

The Madhya Pradesh government suffered a legal setback in the matter of the 'alleged' encounter of eight SIMI activists (that took place near Bhopal in October, 2016) when the Supreme Court issued notices to the Union and State governments. The Court also directed the CBI to give a response in a petition filed by a relative of one of the deceased that seeks a court-monitored probe by an independent agency. It comes as no surprise that the police officers who were part of the encounter do not want the enquiry to move out of the control of the top state authorities who have supported their actions, the fulsome praise flowing down from the Chief Minister himself.

There are those in the BJP who think that the time has arrived for a change of leadership if Narendra Modi and Amit Shah are indeed thinking about retaining power when Madhya Pradesh goes to the polls in November, 2018. Worse news could follow a few months later in the Lok Sabha elections.

On October 2, 2014, just months after taking over as the PM, the Swachh Bharat Mission – a particularly ambitious cleanliness campaign – was launched by Narendra Modi who dramatically declared that 'a clean India would be the best tribute India could pay to Mahatma Gandhi on his 150th birth anniversary in 2019'. He promised to transform sanitation and waste-management in the country.

Three years on, it is clear that enormous efforts have gone into making the Mission a flagship programme of the NDA-II.

According to the World Bank, over the years 1999-2013, the Central and state Governments 'expended INR 150 billion (USD 2.4 billion) on cleanliness campaigns'; much of that money was wasted. The Swachh Bharat Mission proposes to spend several times that volume of funds in just five years.

While there can be no quarrel with Modi's fervent push to re-energize government and voluntary action in an area long-neglected in India's development agenda, the fact of the matter is that, on the plank of effective execution, the signals are, at best, 'very mixed' and that the programme is floundering in several states. Prominent politicians have posed for pictures wielding brooms but, as Bezwada Wilson[6] said, he was yet to see any of them photographed cleaning a latrine!

When this Mission does make a perceptible impact on the ground, the credit will, no doubt, accrue to Modi's vision in launching a national campaign.

The NDA-II had, for months, been on the horns of a dilemma over whether or not to subject the recently retired Comptroller and Auditor General of India (C&AG) – appointed to the constitutional post by UPA II in May 2013– to interrogation in the aborted Agusta Westland VVIP helicopter purchase deal. The matter came into the public domain in India only because of a specific reference to the seizure of certain incriminating documents in the judgment of an Italian Court. The constitutional appointee, as also a key aide of the Congress President (more a family factotum) are among the names mentioned in this behalf.

Between 2003-2013, the C&AG was directly connected in the Ministry of Defence with the processing of a number of defence purchases and with

6 Bezwada Wilson (born 1966) is an activist and one of the founders of the Safai Karamchari Andolan (SKA) that has worked for the eradication of manual scavenging. He was honoured, in July, 2016, with the Ramon Magsaysay Award.

other matters, such as ensuring a chosen line of succession for the post of Chief of the Army Staff (COAS). One commonly-held perception has been that the UPA government made the appointment of the C&AG to 'cover up the misdeeds in defence procurement during its decade in office'.

Two former Chiefs of the Naval Staff and a few retired bureaucrats filed a Petition in Public Interest (PIL) in the Delhi High Court seeking an appropriate direction to declare the C&AG appointment as void since it was made arbitrarily by a procedure that did not withstand the test of constitutionality and also on the ground of nemo judex in causa sua, which is to say that no person shall be a judge in his own cause.

This well-intentioned attempt to obtain a judicial intervention did not bear fruit; a Special Leave Petition was submitted to the Apex Court who might, perhaps, have indicated that the Government of India establish a transparent and non-arbitrary procedure for the C&AG's selection which would replace the sole discretion currently residing with the Executive.

In the Constituent Assembly debates, the C&AG was described as a most important officer under the Constitution and one who must, like Caesar's wife, be above suspicion, Dr Ambedkar observed: 'If this functionary is to carry out the duties which are far more important than the duties even of the judiciary, he should be certainly as independent as the judiciary ...'.

If, after vacillating endlessly, the NDA-II had at last permitted the interrogation of the C&AG, he would probably have had to put in his papers, which should have been a small price to pay for upholding the values of probity and integrity – to which the Modi government stands committed – and for protecting the impartiality of an 'integrity institution'. It would, at least, have shown that the UPA II and the NDA II are not quite the same thing.

An important area in which the Modi government should be contemplating a course correction pertains to the matter of high-level appointments where it has been floundering from one controversy to another. The appointment of a retired administrator with no track record in the realm of scholarship and historical research (but who was, earlier, on Atal Bihari Vajpayee's staff) as the Director of the Nehru Memorial Museum and Library (NMML) is yet another link in the series of ham-handed appointments that are being bullied through, provoking one of the few leading public intellectuals, who was sympathetic to the government, to tender his resignation from the Executive Committee of the NMML.

What is shocking is not just the crass way in which such appointments have been pushed through, but the utter disregard those in power have for liberal middle-class opinion.

The rot is deeper. The delay in judicial appointments and to top posts in the armed forces and making adhoc arrangements, at senior levels, in several departments, all point to an attempt both to screen out those who could become 'inconvenient' and to wait as long as may be necessary to identify and appoint those who show sufficient intellectual flexibility to toe the given line.

Such a sinister dimension to senior government appointments is built on a huge body of bad practices, perfected by previous governments, beginning with Indira Gandhi who started the tradition of making key appointments on the basis of personal loyalty. Most Prime Ministers, thereafter, fine-tuned their own versions of the US presidential system of 'spoils'.

The UPA-II (2009–14) created a vast network of patronage in government outside the civil services framework and outside the purview of the Union Public Service Commission (UPSC) in the form of commissions, independent regulators, ombudsmen, statutory authorities and the like. This patronage network serves three purposes-keeping civil servants on the verge of retirement pliant and malleable while still serving, ensuring that the person remains obliged through his or her tenure, once re-employed (turncoats, such as the UPA-appointed holders of high office notwithstanding) and sending the bureaucracy a signal that loyalty and subservience are essential virtues.

While the UPA-II set up an unprecedented opportunity for extended patronage, the NDA government has not only embraced this tradition, they have improved on it both by adding to the number of posts and by raising the bar for allegiance and loyalty.

A parallel route through which our version of a 'spoils' system has been institutionalized is by making selection for important appointments an opaque process, tightly controlled and managed by the PMO. This ensures that the appointees maintain direct allegiance to the PMO and will do its bidding even if it means compromising on the well-established principles of a Cabinet system of government.

Cronyism in appointments is not new in the Indian administration. There are, however, two disturbing features in the approach of the present government. One, the brute manner in which predetermined choices are foisted even if it involves changing laws and rules and altering procedures and conventions. And secondly, the desperate need to find those with an affinity to the ruling party, regardless of whether they have the requisite qualifications or expertise. Mediocrity in senior-level appointments has become universalized in the NDA II.

A sense of foreboding has found its way into the civil services. The NDA II that had laid much store by its ability to galvanize the bureaucracy to work towards a transformed India has now to reckon with its growing sullenness, a discernible discomfort with the way its affairs are being handled and a heightened sense of fear that stepping out of line or speaking out can prove costly.

After the first three years (2014–17), the general perception is that the bureaucracy stands compromised, the arbitrary use of state power is on the increase, the criminal justice system is in decline and everyday corruption is as bad or worse.

The last round of empanelments for appointment as Secretaries at the Centre has had a demoralising effect. The process of 'empanelment' in the central government has long been questionable but, over the years, some practices and conventions had evolved that had reduced arbitrariness and increased acceptability. This year, the process was turned upside down and about 35 per cent of the officers who were due to be empanelled were being left out because of a drastic overhaul of the way assessments are being made. The change was done ostensibly to make the process merit-based, which was determined not merely on the basis of the Confidential Report (CR) dossier but on the basis of diverse inputs drawn from a variety of sources. It is unclear as to what these inputs were. There are no explanations for why some candidates have been left out or what criteria have been followed, what kind of inputs were obtained to make the assessment or from where they were obtained or what redress an officer has if there is cause to feel unfairly treated. Introducing such uncertainty in career advancement at the end of a career is both inexplicable and whimsical.

For the bureaucracy as a whole, the message is that the authority of the PMO is absolute. Access to the top is filtered through the chosen few whose decisions may (or may not) be based on prior consultation. As of now, therefore, officers will have to live with uncertainty regarding their future, which could be bright if they read the signals right but bleak if they get it wrong. The higher echelons are slowly learning that honesty and objectivity in decision-making no longer matter.

The PMO itself keeps out of the limelight and is unapproachable except for the chosen few.

There is a silver lining in that the Prime Minister is sensitive to the need for having 'economic managers' at the top on the basis of proven credentials and a track record rather than ideological affinities. The appointments of the Vice-Chairman of the Niti Aayog and of the Chief Economic Adviser were merit-based. There may still be light at the end of the tunnel.

On the eve of the presidential election in the United States in November 2016, a former IAS bureaucrat who went on to serve in the Election Commission of India [and who was an Election Commissioner (EC) when a fierce and unseemly controversy raged between the then Chief Election Commissioner (CEC) and another Election Commissioner, the first appointed by the BJP and the second by the Congress] opined that '... what has worked well for India is a fully empowered but fiercely independent and neutral Election Commission'. He might have added that it is also important, in the first instance, to appoint the CEC and the ECs, being constitutional posts, through the recommendations of a duly notified, top-level Selection Committee rather than as the arbitrary choice of the political executive, which is the case with the appointment of the C&AG as well.

A journalist who was chosen for one of the Ramnath Goenka Excellence in Journalism Awards for his book *Gita Press and the Making of Hindu India* created a flutter when he said:

> I have great regard for the Award but I could not come to terms with the fact that I will accept it from a man whose tenure as the political head of the country has been so bad for Indian Journalism.

At this same function in early November 2016, Prime Minister Modi, who was presenting the prestigious Awards, observed:

> Every generation must keep reflecting on the Emergency period in an unbiased manner so that no future political leader can even wish to commit the same sin.

The Prime Minister's words will ring true when, in the remaining term of the NDA II, he is convincingly seen to arrest the increasing use of state power (even routine politics can risk detention) and curb the cult of propaganda.

The way in which Indian civil society's revolt against rampant and widespread corruption has been neutralized is astounding. Scams of an unprecedented magnitude, like Vyapam, have been wiped out of public discussion. The investigating agencies, with hardly any exception, have failed to nail vice and wrongdoing; the long arm of the law has yet to reach the culprits in the major scams. And one is left wondering whether it ever will.

Narendra Modi would have found himself in a better position to more assertively tackle the main tasks before the NDA II if he had, like one of his predecessors, Narasimha Rao, more of a functioning bureaucracy at his disposal at the Centre. The impact that he has been wanting to showcase would have been more visible by now had effective and purposive steps been taken to tone up governance and enforce the accountability of the senior levels in the civil services.

The Prime Minister's initiatives in the sphere of Foreign Policy – commendable as these are – must take account of the undeniable fact of China's rise and a fast deepening China-Pakistan axis. This alignment has the potential to thwart, politically and diplomatically, India's global aspirations where these matter most. The still emerging implications of change of occupancy at the White House will have to be comprehensively addressed.

The strengthening of Indo-U.S. ties need not be accompanied by a nosedive in Sino-Indian relations, the latest trends in which are disturbing, at the very least.

Barely months before the last State elections in Punjab, Uttarakhand, Uttar Pradesh, Manipur and Goa, Prime Minister Modi displayed his appetite for risk through the demonetization of currency notes of two denominations. He undertook a much bigger exercize than the one ordered by the Janata Party Government in 1978.

Demonetization was projected as a potential game-changer through which the Prime Minister made a style statement; he was risk-friendly and has the charisma and authority to convince the people that this was, in reality, a thrust at the rich on behalf of the poor. Later, however, the data released by the Central Statistics Office (CSO) on May 31, 2017 pointed to an economic slowdown, enabling the Opposition to launch a scathing attack.

The growth of Gross Value Addition (GVA) is reported to have declined from 7.9 per cent in 2015-16 to 6.6 per cent in 2016-17; the cost to the economy was 1.3 per cent. Another disquieting feature pertains to core sector growth (a truer measure of industrial activity) that fell from 10.7 per cent in Q4 of 2015-16 to 3.8 per cent in Q4 of 2016-17. Sectors like mining, manufacturing, construction, transport and professional services also declined; of these, the construction sector, which is the second largest job-creating sector, shrunk by 3.7 per cent in 2016-17, indicating job losses.

It did not hit agriculture production, but demonetization is being seen as a cause for the current unrest in rural India. We have witnessed a generalized fall in the prices of agricultural commodities much of whose trading is cash-based, through *mandi* intermediaries, processors and retailers. This traditional capital was delivered a body-blow by demonetization. Till liquidity returns, the ultimate sufferer will be the farmer. In the current deflationary environment, the farmers are the clear losers.

Narendra Modi made another style statement in the appointment of a new Chief of Army Staff (COAS). Two of his predecessors have not exactly covered themselves in glory in connection with their roles in the scam relating to the Adarsh Housing Society, Mumbai, as per the findings of an independent enquiry instituted in this behalf. The COAS between 2002-05 who has been the more strongly indicted, continues to preside over arguably the most influential non-government body in the country today, a public policy think-tank, that is, in some respects, an extension of the NDA-II itself.

This is the Modi way of doing things, which he seems to have consciously avoided earlier. He is a politician of incredible self-belief and feels that he has come up with an out-of-the-box solution to break the unholy nexus of corruption, black money and terrorism that is threatening the very fabric of India. He would, however, need to follow this up by putting more action in place. To begin with, the funding of elections has to be made transparent and above board.

The battle against black money will have been worthwhile if the resultant revenue gains are efficiently utilized. In the first place, as the size of the parallel economy shrinks, the tax base will automatically widen; this will allow the government to reduce rates and boost consumption. Secondly, the additional revenue will allow the government to significantly enhance the efficacy of welfare schemes. Here, the best way forward may be to actualize the idea of a universal basic income, the essence of which is to transfer a sum of money to all families.

The country ranks high in recent estimates of the levels of hunger and malnutrition which have resulted in under-nourishment, wasting and mortality among children. The responses of the UPA-II and the NDA-II have, been skewed and inadequate.

A World Bank assessment on India's performance in respect of ease of doing business shows the country to be lagging behind many of the East African and sub-Saharan African nations in enforcement of contract, largely because of an inefficient judicial system which has failed to keep up with the technological revolution that has changed the pace of delivery of justice, globally. Citing the example of Rwanda, the assessment says that the authorities have implemented the integrated electronic case management system across all courts which allows for an automatic registration of lawsuits, electronic organization and scheduling of cases and automated claims processing.

Narendra Modi is often seen as a forgiving and lenient head of government when it comes to fixing responsibility and penalizing blatant misdemeanour. His immediate predecessor, Manmohan Singh, sent one of the Cabinet members to jail; another UPA minister was headed towards meeting a similar fate, even as others were asked to quit in the face of allegations of serious impropriety.

In the NDA-II, a clean chit appears to have already been given to the then Minister of Coal, Manmohan Singh relating to the precise period when coal blocks were allocated, on verbal or unsigned recommendations, including by his Principal Secretary, a Keralite borne on the Punjab IAS cadre. No UPA minister has been the subject of an FIR, let alone a CBI prosecution.

On the other hand, the then Secretary, Department of Coal, an Uttar Pradesh IAS, was chargesheeted and hauled over the coals (pun intended).

Some positions in the Modi-led setup are still occupied by officials who were active in UPA II and who can decelerate the transformational measures promised by a government whose record, so far, has not been as spectacular as was anticipated when it took office.

A former Lieutenant Governor of Delhi, a UPA favourite, survived in the post for well over two years before finally putting in his resignation.

His successor, with origins in the Union Territories IAS cadre and a BJP appointee, has had no less a chequered association with the political leadership of differing hues, ranging from C.M. Ibrahim (a one-time Deve Gowda loyalist, who was the Minister of Civil Aviation in 1997-98 and is now with the Congress Party)[7] and a senior serving Cabinet Minister in NDA-II, who saw him through, with Deputy Prime Minister Advani's intervention, to the Union Home Secretary's post in the last phase of the Vajpayee government.

Not quite in line and senior enough for the Home Secretary's position, he was, apparently, upset about being shifted by UPA-I to the Ministry of Urban Development exhibiting, thereby, a measure of misplaced self-conviction in being able to carry on, despite the changed circumstances.

The internal security situation is on a slippery slope. Jammu and Kashmir continues to be in the news for the wrong reasons, accompanied by ceasefire violations by the Pakistan army, continuing infiltrations by terrorists, their attacks on security forces and radicalization of the local youth. The BJP's coalition experiment with the PDP has not delivered but the government seems unwilling to acknowledge its failure.

---

7 M.K. Kaw: *An Outsider Everywhere, Revelations by an Insider* (Konark Publishers, 2012, Chapter 24).

The clashes which took place in Mathura (U.P.) on June 2, 2016 in U.P. were but another manifestation of the abysmal depths to which a corruption-ridden administration has sunk in most parts of India over the last thirty years or so. Corrective steps in the field of police reform have been recommended in several Reports which have been gathering dust in the Government of India for decades. The heart-rending pictures of the grieving family of the then Superintendent of Police (City) who was killed, his aged parents and his two very young sons, will haunt me for the rest of my life. It was a supreme tragedy for them.

The situation can be allowed to slide further, only at the nation's peril. The political parties – and their leadership – will have to collectively arrest the deterioration in the maintenance of law and order, in the morale of the civil services, as a whole, in communal harmony and in the security of life and property afforded to the common man, before visions of all-round progress and prosperity are entertained, much less accomplished.

The NDA II has an opportunity to reverse a generally, self-defeating course (with some bright patches here and there) that the country has had to pursue, particularly after the demise of Sardar Patel in December, 1950. As a resurgent nation, we cannot afford to wallow in the luxury of merely recalling the past and eulogizing the Gandhi-Nehru pattern of things, which has dominated most histories of the freedom movement in India. The Gandhi-Nehru equation has, for too long, held captive the imagination and genius of the post-independence generations.

Issues of critical importance, such as those of Jammu and Kashmir, which arose soon after the Partition and have assumed the utmost seriousness, will have to be effectively tackled.

India stood at the crossroads of history in 1947 when she was divided on religious lines. She has, since then, witnessed armed confrontation with Pakistan, including in Kargil in 1999, as also the unceasing terror attacks that have claimed thousands of civilian lives.

Four Prime Ministers – Nehru, Shastri, Indira Gandhi and Vajpayee – have faced the challenge of military conflict with Pakistan, mainly over Jammu and Kashmir, but also in the erstwhile East Pakistan which was as much a product of Partition as the western wing.

Two Prime Ministers, I.K. Gujral (born 1919) and Manmohan Singh (born 1932) in the Jhelum and Muzaffargarh districts respectively of the western Punjab (now in Pakistan) were among the millions displaced in the Partition. Both tried, unsuccessfully, to embrace cordiality with Pakistan.

In the prevailing scenario, India could do without opinions being randomly expressed in its own media, such as by a top general who observed at a conference organized by the Army and the CII that '… Pakistan probably has a better industrial base, as far as defence production is concerned, than our country. In fact, they export defence equipment abroad, definitely more than what we are doing … having indigenous industrial capability is very crucial …'.

Which is not to say that the general's remarks should fall on deaf ears in the Government of India; defence production has remained a hugely neglected sector.

It was disconcerting to read that the Indian Army crashed out of a military competition after its Russia-origin T-90S main battle tank broke down due to mechanical snags, even as the armoured combat vehicles of China, Belarus, Kazakhstan and Russia went ahead to the finals. The Army is known to swear by the T-90S Bhishma tanks which are being made, under licence, in India, after the first consignment was imported from Russia from the year 2001 onwards. On the other hand, the Defence Research and Development Organization (DRDO) are said to be peeved over the Army's reluctance to order the upgraded Arjun Mark-II tanks after inducting the first lot of Mark-I variants, stressing that the indigenous tanks performed better than the T-90S tanks in comparative trials in 2010.

A United India, if it had existed, might already have been a major power, matching China, militarily and economically, and with a permanent seat at the U.N. Security Council. It would have been the natural successor to the British Indian Empire, whose role and profile the Dominion of India did not inherit as one of the two successor-states. Consequently, its capability and capacity to address the issues left behind by the British, such as in the North East, were impaired. But for Partition, there need not have been a huge expenditure, interminably, on arms and armaments that has heavily burdened the sub-continent as a whole.

Today, after a series of coalition governments at the Centre, India is again at the crossroads with a Hindu Nationalist Party that enjoys, for the first time, a clear majority in the Lok Sabha in control of the Government of India; communal tensions have been on the rise.

The Hindu-Muslim divide was not plugged at Partition and, as some contend, may actually be widening in the context, especially, of matters raised in the elections held from time to time. Be that as it may, this cannot be allowed to degenerate into some sort of variant of notions of separate identity or nationhood.

Given Narendra Modi's popularity, across the country, the moment is upon him to decisively emerge as *a* powerful instrument and symbol of the Oneness of India. If there is a sense of intolerance, it will impede economic growth.

The most important challenge confronting the policy makers today is the creation of employment opportunities for the increasing numbers that enter the labour market every year. This calls for the revival of the investment climate on the one hand and structural reforms to incentivize labour-intensive manufacturing on the other.

The government's economic policies have come under direct fire from two very senior, able and experienced members of the BJP. The first, Dr Subramanian Swamy, an acclaimed academic and economist, has said that '...the economy is in a tailspin. Yes, it can crash. We need to do a lot of good things to revive the economy. Even a tailspin can be made to steady. If nothing is done, we are heading for a major depression...'.

Dr Swamy is not the lone critic from the party's own camp. In a scathing criticism, a former Finance Minister, Yashwant Sinha, contends that the distress in the economy is so deep that a revival is unlikely before the next general elections and that the GDP growth for April-June, 2017, as per the old method of calculation, might be even less than 3.7 percent, not 5.7 percent as the government data claims.

For the underprivileged and the downtrodden, the 2019 polls will afford a chance to elect Members of Parliament who sympathise with the plight of the masses and, more importantly, do not sell out the poor and the working class to corporate power and lobbyists.

In thinking that a time-span of nearly four decades in the civil service may be of help in making objective and unbiased assessments, I have felt sufficiently encouraged to embark upon this book and wish to avail the occasion to thank the historians, writers and authors whose research and erudition have been of inspiration and guidance to me.

I have profited from the writings of V.P. Menon, Stanley Wolpert, Chaudhri Muhammad Ali, fourth Prime Minister of Pakistan, Prof L.F. Rushbrook Williams, H.M. Seervai, one of India's most eminent jurists, S.S. Gill, Ayesha Jalal, Ramachandra Guha, Saeed Naqvi, Christophe Jaffrelot and Vinay Sitapati, a biographer of P.V. Narasimha Rao, to mention a few.

My purpose in writing the pages that follow would be amply rewarded if public apathy were to shrink somewhat in relation to the issues that have been raised. It is in the cause of those who must, with all their hopes and fears, live out their days as citizens of the Republic of India and in our countless living bravehearts, that I seek a wider readership.

AUGUST 7, 1947

Mohammed Ali Jinnah flew from Delhi to Karachi to become the first Governor-General of Pakistan. As he stepped into the aircraft, the Viceroy's Silver Dakota, he looked back towards the city in which he had fought for, and won Pakistan; he said: 'I suppose this is the last time I'll be looking at Delhi'. As the aircraft taxied out, he said, 'That's the end of that'.

Arriving at Government House, Karachi, as he walked up the steps he made a statement to Lieutenant S.M. Ahsan, the Naval A.D.C, that was remarkable, 'Do you know, I never expected to see Pakistan in my lifetime. We have to be very grateful to God for what we have achieved'.

QUAID-I-AZAM'S BIOGRAPHY BY HECTOR BOLITHO (1954)

PART I

Road to Pakistan

Gandhi-Jinnah Talks, Bombay, September, 1944

We maintain and hold that Muslims and Hindus are two major nations by any definition or test of a nation. We are a nation of a hundred million and, what is more, we are a nation with our own distinctive culture and civilization, language and literature, art and architecture, names and nomenclature, sense of value and proportion, legal laws and moral codes, customs and calendar, history and traditions, aptitudes and ambitions. In short, we have our own distinctive outlook on life. By all canons of international law, we are a nation.

REPLY OF QUAID-I-AZAM M.A. JINNAH
TO MAHATMA GANDHI ON INDIAN MUSLIMS

❖

A HARSH PERCEPTION OF PAKISTAN was once put across by the late J.N. Dixit, a former Foreign Secretary and, later, a National Security Adviser in the Government of India:

> The reason Britain partitioned India was to fragment Hindu areas into political entities and ensure Pakistan's emergence as the largest and most cohesive power in the subcontinent. Pakistan's ultimate aim is to fragment India. The Pakistani invasion of Kashmir in 1948 and subsequent wars are a part of this continuous exercise ... India has not been decisive and surgical in resisting Pakistani subversion ... Pakistan's long-term strategic objective is to ensure that India does not emerge as the most influential power in the South Asian region ... continued questioning of Indian secularism, democracy and constitutional institutions is a deliberate

> attempt to generate friction within India. Pakistani support to secessionist and insurgent forces in Jammu and Kashmir, in Punjab and in the north-eastern states confirms this impression ....

While it has been widely debated as to whether the British played a significant role in bringing about the Partition of 1947, the fact remains that the division amounted to a dismemberment of their Indian Empire – their greatest imperial achievement – which, in turn, created fissures that have led to divisive movements emerging in several parts of a newly-independent subcontinent. In present-day India, the fissures are all too noticeable.

The British political leadership and the colonial officialdom had good reasons to encourage disunity among Hindus and Muslims. The years 1946 and 1947 saw the conclusion of a long-drawn political struggle, but the communal problem was not successfully resolved. The bitterness of this failure marred the savour of Independence.

The Partition was an early but decisive step towards the collapse of the basic parameters of governance throughout the subcontinent.

The decline has continued, although it was less pronounced in the Nehru, Shastri, Indira Gandhi and Narasimha Rao governments, all of the Congress party.

The humiliation that the Pakistan Army suffered in 1971, resulting in the loss of the eastern wing and of some 90,000 of its officers and men who were held as prisoners of war in India left a deep scar on its psyche. Considering also that the Pakistan Army has controlled the country's foreign, nuclear and India policies through either direct military rule or through proxy civil rule, their strategic mission of bleeding India through a thousand cuts carries an element of brutal revenge.

The Pakistan Army recognizes that disparity in the size of the economies and the military makes direct confrontation with India unequal. They, therefore, embarked on a nuclear weaponization programme. In his book, *Eating Grass: The Making of the Pakistan Bomb*, Brigadier Firoz Khan (retired) of the Pakistan Army mentions that 1971 and the never again paradigm that emerged after the defeat in the eastern wing proved pivotal in the decision to build the nuclear bomb.

In analysing Dixit's contentions, those in authority in India at the time would have reflected upon the need for the Indian State to upgrade and augment the efficiency of its instruments of governance and of government's strategy to pursue the relevant objectives. If we want peace with the Islamic

Republic next door, India has to continue proving that she is militarily, economically and diplomatically stronger; only this can convince that country's rulers to abandon their designs for a greater Pakistan which, they think, would be powerful enough to match India in every way.

Partition was not an accident and it became a reality extremely quickly. The concept of Pakistan was employed by M.A. Jinnah as a threat to bring the Congress to the negotiating table on the Hindu-Muslim question. It was not a legal possibility as an offer until April 1947 but was signed and sealed on 3rd June 1947 and delivered by the British Parliament in July 1947.

Attendances of the British Prime Minister in the House of Lords are rare. It happened when Clement Attlee, having steered the Indian Independence Bill through the Commons on July 10, 1947, visited the Lords six days later to hear peers debate the legislation that would end British rule in India.

Speakers in the Lords included the 2nd Baron Sinha of Raipur, Aroon Kumar Sinha, son of Satyendra Prasanno Sinha, the first Lord Sinha[1]. The Earl of Selborne predicted: 'One thing we can be sure of, and that is that there cannot be democracy in India. There was never any hope of democracy in India in the Anglo-Saxon and Scandinavian sense of the term, because the conditions which make democracy possible do not exist'.

There are many who believe that Pakistan is an inevitable resultant of early history and modern needs – a resultant in which British policy was a complicating, not an initiating, factor. In present-day Pakistan, the memory of the past is strong. Many of the leading families trace their descent to soldiers and administrators who came in the train of conquerors through the northern passes; few can forget that until the break-up of the Mughal Empire, Muslims ruled a Hindu country and, but for the British, might have continued in that position. In the erstwhile East Pakistan (now Bangladesh), racially so different, the tradition of Muslim rule remains very much alive, as lately evident in the communal incidents which periodically occur, the ghastly violence in Dhaka and threats even to the Ramakrishna Mission.

The way to better understanding between the Muslims and the British was paved by Sir Syed Ahmed Khan (1817–98) who has been called 'the

---

1 The 1st Baron Sinha (1863–1928) was a legal luminary and the first (and last) Indian to be elevated to the peerage, becoming a member of the House of Lords in 1919. The following year, he was appointed Governor of Bihar and Orissa, again the first Indian to fill such a high rank in the administration of British India.

first Pakistani'. He was assisted by others like Sahibzada Aftab Ahmed Khan who was the Vice Chancellor, Aligarh Muslim University (AMU) between 1924–26; his grandson, Sir Syed Ross Masood, was the Vice Chancellor between 1929–34.

The year 2017 marks the 200th birth centenary of Sir Syed (1817–1898).

For the Muslims, a critical moment was reached when a Delegation led by Sir Sultan Muhammad Shah Aga Khan III (1877–1957), alongwith Nawab Viqar-ul-Mulk (1841–1917), Nawab Salimullah Khan of Dacca (now Dhaka)[2] and other dignitaries petitioned the Viceroy, Lord Minto, at Simla (now Shimla) in 1906 about their political rights and interests. As the head of the Nizari Ismaili Muslims, a sect of Shia Islam, the Aga Khan enjoyed enormous prestige and influence. The separate electorates emanating from the Morley-Minto Reforms of 1909 were a precursor to claiming a separate identity for the Indian Muslims. In the fullness of time, the Aga Khan was to say of Jinnah: '… I am convinced that he was the most remarkable of all the great statesmen that I have known. It puts him on a level with Bismarck'.

The Pakistan connection continued through his son, Prince Aly Khan (1911–60) who was passed over in the succession and was Pakistan's Permanent Representative to the United Nations in the late fifties.

During 1930s and 1940s, the idea of Pakistan entered more deeply into the Muslim consciousness. This was due, in part, to the growing gulf between Hindu and Muslim political ideas and about sharing of the power which the British were steadily handing over. Other forces were also at work. Muslims who were not entirely convinced by what was soon to be termed 'the two nation theory' were, nonetheless, seriously concerned about how they would fare in a future India dominated by a Hindu majority.

In the inter-war years, Mahatma Gandhi progressed towards assuming a predominant role in the Congress, even as Bal Gangadhar Tilak, C.R. Das and Lajpat Rai departed the scene in the decade of the 1920s.

Under Gandhi's leadership, the Congress steadily grew into a party of the masses. A few like Jinnah and Sir Tej Bahadur Sapru, a liberal, were alarmed by his style and the religious idiom employed in his political agitation. But the tide was with Gandhi.

---

2 Nawab Sir Salimullah Khan (1871–1915) was a staunch supporter of the Partition of Bengal. In December 1906, the All India Muslim League (AIML) was officially founded after the All India Mohammedan Educational Conference had met at Ahsan Manzil, the residence of the Dacca Nawab Family.

Before him, Aurobindo Ghose's nationalism was woven around the concept of the mother goddess, Kali, to whom the patriotic poem which became an anthem – 'Vande Mataram' – was dedicated by the celebrated novelist, Bankim Chandra Chattopadhyay. Now, with Gandhi at the helm, a catalytic event was provided by Europe which, in India, took the shape of the Khilafat movement, a struggle launched by Muslim leaders and religious teachers to oppose the abolition of the Turkish Caliphate in the aftermath of World War I. The Movement was radicalized by the Ali brothers, Maulana Shaukat Ali and Maulana Mohammed Ali, and Gandhi saw this as a heaven-sent opportunity to harness Muslims to the cause of Indian Independence. He came out in support of the Khilafat on a platform of Hindu-Muslim solidarity.

Gandhi had launched a campaign of Satyagraha, linked both with the Khilafat movement and with the cause of Swaraj. On April 13, 1919 occurred the massacre of Jallianwala Bagh in Amritsar which did much to alter the course of history. Rabindranath Tagore renounced his knighthood. Soon afterwards, Gandhi suspended the campaign because, he said, the people were not yet ready for satyagraha. However, he continued to mobilize Hindu support for the Khilafat, spearheaded by Maulana Mohammed Ali and Maulana Shaukat Ali – the Ali Brothers – and backed by the Jamiat-ul-Ulema-i-Hind.

In September 1920, the Muslim League met in special session at Calcutta, alongside the Congress, with Jinnah presiding. He denounced the 'outrageous' terms imposed upon Turkey and the plunder of the Ottoman Empire under the guise of Mandates. But he was not ready to go along with non-cooperation and opposed Gandhi who was, however, supported by Shaukat Ali, Fazlul Huq[3] and some other prominent Muslims. If the Muslims were in two minds, so too were the Congress leaders.

The death of Lokmanya Tilak, who had led the movement for 'working the Reforms[4] for what they are worth', left Gandhi in the ascendant. When the Congress met in full session at Nagpur in December 1920 (again alongside the League), a Resolution on non-cooperation was carried by almost unanimous acclaim. In the midst of all this, one man 'stood up to be counted' in opposition – M.A. Jinnah.

At a considerably later date, Jawaharlal Nehru offered his own analysis, as follows:

---

3 A.K. Fazlul Huq (1873-1962) was popularly known as Sher-e-Bangla and was appointed Premier of Bengal in 1937 as head of the Krishak Praja Party (KPP).

4 The Montagu-Chelmsford Reforms of 1919 did not satisfy political demands in India.

> A few old leaders dropped out of the Congress after Calcutta and among these a popular and well-known figure was Mr. M.A. Jinnah … He had been largely responsible in the past for bringing the Muslim League nearer to the Congress. But the new developments in the Congress, non-cooperation and the new constitution which made it more of a mass organization, were thoroughly disapproved of by him. He disagreed on political grounds, but it was not politics in the main that kept him away … Temperamentally, he did not fit in at all with the new Congress. He felt completely out of his element in the Khadi-clad crowd demanding speeches in Hindustani … So he drifted away from the Congress ….

Nehru was not entirely right in his facts – Jinnah remained in the Congress for a few years more. But there is substance in his assessment of Jinnah's early distaste for mass politics.

The divergence between Gandhi and Jinnah was as much in political perception as in moral posture. In 1928, Jinnah said to his friend, Diwan Chaman Lall,[5] that 'if only Gandhi had a touch of Lenin in him, the history of the last few years would have been different'. Much earlier, in 1921, he had written to Gandhi: 'I shudder to contemplate the consequences of your programme'. The consequences were a bitter harvest in the shape of the holocaust of 1947.

In November 1932, in London, the future founder of Pakistan read H.C. Armstrong's biography of Mustafa Kemal Ataturk (1881–1938) entitled *Grey Wolf* and seemed to have found his own reflection in the story of Turkey's great modernist leader. It was all he talked about for a while at home, even to Dina[6] who nicknamed him 'Grey Wolf'[7].

Among others, Hakim Ajmal Khan (1868–1927) and Dr Mukhtar Ahmed (M.A.) Ansari (1880-1936) supported Gandhi in the Khilafat movement; while keeping their links in the Muslim League, they were also aligned with him in the Congress. Both were Chancellors of the Jamia Millia Islamia University.

---

5 Diwan Chaman Lall (1892-1973) was a founder and first General Secretary of the All India Trade Union Congress (AITUC), a Member of the Constituent Assembly and, later, of the Rajya Sabha.

6 Dina Wadia, Jinnah's daughter and only child (born August 15, 1919) who lives in New York. The Chairman, Bombay Dyeing, Nusli Wadia, is her son.

7 Stanley Wolpert: *Jinnah of Pakistan*, OUP, 1984 (p.130).

With Gandhi's call, several disparate struggles found a new legitimacy for their actions. Then suddenly, in February 1922, he ordered suspension of the movement after violence took place at the village of Chauri Chaura in what is today's Uttar Pradesh. He did this without consulting the Congress colleagues or his Muslim partners who had brought out their followers and whose sacrifice was greater, as compared to all other communities.

It was a blunder of Himalayan proportions. Gandhi had gone into a nationwide struggle with little preparation and even less teamwork from his colleagues. In the event, he lost the support of the Muslims who never really trusted him (or the Congress) again. The parting with the Ali brothers was bitter. More fundamentally, it marked a step towards the goal which later found a measure of clarity in the form of the Pakistan Resolution adopted by the All India Muslim League (AIML) at Lahore in 1940.

A few years earlier, Jinnah had returned from Britain to take charge of the League.

The long-term effects of Chauri Chaura were serious, Gandhi had created a viable national platform, bringing together the two disparate 'nations' around an anti-imperialist issue. The British were disturbed and the Viceroy, Lord Reading, seemed inclined to offer negotiations which a moderate leader such as C.R. Das would have been happy to accept. By suspending the movement, Gandhi unilaterally took the pressure off the British. Had this not happened (and with the principle of Home Rule having been conceded in the Montagu-Chelmsford Report of 1918 which formed the basis of the Government of India Act, 1919), India could have secured Home Rule in the mid-twenties and the issue of Partition demolished for good.

An idealist band of young nationalists like Chandrashekhar Azad (1906-31) and Bhagat Singh (1907–31), who were prepared to offer the supreme sacrifice, were alienated from the Congress for good.

Huseyn Shaheed (HS) Suhrawardy, a later day Prime Minister of Pakistan, who, like Subhas Bose, regarded C.R. Das as his political guru, writes:

> The brunt of all elections in Bengal on behalf of the Muslim League had fallen upon me in my capacity as secretary of the Bengal branch of the AIML since 1937. Entering politics in 1920, I became a member of the Bengal Legislative Assembly and joined the Khilafat organization and was the secretary of the Calcutta Khilafat Committee for a number of years. In the initial stages I was loosely associated with the Congress and was the Deputy Mayor of Calcutta with Deshbandhu C.R. Das as Mayor. He

> was the greatest Bengali, may I say Indian, scarcely less in stature than Mahatma Gandhi, I have ever had the good fortune to know. He was endowed with wide vision, he was wholly non-communal, generous to a fault, courageous and capable of unparalleled self-sacrifice. His intellectual attainments and keen insight were of the highest order. As an advocate he commanded fabulous fees which he laid at the feet of his country. Towards the end of his days, he renounced his profession, devoted himself to politics and the service of his country and died a pauper overwhelmed with debts. I believe with many that had he lived he would have been able to guide the destiny of India along channels that would have eliminated the causes of conflict and bitterness, which had bedevilled the relationship between Hindus and Muslims which, for want of a just solution, led to the Partition of India and the creation of Pakistan.[8]

Suhrawardy, in turn, was a mentor of Sheikh Mujibur Rahman who led the Awami League to victory in the elections in the still undivided Pakistan in 1970.

When Sri Aurobindo was acquitted in the Alipore Bomb case in May 1909, C.R. Das was his defence counsel. Sri Aurobindo recalled that he was 'visited' by Swami Vivekananda in the Alipore jail and that '... I was hearing constantly the voice of Vivekananda speaking to me for a fortnight in the jail in my solitary meditation and felt his presence'. Das took no fees in this matter and himself paid about Rs.15,000/- (a princely sum in those days) to defray the expenses. In the following months, Sri Aurobindo chose to pursue the path of a spiritual reformer which took him to Pondicherry, then a French colony, in 1910 and where he passed away forty years later.

The unprecedented gathering at Das' funeral and the depth of emotion of the people who called him 'the uncrowned king of Bengal' prompted Rabindranath Tagore (1861–1941) to pen a couplet that has immortalized the person to whom the words were offered: 'You had brought with yourself a life-without-an end, as you depart you donate the same' [English translation from Bangla].

The revolutionary spirit did not wane with Sri Aurobindo's passage to a spiritual world, in fact it gained fresh energy through the infusion of scores of

8 *Memoirs of Huseyn Shaheed Suhrawardy, with a brief account of his life and work* [Edited by Mohammad H.R. Talukdar, Foreword by Kamal Hossain], Oxford University Press, 2009 (p. 102).

young men and women, extraordinarily brave, in several parts of the country. However, in a Congress (more precisely, Gandhi–Nehru) context, the impact of their patriotism was restricted to the margins.

For many years, Bhagat Singh and his revolutionary compatriots were not alone in being consigned, as it were, to the footnotes of more than one narrative of the freedom struggle. A similar treatment was reserved for innumerable others like Chandrashekhar Azad, Ram Prasad Bismil (1897–1927) and Ashfaquallah Khan (1900–27) of the Hindustan Socialist Republican Association (HSRA) who spearheaded the Kakori Conspiracy, Madan Lal Dhingra (1883–1909), Khudiram Bose (who was under 19 years of age when he was hanged in 1908), the trio of Benoy, Badal and Dinesh, Surya Sen and his associates (Chittagong Armoury Raid) and Bina Das of the Chhatri Sangh, a womens' revolutionary organization in Calcutta, to mention only a few.

Also largely forgotten in the pages of history is the Ghadar Party which was founded in 1913 by Indians in the United States and Canada with the aim of securing India's independence from British rule. A nationalist revolutionary of great intellectual ability, Lala Har Dayal (1884–1939) acknowledged Lala Lajpat Rai as his guru and had connections with Shyamji Krishna Varma (who established India House in London for Indian students and freedom fighters), Vinayak Damodar Savarkar, Madam Bhikaji Cama and Bhai Parmanand of the Arya Samaj. According to Swami Rama Tirtha, Har Dayal[9] was the greatest Hindu who ever came to America, a great sage and saint, whose life mirrored the highest spirituality as his soul reflected the love of the 'Universal Spirit' whom he tried to realize.

During World War I, Rash Behari Bose (1886–1945) became a leading figure of the Ghadar Revolution that attempted to trigger a revolt in India in February 1915. Most of the revolutionaries were arrested but Bose managed to hoodwink the British intelligence and reached Japan.

A very young member of the Party, Kartar Singh Sarabha (1896-1915) was hanged at the Central Jail, Lahore for his role in the Ghadar Conspiracy. His life was of great inspiration to Bhagat Singh. During his trial, the judges were impressed by his courage; he wrote a popular song and it is said that he died singing it:

---

9 Lala Har Dayal (1884-1939) was an acclaimed Indian nationalist revolutionary. A Mathur kayastha of Delhi, he was influenced, among others, by Bhikaji Cama and Veer Savarkar. Quite belatedly, the India Department of Posts issued a Commemorative Stamp in his honour in 1987, as part of the series: 'India's Struggle for Freedom'.

Serving one's country is very difficult,
It is so easy to talk,
Anyone who walked on that path,
Must endure millions of calamities

In the words of the Ghadar Party's founding president, Sohan Singh Bhakna (1870–1968) who served sixteen years of a life sentence: 'We were not Sikhs or Punjabis. Our religion was patriotism'.

Bal Gangadhar Tilak predeceased Das by five years. A study of the relationship between Tilak and Jinnah reveals facets of their personalities about which not enough is known to the historians of modern India. Theirs was a comradeship forged in particularly difficult days of the freedom struggle and it held promise for addressing the Hindu-Muslim question and upholding Indian unity. Jinnah defended Tilak at his trial in 1916 on sedition charges and ultimately secured his acquittal.

Jinnah was part of the group of 'moderates' in the freedom movement who preferred to petition the British to share power with the Indians. Tilak, on the other hand, had started the Ganesh and Shivaji festivals to create a mass base for the movement. The moderates opposed what they perceived as the intrusion of religion in politics, as also Tilak's stand on several social issues. None of this seemed to matter to Jinnah. What mattered to him was Tilak's endeavour to uphold the freedom of the press. He saw in Tilak a relentless campaigner who was firm in his conviction that it was through education and through the press that various sections of opinion could be mobilized to challenge the colonial rule. In this respect, both Lokmanya Tilak and Mahatma Gandhi were among the most effective 'communication strategists' in the struggle for Independence.

After Tilak's death, Jinnah continued to associate closely with political leaders of differing persuasions; had Tilak lived longer, Jinnah may not have had to abandon his hopes of working jointly with Congress to achieve freedom for a united India, but which he was compelled to do after the 1937 elections held under the scheme of provincial autonomy.

As one of the first proponents of Swaraj, Tilak built an alliance with Bipin Chandra Pal and Lala Lajpat Rai and rejected the Gandhian approach of total *ahimsa* (non-violence) in politics. The triumvirate of Lal Bal Pal had no faith in protests in the form of Non-Cooperation with the Raj.

The revolutionary Urdu poet, Maulana Hasrat Mohani, was an ardent admirer of Tilak. His biographer records: '... Once while discussing about their favourites amongst the national leaders, many students named Sir Syed Ahmed Khan as their guide ... some named Dadabhai Naoroji or Surendranath Bannerjee; Mohani, however, mentioned Bal Gangadhar Tilak as his mentor and guide...'.[10]

During the twenties, Jinnah cooperated actively with Malaviya and Lajpat Rai with both of whom he had close personal relations; Lajpat Rai's biographer says:

> It was not only for enlisting Hindu support to the Nehru scheme that Motilal had to lean heavily on Lalaji; for even securing the support of an outstanding Muslim leader like Jinnah ... Lalaji's contribution would be found to outweigh that of any other Congress leader. Lalaji strove for a united stand against the Simon Commission and secured full support from Jinnah .... They had worked together in the pre non-cooperation days and though Jinnah left the Congress when Gandhi came into power, they had once again to work with each other when Lalaji went to the Legislative Assembly and they were often seen discussing things not on the Assembly agenda but the broader aspects of the Hindu-Muslim relationship. They did not always see eye-to-eye and sometimes differed sharply and publicly criticized each other ... but it was always possible to know where the differences lay and to what extent they could work together, the boycott of the Simon Commission being an instance in point. During the Assembly session, Jinnah would frequently walk into Lalaji's room without an appointment and unannounced. Sometimes he would do so several times in the course of the same day. Lalaji visited him likewise and very often they both would rise from a talk and go together to Malaviyaji to continue the discussion. There were no formalities ...[11]

Madan Mohan Malaviya presided over three sessions of the Indian National Congress (Delhi 1918 and 1932 and, Calcutta 1933), Lajpat Rai presided at

---

10 Muzaffar Hanafi: *Hasrat Mohani* (National Book Trust of India, 2004, p. 26),

[Maulana Hasrat Mohani, 1875–1951, created the slogan '*Inquilab Zindabad*' and first used it at a labour rally in Calcutta in 1928. As early as 1921, eight years before the Congress pushed for *purna swaraj*, the Maulana demanded complete freedom – *mukammal azadi* – for India. He wrote romantic poems and professed devotion to Lord Krishna].

11 Feroz Chand: *Lajpat Rai, Life and Work* (Publications Division, Ministry of Information & Broadcasting, 1978).

Calcutta (special session) in 1920 and C.R. Das at Gaya in 1922. Malaviya was also actively associated with the Hindu Mahasabha; he left the Congress in 1934.

Tilak, Lajpat Rai and Malaviya, right-wing nationalists, represented, each in his own way, a Hindu orientation. Their commitment to communal harmony was, however, never in doubt.

A Hindu bent of mind was later in evidence in the Congress in the persona, among others, of Sardar Patel, Dr Rajendra Prasad, Rajarshi P.D. Tandon, Pandit G.B. Pant, Dr Sampurnanand, Lal Bahadur Shastri, K.M. Munshi and Morarji Desai, all steadfast nationalists who received the respect of large sections of the Muslim community.

After C.R. Das fell mortally ill in 1924, Motilal Nehru, as head of the Swarajist faction within Congress, was Gandhi's only competitor for leadership of that organization. In August that year, Gandhi wrote confidentially to Motilal to inform him that he was 'prepared to facilitate your securing the Congress machinery, actually assisting you to do so', claiming 'no interest in anything but promoting a peaceful atmosphere … if you are not prepared to take over the whole of the Congress machinery, I am quite prepared to facilitate your taking over those Provinces where you think you have no difficulty in running it'[12].

Almost as an afterthought, in the same letter, Gandhi named those who had been insistent that he (Gandhi) should become president himself.

In certain quarters, the hostility to Gandhi was not new. It took a serious turn in 1934 when he faced demonstrations in Poona (now Pune) during a tour for the emancipation of *Harijans* (Dalits). Opposition came, for instance, from Periyar E.V. Ramaswamy (1879–1973) who had joined the Congress in the then Madras Presidency in 1919 but resigned in 1925 when he felt that the party was only serving the interests of the Brahmins. In 1939, he became the head of the non-Brahmin Justice Party[13] and, in 1944, he changed its

12 Stanley Wolpert: *Jinnah of Pakistan*, OUP, 1984 (p. 84).

13 The Justice Party (South Indian Liberal Federation) was active in provincial politics. Raja Sir Ramakrishna Ranga Rao (1901–1978) of Bobbili (in present-day Andhra Pradesh) was the Premier in the then Madras Presidency on two occasions between 1932–37 and was succeeded for a few months by Sir Kurma Venkata Reddy Naidu (1875–1947) who was the last from the Justice Party to hold the post. Another senior leader, Sir A. Ramaswamy Mudaliar (1887–1976) was a Member of the Viceroy's Executive Council during World War II and was appointed to Prime Minister Churchill's War Cabinet in 1942.

One of the Justice Party's founder-members, Sir Annepu Parasuramdas Patro, an Oriya, from Ganjam district was a minister and resigned from the Madras Legislative Council when Ganjam district and parts of Vizagapatnam district were officially transferred to Orissa (now Odisha).

name to Dravidan Kazhagam. While continuing the Self-Respect Movement, Periyar was also championing an independent Dravida Nadu.

In his references to Gandhi, he said that, with all his good qualities, the Mahatma '... did not advocate the eradication of the Varnasrama Dharma structure but saw in it a task for the humanisation of society and social change possible within its structure. The consequence of this would be continued high-caste leadership ...'. He found a lieutenant in Conjeevaram Natarajan (C.N.) Annadurai who established his linguistic skills in the first anti-Hindi agitation of 1937–39, launched against the compulsory study of Hindi in schools.

Periyar's impact on Tamil politics remains palpable. A breakaway group, the Dravida Munnetra Kazhagam (DMK) led by Annadurai pulled the carpet from under the Congress and scripted the political empowerment of backward classes. Consequently, one or the other Dravidian party has ruled Tamil Nadu for the last fifty years. On the other hand, Periyar's movement also triggered the de-brahminisation of the Congress and bolstered the chief ministership of K. Kamaraj which commenced in 1954.

The break between Periyar and Annadurai came when Periyar declared August 15, 1947 as a day of mourning. Annadurai was one of the first leaders of post-independence India who did not play a role in the freedom struggle.

Gandhi was the Congress President at the Belgaum Session in 1924 and this was the only time he formally headed the party. He was preceded by Abul Kalam Azad (the youngest President) at the Special Session in Delhi in 1923 and succeeded by Sarojini Naidu (the first Indian woman president) at the Kanpur Session in 1925.

The recommendations of the Motilal Nehru Report were ignored by the British in 1928 but not by the Muslim League. Objecting to the abandonment of the promises for communal representation made in the 1916 Congress–League Pact at Lucknow, the League endorsed Jinnah's Fourteen Points, an alternative constitutional draft. The episode was an important rupture between the shared anti-colonial objectives of both the parties.

Towards the early thirties, the Congress presidency was slowly, but surely, passing on to a younger generation, mainly the Mahatma's direct disciples, once described by Jawaharlal Nehru as 'Us Five', namely, Patel, Rajendra Prasad, Azad, Rajagopalachari (Rajaji) and himself. It was also becoming clear that Nehru was, indeed, the chosen one. One might say that by the stage of Subhas Bose's forced exit in 1939, Gandhi, Nehru and Patel were, the inner ring in Congress' decision-making echelons. The Mahatma's unwavering preference for the younger Nehru may well have had something to do with the constructive role played by Pandit Motilal in facilitating the rapid spread of Gandhi's influence in northern India, in particular the United Provinces.

In an article 'who should wear the crown' in September 1929 in *Young India*, Gandhi wrote: 'Those who know the relation that subsists between Jawaharlal and me, know that his being in the chair is as good as my being in it'. To the Congressmen who still persisted that he take office, Gandhi expressed his inability, saying that his hands were too weak to hold the reins of the Congress.

Gandhi went so far as to intervene in *l'affaire* Syed Hussain (involving Motilal Nehru's older daughter) so as to protect the family name.

Quite early on, Nehru realized that without Gandhi's support he could not achieve power over Congress and without the Congress behind him, he could never rule India. By the late thirties, Nehru began to see Subhas Bose as the one obstacle to his own rise as India's man of destiny. Gandhi was old, sought no office and none of his principal lieutenants, like Patel, Rajaji or Rajendra Prasad, was popular enough.

The break between the two men came after Bose's re-election to the party presidency at the Tripuri Congress in 1939. Bose soon found that he had little support in the Working Committee, twelve of whose members resigned after consulting Gandhi. The resignation of Vallabhbhai Patel and some others was not surprising and Bose took this in his stride. But he did want Nehru, his brother, Sarat Bose, Narendra Deva and JP, the Congress socialists, in a left-wing Working Committee that would call on the country to rise up against the hard-pressed British Government with the demand for complete *Swaraj*. With this in mind, he had been urging Nehru to join forces with him to launch a massive non-cooperation movement.

Given Gandhi's opposition and displeasure (his own presidency nominee was defeated), the road ahead could not be expected to be easy for Bose. In the event, he himself had to quit. While the parting of the ways distanced Nehru from his closest colleagues in the Left, from JP and nearly all of the leading socialists, it was Bose who felt betrayed. Writing bitterly to Nehru, he gave vent to his views:

> Ever since I came out of internment in 1937, I have looked upon you as politically an elder brother and leader and have often sought your advice. When you came back from Europe last year, I went to Allahabad to ask you what lead you would give us ... you put me off by saying that you would consult Gandhiji and then let me know. When we met at Wardha after

> you had seen Gandhiji, you did not tell me anything ... Twelve members resigned. They wrote a straight-forward letter ...But your statement – how shall I describe it? I shall ... simply say that it was unworthy of you ... When a crisis comes, you often do not succeed in making up your mind ... you appear as if you are riding two horses ... I may tell you that since the Presidential election, you have done more to lower me in the estimation of the public than all the twelve ex-members of the Working Committee put together ... In my humble opinion, considering the situation in India and abroad, the one problem – the one duty – before us is to force the issue of Swaraj with the British Government ... You have told me more than once that the idea of an ultimatum does not appeal to you ... I fail to understand what policy you have with regard to our internal politics ... For some time past, I have been urging everybody ... that we must utilize the international situation to India's advantage ... but I could make no impression on you or on Mahatmaji, though a large section of the Indian public approved of my stand ... Another accusation you made ... was that I adopted an entirely passive attitude in the Working Committee ... Would it be wrong to say that usually you monopolised most of the time of the Working Committee? ... To be brutally frank, you sometimes behaved in the Working Committee as a spoilt child and often lost your temper ... Sardar Patel ... had a clever technique for dealing with you ... Let you talk and talk and ... ultimately finish up by asking you to draft their resolution. Once you were allowed to draft the resolution, you would feel happy ... Rarely have I found you sticking to your point till the last ... As a doctrinaire politician you have decided once for all that a Coalition Ministry is a Rightist move ... What is the use of your sitting in Allahabad and uttering words of wisdom which have no relation to reality? ... Regarding Bengal, I am afraid you know practically nothing. During two years of your presidentship, you never cared to tour the province ... We should have ... a [Muslim League] Coalition Ministry ...[14]

Subhas Bose did not possess Nehru's refinement, he did not possess the sure touch of a master of political guile and he made some big mistakes such as in not trying to adjust, howsoever loosely, with Mahatma Gandhi.

---

14 Stanley Wolpert: *Nehru, A Tryst with Destiny*, OUP, 1996 (p. 252-253).

He is known to have accused Nehru in February 1939 as having done more to lower me in the estimation of the public than all the twelve ex-members of the Working Committee put together.

In 1960, the senior socialist leader, Ram Manohar Lohia (1910-67) wrote:

> I am not too sure today that Gandhiji was not to blame in the Subhas affair. Gandhiji ... was, more often than not, on the less radical side in the internal disputes in the Congress Party ... This may have been occasioned by the fact that the more radical person or wing in the Congress was the less pliable in respect of non-violence and other Gandhian beliefs ... I was then neutral because I preferred Gandhiji to Subhas Bose but did not like Gandhiji's men ... I have often wished to give to Subhas Bose after his death what I withheld from him in his life. Subhas Bose was the embodiment of the ... spirit ... we need most in our national life ... His aim was clear, he accepted neither defeat nor the withdrawal of lassitude, and he tried to act in all situations ....[15]

The issue has been raised as to whether Subhas Bose would have stood a better chance of negotiating and settling the Hindu-Muslim question with Jinnah? Considering that the play of the relationship between Gandhi and Nehru on the one hand and Jinnah on the other only worsened over the years, Bose, at any rate, was a Congressman whom Jinnah neither disliked nor distrusted. As the Congress President, Bose met with Jinnah in 1938. Contrary to Nehru's hard-to-understand attitude, Bose was not averse to forming coalition ministries with the League; he was also perceived as carrying forward the political legacy of C.R. Das who commanded great respect with the Muslim leaders of Bengal. His brother, Sarat, and he could certainly have contributed to preventing the eventual division.

As a secularist, Nehru thought that there was no such thing as a minorities' problem in India. He did not have much to tangibly offer to the Muslims; his Mass Contact campaigns in 1937 and 1938 caused such unease in Muslim League circles as to induce Jinnah to launch a counter-offensive. While the U.P. Muslims had personal affection for Nehru whom they considered their friend, an idealist in politics who had been caught in the snare of 'Communalist Hindus', the programme of Muslim Mass Contact was singularly foolish.

15 Ram Manohar Lohia: *Guilty Men of India's Partition* 1960 (p. 98-99).

It was launched to establish direct contact with the Muslim masses without the mediation of Muslim organizations and there was opposition to this within the Congress itself. Muslims raised the cry of 'Islam in Danger', inferring that the Congress was determined to wipe them out. Seized with a fear complex, they gave support to the Muslim League which, Nehru believed, was a reactionary body for safeguarding the vested interests of the Muslim upper classes and the loyalists.

In the provincial elections set for early 1937, the Congress had several advantages over the Muslim League. The first was a pre-existing national organization that was largely Gandhi's work; it stretched right across the country and reached down to the village level. The second was a coherent national programme. At this point, the socialist wing of the Congress was in the ascendant, and a vote for the Congress represented a clear choice for agrarian reform, self-government and inter-communal unity. The League had no such political machinery, much less money and its platform was narrower, being confined to rights for Muslims and a rejection of Congress rule.

Matters did not start well for the Muslim League. Across the eleven provinces of British India, the League formed no governments at all and only had a share in a coalition in Bengal with A.K. Fazlul Huq's Krishak Proja Party. The Congress, however, formed seven ministries. This was bad enough for Jinnah but the outcomes of the individual contests were even more discouraging in that the League had also failed to win anything like a majority of the provincial assembly seats reserved for Muslims. Out of 482, it won only 109, even as the Congress secured all the general seats open to it, plus about 60 of the reserved seats, making a total of 716. On this showing, the League was not only *not* an All India Party, it was not even one with much of an appeal to the Muslims.

A senior British ICS who was the Secretary to the Governor of the United Provinces, Sir Harry Haig, in 1937, was asking: 'What has that fellow Jinnah got to do with U.P. Muslims; who is he in U.P. anyway?'

It remains Jinnah's astonishing feat that within the next eight years or so, all these perceptions were reversed and the weaknesses addressed. During this period, Jinnah turned the Muslim League into a coherent and potent political force that could no longer be excluded from national politics.

Along the way, help first came for Jinnah from an unlikely source, the Congress, who were the clear winners. Jinnah, however, did not accept this and he asked that some League members be brought into the new provincial governments. He was rebuffed; the determination with which the Congress rejected Jinnah's overtures has been traced more to the influence of Nehru than of Gandhi. It is fair to say that a Congress-League coalition, if only in the United Provinces, would have saved the day for the future of the Hindu-Muslim relationship. The almost complete exclusion from political office was a deep shock to the Muslim League, especially after years of power sharing, minority safeguards and coalitions. The stark application of '*first-past-the-post*' elections did not augur well for a bridging of the Hindu Muslim gulf and was seen as yet another display of Congress' arrogance, as exemplified by Nehru's outlook and approach.

In a succinct analysis of the events as they unfolded in 1937, Professor Mohammad Mujeeb[16] writes:

> … I was at home in Lucknow when the draft of the agreement proposed by Maulana Azad on behalf of the Congress was sent to Choudhry Khaliquzzaman. My immediate reaction on reading it was that the Muslim League was being asked to abolish itself. This was an attack not on the persons who wanted to become ministers but on the whole class that had painfully organized itself and was still feeling very shaky. Jawaharlal Nehru made matters still worse by writing to the Muslim League president that there were only two forces in India at that time – British imperialism and Indian nationalism … it was very poor statesmanship that transformed a difference of opinion over a ministerial position or two into a national struggle in which a class (the Nawabs, Rajas, Taluqdars and the Khan Bahadurs) felt that it was fighting for its life.
>
> It would not have shattered Nehru's prestige if, because of him, the Muslims had got one ministerial post more than they were entitled to, and if Khaliquzzaman had been made a minister, the League in U.P. would most probably have dissolved of itself … Khaliquzzaman was not a full member of the (landed) class because he lacked the requisite property qualification. There would have been resentment against his appointment … and he would either have had to resign or to work against the class which it was his ambition to represent and lead ….

16 Professor Mohammad Mujeeb (1902–1985), eminent scholar, educationist and Vice Chancellor, Jamia Millia Islamia, Delhi (1948–1973).

Nehru cleared the path for Khaliquzzaman to become the champion of an insulted and injured community.

The late Raja of Mahmudabad, Mohammad Amir Ahmed Khan (1914–73), was a prominent leader of the Muslim League during the Pakistan Movement and, in 1937, the youngest member of its Working Committee. He believed that '... The idea of a separate Muslim State in India stirred the imagination of the Muslims as nothing else had done before'.

The Raja says that when he became a staunch supporter of Jinnah, he did not realize that before long the League and the Congress would be poles apart and that

> I still thought that the two organizations were like two parts of the same army fighting a common enemy on two fronts. With all my nationalistic tendencies and my association with the Congress and other progressive political workers and leaders, some of whom I personally knew and admired, I might have joined the Congress. But my enthusiasm cooled down when to my great disappointment I found that instead of trying to understand the League politics, Jawaharlal Nehru showed nothing but contempt for the Muslim League and its leader to whom I had given undivided loyalty. The more Nehru spoke contemptuously and violently about the League and Jinnah, the more I disliked the Congress. This feeling was shared by a large number of the Muslims I knew who, but for this, would have shown less antipathy to the Congress. There was a general feeling that Nehru and Jinnah were talking at each other and that there was not much substance to this personal political dialogue.

Sir Muhammad Iqbal (1877–1938), widely known as *Allama Iqbal*, commands admiration in India for his poetry, especially the '*Tarana-e-Hind*', a patriotic song, and his literary achievements; he is commemorated in Pakistan as the ideological founder of the State. Iqbal was elected President of the Muslim League at its Session in Allahabad in December 1930 when he outlined a vision of an independent unit for Muslim – majority provinces in north western India.

Allama Iqbal's verse had a witty side. When Akbar Allahabadi[17] sent a box of the choicest *Langra* mangoes to him in Lahore, Iqbal replied by way of a couplet:

17 Akbar Hussain Rizvi (1846-1921), popularly known as Akbar Allahabadi; is famous for humour and satire in his Urdu poetry.

'Asar hai teri aijaz e masihaee ka ae Akbar
Allahabad se Langra chale, Lahore tak pahunche'

[This, Akbar, is the miracle of your healing powers – like those of Jesus. Langra – the lame-travelled from Allahabad and has reached Lahore]

Gandhi received some initial acclaim from Iqbal but the admiration faded away. The two met at the Amritsar session of the Khilafat Movement in 1919 and, later, during the Second Round Table Conference in London in 1931 where Iqbal was disappointed by, as he perceived it, Gandhi's 'negative stand' on conceding constitutional safeguards to the minorities in India.

According to Iqbal[18] '... The British as a Western people cannot but conceive political reform in India as a systematic process of gradual evolution. Mahatma Gandhi, as an Eastern man, sees in this attitude nothing more than an ill-conceived unwillingness to part with power ...'. In Iqbal's view, the communal issue was the only real problem in India (and not the inherently temporary British colonial rule).

Iqbal's letter of November 29, 1920 to Gandhi declining the offer of Vice-Chancellorship of the Jamia Millia Islamia (then at Aligarh) is instructive:

> ... I regret very much my inability to respond to the call of those for whom I have the highest respect. While I am a strong supporter of National Education. I do not think I possess all the necessary qualifications for the guidance of a University which requires a man who would steer the infant institution through all the struggles and rivalries likely to arise in the earlier stages of its life. And I am, by nature, a peacetime worker ... Situated, as we are, Political Independence must be preceded by Economic Independence and in this respect the Muslims of India are far behind other communities ... Their principal need is not Literature and Philosophy but Technical Education ... I am not an expert on the Shari'a but it is my conviction that in ... the question of education the law of Islam cannot fail to give us a suitable line of action ....[19]

Never close to the Muslim leaders of the Congress, Iqbal was also disillusioned with the politicians of the Muslim League owing to the factional

18 Presidential Address at the Muslim Conference in Lahore, 1932.

19 *Iqbal, an Illustrated Biography* [Iqbal Academy, Pakistan, 2006].

conflicts that plagued the League in the 1920s. He engaged in personal correspondence with Jinnah who, he believed, was the only leader capable of drawing the Indian Muslims to the League and maintaining party unity to confront the British and the Congress.

In a letter to Jinnah in May 1937, Iqbal advised that he must leave behind the 'old League' of the higher classes, or he would forever lose 'the masses who have so far, with good reason, taken no interest in it'. Iqbal urged an appeal to 'the law of Islam' which, upto that point, ran counter to Jinnah's entire career. Within months, Jinnah said at a conference in Allahabad in January 1938: 'I am proud to be a communalist', by which he meant that he was proud to have been fighting for the Muslims of India.

'Leave the Muslims alone,' he warned, directing his words at Jawaharlal Nehru whose Congress Party had members of all the communities in its ranks. Nehru's reply was: 'What does the Muslim League stand for? Does it stand for the Independence of India?' And he himself went on to answer the question: 'It represents a group of Muslims, no doubt highly estimable persons, in the higher regions of the upper-middle classes having no connection with the Muslim masses and few even within the lower-middle classes.' His last sentence was acerbic: 'May I suggest to Mr Jinnah that I come into greater touch with the Muslim masses than most members of the League?'

Jinnah neither forgot these words nor forgave Nehru. He reacted by trying to muster the support of the Muslims in the different provinces. The exclusion of the League from the Congress government in the United Provinces after the 1937 elections had already reaped him a rich harvest. Influential leaders, like Khaliquzzaman, who had worked for an understanding between the Congress and the League, were now firmly with Jinnah; so was Nawabzada Liaquat Ali Khan, who was to become Pakistan's first prime minister. His headgear came to be known as the 'Jinnah cap'; it was distinctively different from the khadi 'Gandhi cap'. Anything different, anything that made him convey a separate identity, was to Jinnah's liking.

With the UP in his bag, Jinnah went to Calcutta where the two Muslim leaders were vying for supremacy. He was able to get Dacca's United Muslim League Party to his side. But Fazlul Huq, the Bengal premier, and his Krishak Proja Party were a hard nut to crack. Huq first joined the League but left it to carve out a separate entity. When he realised that he would lose the government, he joined the League.

Jinnah could not work out the same arrangement in the Punjab where Sir Sikandar Hayat Khan[20], the Premier was too powerful and too strongly entrenched to be taken lightly. His Unionist Party, which had a majority in the Punjab legislature, included Hindus and Sikhs. Jinnah struck a compromise. For Sir Sikandar's acceptance of his leadership, Jinnah gave full autonomy to the Unionist Party. It was a strange arrangement, but it was the price he had to pay.

Even so, Sikandar's successor, the last Unionist premier, Sir Khizar Hayat Khan Tiwana, held out against the Muslim League till as late as March 1947.

In the twenties and thirties, the Congress leadership did not reach out to such eminent Muslims in the Punjab as Sir Mian Muhammad Shafi and Sir Mian Fazl-i-Hussain.

By now an inveterate separatist, Jinnah said in his presidential address to the Lucknow meeting of the Muslim League in 1937 that the Congress provincial governments 'were pursuing a policy which is exclusively Hindu' and that 'the Muslims cannot expect any justice or fair play at their hands'. He declared: 'The present leadership of the Congress, especially during the last 10 years, has been responsible for alienating the Mussalmans of India.'

A year later, he appointed an 'Inquiry Committee' to report on the omissions and commissions of the provincial Congress governments. The Pirpur Report (the head of the Committee was Raja Sayed Muhammad Mehdi of Pirpur in Faizabad district, U.P.) concluded that the Congress failed 'in spite of its oft-repeated resolution of guaranteeing religious and cultural liberty to the various communities, because its actions are not in conformity with its words'. Another Muslim League Committee, in the *Shareef Report*, gave an account of 'atrocities perpetrated by Hindus at various places in Bihar'. While these reports were exaggerated, they, perhaps, reflected the mood of the Hindus at the time. After centuries of subjugation, first by Muslims and then by the British, they might have felt emancipated, even though enjoying only limited self-rule.

Maulana Azad criticized the Pirpur Report in his memoirs 'India Wins Freedom' but he also mentioned the two developments at the time that left a very negative impression about the attitude of the Provincial Congress Committees. Azad speaks of how K.F. Nariman, a Parsi and a leader of the Congress in Bombay, was denied the premiership; the position was given to

20 Sir Sikandar (1892-1942) was the Unionist Premier of the Punjab between 1937-42 and opposed the Quit India Movement. He believed in cooperating with the British to preserve the unity of the Punjab and was well-known to be non-communal in temper and outlook.

B.G. Kher. Similarly, in his view, Dr Syed Mahmud should have been Bihar's first Congress premier but Sri Krishna Sinha was asked to head the government.

Jinnah used the Pirpur and Shareef Reports to highlight the differences between the Hindus and the Muslims and made it appear as though the Congress governments were wreaking vengeance on a 'helpless Muslim minority'.

In the Central Provinces & Berar, an initiative in the field of Elementary Education – the Vidya Mandir Scheme – was taken in 1937 by Ravi Shankar Shukla, Education Minister in the newly-installed Congress ministry who became the Premier in 1938. The new government soon faced criticism regarding the treatment of Muslims whose grievances mainly related to the Education Department and the Vidya Mandir Scheme, alongside complaints over the neglect of Urdu and compulsory participation in the singing of 'Vande Mataram'. This had implications for Hindu-Muslim relations in the province and between the Congress and the Muslim League at an All India level.

After the Congress ministries were formed in 1937, the charges of corruption against the ministers constrained Gandhi to say ' … I would go to the length of giving the whole Congress a decent burial rather than put up with the corruption that is rampant'[21].

By now, Jinnah had fully joined issue with Gandhi and Nehru. When Gandhi wrote to him to ask: 'Are you still the same Mr. Jinnah … the staunchest of nationalists and the hope of both Hindus and Muslims?' he replied: 'Nationalism is not the monopoly of any single individual and, in these days, it is very difficult to define it.'

In response to Nehru's letter of April 16, 1938, saying that 'the Muslim League is an important communal organization … but other organizations, though they might be younger and smaller, cannot be ignored,' Jinnah said: 'Your tone and language display the same arrogance and militant spirit, as if the Congress is the sovereign power. Unless the Congress recognizes the Muslim League on a footing of complete equality and is prepared as such to negotiate for a Hindu-Muslim settlement, we shall have to wait and depend upon our inherent strength.'

With the outbreak of World War II came the resignation of the Congress ministries in October 1939, another 'Himalayan blunder'. This was celebrated by the Muslim League as a 'Day of Deliverance and Thanksgiving'. For the ensuing five years, Congress was in the wilderness and Jinnah had an open field; he was now in a position to state:

21 D.G. Tendulkar, Vol. V, p.94 (his biography of Mahatma Gandhi is in eight volumes).

> Upto the time of the declaration of the war, the Viceroy never thought of me, but of Gandhi and Gandhi alone ... Therefore, when I got this invitation from the Viceroy, along with Mr Gandhi, I wondered ... why I was so suddenly promoted and ... concluded that the answer was the All India Muslim League, whose President I happen to be. I believe that was the worst shock that the Congress High Command received, because it challenged their sole authority to speak on behalf of India.

Soon after the passage of the Pakistan Resolution at Lahore in March 1940, doubts were raised in regard to its impact on the Muslims outside the Muslim – majority areas. These doubts were aired, amongst others, by the Karachi-based Sir Abdullah Haroon (1872–1942) who had organized the Muslim League in Sind and by the Nawab of Chhatari (1888–1982)[22] who wrote to Jinnah in October 1940 that 'even the Lahore Resolution will not solve the problem because the Muslims in the minority provinces will suffer in any case'. Jinnah assured Chhatari that the Resolution made it quite clear that we cannot leave the Muslims in the Hindu provinces to their fate and asked him to come out 'with a definite scheme of his own' which he promised to consider before making a final decision in this regard.

Choudhry Khaliquzzaman, who had seconded the Lahore Resolution (with Jinnah in the chair) stayed on after August 1947 as a Member of the Constituent Assembly of India. His movement to Pakistan displeased the Quaid who was reluctant to even grant an audience. He briefly served as Governor of the then East Bengal in 1953-54; in his memoirs entitled *Pathway to Pakistan* (1961) he said that Jinnah bade farewell to the two-nation theory in his famous speech at Karachi on August 11, 1947.

In that speech to the Pakistan Constituent Assembly, Jinnah said:

> If you change your past and work together in a spirit that every one of you, no matter to what community he belongs, no matter what relations he had with you in the past, no matter what his colour, caste or creed, is first, second and last a citizen of this State with equal rights, privileges and obligations, there will be no end to the progress you will make ... You are free, you are free to go to your temples, you are free to go to your mosques or to any other place of worship in this State of Pakistan. You may belong

22 Nawab Sir Muhammad Ahmed Said Khan of Chhatari; Acting Governor, United Provinces (April-November, 1933) and Premier, United Provinces (April-July, 1937).

> to any religion or caste or creed – that has nothing to do with the business of the State … We are starting with this fundamental principle that we are all citizens and equal citizens of one State … Now, I think we should keep that in front of us as our ideal and you will find that in course of time, Hindus would cease to be Hindus and Muslims would cease to be Muslims, not in the religious sense because that is the personal faith of each individual, but in the political sense as citizens of the State.

Jinnah smothered doubt and dissent, thinking that he would pull off a loose Federation without making concessions in advance of the negotiations. However, when he reached the negotiating table in 1946, the idea of a Federation fell through.

The failure of the Cripps Mission in 1942 – not on the plans for post-war constitutional arrangements but on the powers of the Defence Member of the Viceroy's Executive Council and the status of the Council itself – left the Congress in a limbo. At this juncture, while top leaders such as Patel, Rajendra Prasad and Kripalani had put their faith in the Mahatma, Nehru, C. Rajagopalachari (Rajaji) and Azad were unsure when Gandhi chose the most drastic action one could think of – a final, non-violent movement to make the British Quit India, rather like the Dandi March, his last great effort. He did not seem to recall that the Irwin-Gandhi *Pact* did not concede any of the demands for which the Dandi March was launched in the first place.

It was to save the Pact that Gandhi probably felt constrained in intervening effectively with the Viceroy to seek commutation of the death sentences of Bhagat Singh, Sukhdev and Rajguru. He only sought a postponement and again raised the matter, seemingly under pressure, but perfunctorily. In the event, all three were hanged at Lahore. For this, demonstrations and black flags greeted the Mahatma and Vallabhbhai Patel, the president-elect, at the Karachi Congress in March 1931.

A prominent Congress Muslim, Asaf Ali, who respected Gandhi 'for his saintly life' did not agree with the call of Quit India. He was later to observe: 'Were only Jawaharlal adamant, the disaster could have been staved off. But Jawaharlal succumbed, and Maulana was knocked on the head. The rest of us after that did not count'.

Asaf Ali was included in the Interim Government led by Nehru in September 1946 of which Azad was not a member. Afterwards, he was India's first Ambassador to the United States.

It is correct to say that if outside the Congress only Jinnah [and a few others like Vinayak Damodar (Veer) Savarkar and Syama Prasad Mookerjee of the Hindu Mahasabha and B.R. Ambedkar] could stand up to Gandhi, within it only Nehru could. But Nehru, as Nirad Chaudhuri opined, lacked the mettle. The result was that with Congress leaders in prison. Jinnah could go about, unhindered, in strengthening the League organizationally.

Rajaji was one of the few in the Congress leadership to appreciate the seriousness of the issues put across by the Muslim League. His approach was criticized within the party, so much so that Rajaji had to temporarily leave the Congress, as advised by Gandhi. He did not, therefore, participate in the Quit India Movement and, staying out of prison, devised a proposal – the CR Formula or the Rajaji Formula, as it came to be known – which recognized the Demand for Pakistan, in principle, as a basis of negotiations with the Muslim League.

As early as in December 1923, Lala Lajpat Rai (1865-1928) had been criticized for raising the possibility of a division on religious lines.

After his release from detention at the Aga Khan Palace in Poona (now Pune), Gandhi held talks with Jinnah in Bombay in September 1944 when he brought up the elements of the CR Formula as a means to resolve the deadlock. His efforts could not cut much ice.

The offer of a dialogue was compounded with Gandhi addressing the head of the Muslim League by the title that Jinnah's followers had given him, *Quaid-e-Azam* (or Great Leader). So upset was Abul Kalam Azad when he heard of this that he called the discussions with Jinnah a great political blunder.

Azad wrote: 'When Indian Muslims saw that Gandhiji also addressed Jinnah as Quaid-e-Azam, they felt that he must really be so ... I told my colleagues that Gandhiji was making a great mistake ... Jinnah exploited the situation fully and built up his own position ...'.

The breakdown of the Gandhi-Jinnah talks pleased the Unionists, the Sikhs and the Hindu Mahasabha. Gandhi himself had not expected much from the talks '... so if I return empty-handed, I shall not be disappointed'. But by talking to Jinnah soon after the latter's failure to bring the Unionists to heel and by letting him occupy the dominating position of one who spurns what is offered to him, Gandhi helped Jinnah to recover some of the prestige he had lost in the Punjab.

When Maulana Azad was the Congress President and in jail at the Ahmednagar Fort (alongwith other members of the Working Committee), an initiative was taken by Bhulabhai Desai, a leading lawyer, who led the Congress in the Central Assembly, and Nawabzada Liaquat Ali Khan, the Deputy Leader of the Muslim League in the Assembly, to reach a settlement which came to be known as the Desai-Liaquat Pact of 1945. The idea was to strive for the formation of a coalition government at the Centre based on parity between Hindus and Muslims, simultaneously sidestepping the demand for a separate Pakistan and ending the Quit India movement.

Bhulabhai, a friend of Azad, had the best credentials to negotiate an understanding with the League. It was confirmed by Azad and by the Mahatma's Secretary, Pyarelal, that Gandhi had not only verbally approved the proposals, he had sent written intimation to Bhulabhai in this regard. As the events unfolded, the main Congress leaders forsook Bhulabhai and he was refused a ticket for the ensuing elections. This affected his health. In his *India Wins Freedom* (1959) which is dedicated to Jawaharlal Nehru, Friend and Comrade, Azad writes:

> I visited Bombay … and as usual stayed with Bhulabhai. He was in bed and when I asked him how he felt he was so moved that he began to weep. His deepest regret was that Gandhiji, who knew all the facts, had not defended him against his critics … I described the incident to Gandhiji but I found that by now he had heard so much against Bhulabhai that his heart was turned against him …

Bhulabhai Desai was partial (not unlike a few prominent Congressmen) to the good things of life and shone well in social circles, but he died a deeply dejected person. Before he passed away in May 1946, he had lived his finest hour, as an outstanding defence counsel at the INA trials. While he will be remembered for his extraordinary performance at the trials, his brilliance in the courts and as a indefatigable fighter for India's freedom, it is also true that his effort to address the Congress-League impasse (which had the potential to provide an opening) was very critically viewed in his own Party, including by Sardar Patel.

The Congress leadership faltered.

Jinnah was a person over whom Gandhi had no power; Lord Meghnad Desai writes:

> … Gandhi tried to get under Jinnah's exterior persona by offering to talk in Gujarati, their common language. The shrewd lawyer that Jinnah

> was, he saw the trap and refused ... Jinnah's entire approach had been that a guarantee by anyone in the Congress, including Gandhi, was worthless ...[23]

After the release of the Congress leaders from jail in June 1945, an initiative was taken by Wavell to invite and discuss with them, the Muslim League and the Premiers of the Provinces the way forward to break the constitutional deadlock. The Conference at Simla failed and while Wavell pinned the blame on 'Jinnah's intransigence about Muslim representation and Muslim safeguards', he also added that '... the deeper cause was the real distrust of the Muslims, other than Nationalist Muslims, for the Congress and the Hindus. Their fear that the Congress, by parading its national character and using Muslim dummies will permeate the entire administration of any united India is real, and cannot be dismissed as an obsession of Jinnah ...'.

A British Parliamentary Delegation led by Professor R. Richards of the Labour Party and comprising, among others, Arthur Bottomley (who was later Secretary of State for Commonwealth Relations between 1964–66 in Harold Wilson's Labour Government), Woodrow Wyatt, Godfrey Nicholson, Reginald Sorensen, Krishna Menon's India League comrade and the Earl of Munster was in India in the beginning of 1946 to study the constitutional questions that needed to be resolved. Years later, in 1995, when working with the Indian High Commission in London, I was seated next to Arthur Bottomley (by now a life peer) at a dinner in the House of Lords when he regaled the gathering with accounts of his interactions with Nehru; he told me that he held the Indian Prime Minister in very high esteem and had an autographed picture on the mantelpiece at his London home.

In 1995–96, in London, I was in conversation with the Earl of Listowel, the last Secretary of State for India and Burma and a hereditary Labour peer, at luncheon meetings hosted by the High Commissioner, Dr L.M. Singhvi, at India House. Gentle and warm-hearted, Lord Listowel[24] was then in his early nineties but had a sharp memory. He remembered that after the Labour Party's election victory in 1945, the India Committee of the Cabinet recommended independence for the subcontinent within the lifetime of the Government and that whilst, during the war, Attlee had been careful to represent Churchill's

23 Meghnad Desai: *The Rediscovery of India* (P. 240).

24 William Francis Hare, 5th Earl of Listowel (1906–1997).

conservative views ('very much His Master's Voice'), once Prime Minister himself, he ensured that the Cabinet adopted the liberal recommendations of the Committee he still chaired.

Lord Listowel recalled that Stafford Cripps[25] was the India Committee's most dominant member; it was Cripps, rather than Attlee, who first suggested Mountbatten as Viceroy. Sometime after Lord Wavell had left India, it was Listowel who confirmed to the former Viceroy that the latter had been uncompromising in discussions with Cabinet Ministers and had annoyed them.

Elections on the basis of the Government of India Act, 1935 were spread out over the winter of 1945–46. In this contest, the Muslim League won most of the Muslim seats, 428 out of 482 and all thirty of the reserved seats in the Central Legislative Assembly, seriously denting the Congress' claim to represent all Indians. In the Provincial Assemblies, even as the Congress won the great majority of the non-Muslim seats, the League captured a majority of the Muslim seats, except in the NWFP.

Jinnah was now a mass leader and he asked for a loose Federation, as opposed to the Congress demand of a unitary Constitution.

The Parliamentary Delegation preceded the Cabinet Mission which arrived in March 1946. It was headed by Lord Pethick-Lawrence who had succeeded Leo Amery as Secretary of State for India in Attlee's government but the real leader was Stafford Cripps, a friend of Nehru and of the Congress Party. This could not but be expected to make Jinnah suspicious of him, both in 1942 and in 1946.

Azad[26] remained the Congress President during the war years but now, with freedom in sight, it was Nehru who took over. Sardar Patel had a strong claim. Azad was close to Nehru but in his frank and freely expressed account in *India Wins Freedom* published several years later, he regretted not backing Patel. He might also have felt sorry for himself since the Congress President

---

25 Sir Richard Stafford Cripps, CH, PC, FRS (1889–1952) rejoined the Labour Party in 1945 and served in the Attlee government as President of the Board of Trade and as Chancellor of the Exchequer. He did not succeed in his efforts – the Cripps Mission – to resolve the war time crisis in India, as his proposals were too radical for Churchill and too conservative for the Congress.

26 Maulana Azad, a renowned scholar and Urdu writer, was born in Mecca in 1888. He was in the forefront of the freedom struggle and, as the Congress President, handled the critically important negotiation with the British Cabinet Mission in 1946. His birth anniversary is observed as National Education Day.

would become the country's Prime Minister. However, Azad would have realized that it was no longer politically practicable for a Muslim to occupy that position. In any case, Gandhi had chosen Nehru over Patel.

The memoirs of Asaf Ali, another friend of Nehru, reveal how marginalized Azad felt in the decision-making levels of the Congress: 'Personally I (Asaf Ali) think it is time that merciless self-criticism was undertaken by nationalist Muslims and Hindu Congressmen. Indian Muslims as a bulk are dissatisfied with the policies of the Congress, howsoever well intentioned they may have been ... certain persons (that is Jinnah) and policies are like the red rag to him (Nehru) and the very mention of them sends him into an unreasonable outburst of passion, expressed more in his tense face ... He (Nehru) was frankly not hopeful of any deal with Jinnah who, he thought, was not aware of the world forces and economic developments ... Even in prison, Patel made no secret of his contempt for Congress Muslims ... time and again speaking in a manner ... indicating that Syed Mahmud, I and even Maulana don't come upto their mark ...'.

Nehru, Jinnah, Sardar Baldev Singh and others travelled together to London in December 1946 for a final round of discussions with Prime Minister Attlee and his colleagues; these proved of no avail.

Azad's anxieties could not but extend to the difficulties he foresaw for the Indian Muslims if Partition became a reality. Often at the receiving end of Jinnah's invective (he was called a Congress showboy), Azad continued to proclaim his faith in Hindu-Muslim unity:

> I am proud of being an Indian. I am part of the indivisible unity that is Indian nationality. I am indispensable to this noble edifice and without me this splendid structure is incomplete. I am an essential element, which has gone to build India. I can never surrender this claim.

In his presidential address at the Ramgarh Congress in 1940, Azad spoke vehemently against the two-nation theory and exhorted the Muslims to preserve a united India:

> ... Islam has now as great a claim on the soil of India as Hinduism .... Just as a Hindu can say with pride that he is an Indian and follows Hinduism, so also we can say with equal pride that we are Indians and follow Islam .... The Indian Christian is equally entitled to say with pride that he is an Indian and is following a religion of India, namely, Christianity ....

Strangely enough, B.R. Ambedkar[27], who had foreseen that the creation of a separate nation-state would lead to untold hardship, mass migrations and widespread destruction was not a major participant in the negotiations that were going on. His book *Pakistan or the Partition of India* which appeared in 1940 explicitly discussed the scenario of large-scale human movements across new borders becoming inevitable if a formal division was to be carried out.

In the many writings on Partition, both before and after the event, Ambedkar's warnings have gone largely unnoticed. Totally inadequate preparations were made by the authorities to foresee and forestall the upheaval and the carnage. The Punjab Boundary Force was an unmitigated failure. In point of fact, even the least that should have been done was overtaken by Mountbatten's extreme haste to effect the British withdrawal.

Ambedkar had long been a target of Gandhi's dislike. At the time when the discussions with the Cabinet Mission began, Gandhi is believed to have put across three points to Lord Pethick-Lawrence[28], namely, the release of all detenus, the abolition of salt tax and the removal of Ambedkar from the Viceroy's Executive Council. On 1 August, 1946, he wrote (in Gujarati) to Sardar Patel:

> The main problem is about Ambedkar. I see a risk in coming to any sort of understanding with him, for he has told me in so many words that for him there is no distinction between truth or untruth or between violence and non-violence. He follows one single principle, viz. to adopt any means which will serve his purpose. One has to be very careful indeed when dealing with a man who would become a Christian, a Muslim or Sikh and then be reconverted according to his convenience. There is much more I could write in the same strain.

Ambedkar himself was unsparing in his public attacks on Gandhi whose antipathy, however, was mainly expressed in private.

A major cause of the antipathy arose from the Communal Award announced by Prime Minister Ramsay MacDonald in August 1932 granting separate electorates in British India for the Forward Castes, the Lower Castes,

---

27 Bhimrao Ramji (BR) Ambedkar (1891-1956), popularly known as Baba Saheb, was a front-ranking jurist, economist and social reformer who campaigned against discrimination towards Dalits and is regarded as a principal architect of the Constitution of India.

28 Frederick Pethick-Lawrence, 1st Baron Pethick-Lawrence (1871-1961), Secretary of State for India and Burma (1945-47).

Muslims, Buddhists, Sikhs, Indian Christians, Anglo-Indians, Europeans and the Untouchables (the Depressed Classes) who are today referred to as Dalits. The principle of weightage was also applied.

The Award was criticized by Gandhi (who was in the Yerwada Central Jail, Poona, in the then Bombay province) but welcomed by Ambedkar and by many of the minorities communities. Gandhi's opposition was on the ground that the Award would disintegrate Hindu society. According to Ambedkar, while Gandhi was ready for separate electorates for Muslims and Sikhs, he was against the same for the Depressed Classes. Gandhi commenced a fast-unto-death in the jail from September 20, 1932 which ended four days later through a compromise – the Poona Pact – which envisaged a single Hindu electorate, with the Depressed Classes having seats reserved within it. Electorates for all the other communities remained separate.

The Poona Pact was signed by Pt. Madan Mohan Malaviya, Ambedkar and a few other Dalit leaders.

After the Poona Pact, Ambedkar never trusted Gandhi or the Congress.

In 1945, when Ambedkar was a Member of the Viceroy's Executive Council – the first 'untouchable' to occupy such a coveted position – he authored a severe indictment entitled: *What Congress and Gandhi Have Done to the Untouchables* in which he recalled the 1937 provincial elections (held under the terms of the Poona Pact) and hinted that the Congress had won seats at the expense of his associates; he denounced Gandhi's 1932 fast saying that 'there was nothing noble in the fast'.

Around this time, Ambedkar expressed the opinion that '... if the Mussalmans are bent on having Pakistan then it must be conceded to them'.

An article that was contributed by me in the *Times of India* in 1978 on whether the Partition was avoidable dwelt upon the possibility of an All India Federation for the setting up of which there was provision in the 1935 Act if at least half the Princes, governing at least half of the states' subjects, agreed formally to accede to it. Over the years, much has changed in our understanding and appreciation of events and personalities. India's well-known modern historian, Ramachandra Guha, has written extensively on the subject.

The ruling elite of the Empire had planned for the flourishing of an Indian Dominion to be the surest proof, eventually, of their might and virtue. Writing in the *Daily Mail* in 1930, Winston Churchill offered the view that the Raj was bestowing on India 'health, tranquillity and a ceaseless forward march to civilization ...'.

At the same time, the elite were attaching their names to a series of Reforms and Declarations, each one of which ended up delaying meaningful changes to colonial rule. In the last thirty years (1917–47), the Montague–Chelmsford reforms, to begin with, introduced the prospect of self-governing institutions but did not explain the powers such institutions would have and indicated no timeline as to their gradual development. The 1929 Irwin Declaration promised Dominion Status but without any timeline.

It is a plausible conclusion that the British did not want to leave or even contemplate that option. Having dismissed the idea of Partition as 'silly', even though 'it would be a pity to throw too much cold water on it at the moment', Viceroy Linlithgow was, as late as in 1942, still imagining a future of 'some scheme of government imposed by ourselves with, of course, the inevitable corollary that we shall remain there to hold the balance'.

Lord Linlithgow succeeded Lord Willingdon as Viceroy in March 1936; a Conservative, right of centre, he was convinced that a Federation of the Provinces and the States was the only way a united India could achieve Dominion Status within the British Commonwealth. He tried to push the pace, but was restrained by the Secretary of State for India, Lord Zetland; he also went wrong in setting up a special team of senior members of the Political Service – Sir Arthur Lothian, Sir Francis Wylie and Sir Courtenay Latimer – to explain Federation to the Princes, rather than making the Political Department responsible for selling the proposal to them, through the Residents and Political Agents whom they knew and, more or less, trusted. The approach did not work. Of the eleven Princes Wylie saw, not one was willing to federate.

Another problem was the attitude of the Congress which asked for complete Independence, not Dominion Status. It did not want Federation with the possibility of an alliance between the Princes and Muslims and set terms which it knew the princely order would not accept – no state would be allowed to join that was not run by an elected government and states' representatives in the Federal Assembly would be elected, not appointed by the Rulers. Only in the Rajputana States, where a strong lead was given, did the necessary fifty per cent of the Rulers sign. In retrospect, it would seem that the Princes, properly handled, were not beyond persuasion.

An All India Federation might, if it had come about, been a viable solution. Beginning with a weak Centre dealing with defence, external affairs, communications and currency, the Federation could, over time, have developed into a closer and stronger union with considerable autonomy for the Provinces. More importantly, a Federation structure would have forced the debate and deliberation about minorities' rights and safeguards to proceed along constitutional channels. The Muslim League was still an evolving entity with an elitist core and with the Princes very much on the scene to constrain the politicians, the Federation may have halted the division which eventually came.

A Federation would have afforded a more or less perfect scenario for the British to stay on, to hold the balance. They found themselves bolstering the Muslim League even while abhorring the idea of Partition. Whenever it was expedient, Divide and Rule won the day. The end of the Raj always seemed, as Linlithgow said even in the final years, 'very remote'.

There has been wide discussion in India and abroad about the chance lost with the Cabinet Mission Plan. Maulana Azad was the lone political figure who openly stated that the Congress threw away this last opportunity to have a united India. He remarked that while 'Jawaharlal's mistake of 1937 was bad enough, the mistake of 1946 proved even more costly',[29] an assessment which is entirely correct in terms of human life alone.

The Cabinet Mission had rejected outright Jinnah's demand for Pakistan and, instead, adopted a three-tier zonal scheme with a Federal Centre for Defence, Foreign Affairs and Communications. Included in the Mission's Plan were provisions for the establishment of a Constituent Assembly to work out details and for the immediate formation of a provisional government in New Delhi. In the face of the Cabinet Mission's refusal to countenance an independent Pakistan, the Muslim League accepted the Plan without reservations or conditions, Jinnah, however, making it clear that the acceptance was dictated by the British decision and only as a result of his inability to extract more from the Mission.

The Congress, on the other hand, procrastinated, discussed and hemmed and hawed for several days, despite the efforts of Maulana Azad who sought a compromise with the Muslim League. Even though the Congress Working Committee finally accepted the proposals, approval was hedged round with reservations relating to the formation of the provisional government.

The Mission's Plan had never appealed to Nehru. In the first week of July 1946, he voiced his doubts at Jhansi in the United Provinces; three days later, at a Press Conference, in reply to questions 'whether the

---

29 Maulana Azad: *India Wins Freedom* (Orient Longman, 1959) p. 162.

Congress had accepted the Plan, *in toto*, including the composition of the Interim Government', he said that the Congress would enter the Constituent Assembly 'completely unfettered by agreements and free to meet all situations as they arise'. Pressed further, he emphatically clarified the position with the unambiguous declaration that 'the Congress had agreed only to participate in the Constituent Assembly and regarded itself free to change or modify the Cabinet Mission's Plan as it thought fit.'[30]

These were novel propositions which had not been envisaged by the Cabinet Mission on its departure from India. Maulana Azad was, later, to say that, in his view, Nehru was wrong because the Congress was not free to modify the Plan.

The Congress Working Committee, in a serious dilemma, hastily met to reiterate its original stand but the damage had been done. Now, once again, the whole Muslim question was pushed into the foreground, with the stress laid on the utmost need for an independent Pakistan as the only salvation for the Muslims.

The real issue with the Plan was in respect of how the Constituent Assembly would have framed the Constitution. Unlike the 1935 Act under which an All India Federation could have taken shape by 1938 (if the Princes had fallen in line), Indian politics had been seriously vitiated and communalized by 1946. For the Cabinet Mission Plan to succeed, the Congress would have had to unreservedly enter the realm of power-sharing and Nehru and Patel would have had to give up on their goal of a Congress Raj succeeding the British Raj.

It was feasible for a United India to be preserved, even though the sub-continent would have looked quite unlike what Pakistan, India and Bangladesh are today.

On July 8, 1946, when the Cabinet Mission had left, Wavell apprised King George VI of the work that was done during its stay in India and what he believed were some of the achievements of the Mission. He wrote also about the leading players on the Indian side.[31]

Jinnah is described as

> straighter, more positive and more sincere than most of the Congress leaders ... he is a curious character, a lonely, unhappy, arbitrary,

30 Maulana Azad: *India Wins Freedom* (p. 155).

31 Wavell: *The Viceroy's Journal* (Edited by Sir Penderel Moon, OUP, 1973), Appendix VIII, p. 493-496.

> self-centred man ....The Congress President, Azad ... is a gentleman and stood for good sense and moderation as far as he was able, in spite of poor health and a naturally weak character ... up against Gandhi, he was as a rabbit faced by a stoat .... I have seen much of Nehru and cannot help liking him. He is sincere, intelligent and personally courageous. But he is unbalanced ... and also lacks the political courage to stand up to Gandhi when he knows he is wrong .... Sardar Vallabhbhai Patel is the recognized 'tough' of the Congress Working Committee and by far the most forcible character amongst them. I have a good deal more respect for him than for most of the Congress leaders, and he is probably the only one of them capable of standing upto Gandhi ....The rest of the Congress Working Committee are poor stuff, except possibly one of the younger ones, Mahatab, Premier of Orissa, who is earnest and likeable ....

Following the 'virtual demise' of the Cabinet Mission Plan, an irreversible hardening was in evidence in Jinnah's stand, culminating in the call for Direct Action on August 16, 1946, the day of the 'great Calcutta killings', which left nearly six thousand Hindus dead. A month earlier, Jinnah had, after the Direct Action Resolution was passed, addressed the Muslim League: 'What we have done today is the most historic act in our history. Never have we in the whole history of the League done anything except by constitutional methods .... But now we are obliged and forced into this position. This day we bid goodbye to constitutional methods ... the time has come for the Muslim nation to resort to direct action. I am not prepared to discuss ethics. We have a pistol and are in a position to use it'.

Dr Syama Prasad Mookerjee organized his followers to foil the plan to oust the Hindus from Calcutta.

To Wavell it seemed imperative that the British, before departing, should somehow bring the two opposing sides together in the government so that they fought out their differences in the debating chamber rather than the back-alleys; he felt that he would be abdicating his responsibility if he allowed Congress to form a government and impose its will, so long as there was a remote chance that the Muslim League could be persuaded to cooperate.

For this approach, the Viceroy was accused of being pro-Muslim. Nehru (who had powerful connections in the Labour Party) made sure of pointing out, in successive letters to his friends in Britain, that while Wavell was an honest and sincere man he was a weak man too and had lost all flexibility of mind in his desire to appease Jinnah and the Muslim League. This, according to Nehru, was mainly because of some of the ICS advisers – he termed them the 'English mullahs' - one being Sir Francis Mudie (ICS, UP, 1914), the Governor of Sind in 1946–47. His advisers, Nehru maintained, had succeeded in persuading the Viceroy that no Interim Government should be formed unless the Muslim League came into it.

While there was much substance in the charge that Sir Francis Mudie was anti-Congress and an unwavering supporter of Jinnah and Pakistan, it is, nonetheless, interesting to refer to a letter he wrote, as the British Minister at Belgrade in the then Yugoslavia to Hector Bolitho in August 1953:

> … It is difficult to say why I was fond of Jinnah. He was … cold-at least that was the impression he gave, but I never found him harsh …. His great hold on the Muslims of India was due to his reputation for absolute strength and integrity and any compromise might have been interpreted as a sign of weakness. It might even have been suggested that he had been bought.
>
> I probably knew Jinnah better than any other British officer in India. I was certainly the only British civilian who knew him at all well. I met him first in 1936 when we were both members of the old Legislative Assembly and we started with a most heated controversy … I knew him later again when I was Home Member of the Government of India …. It was then that I got to understand the case for Pakistan, though like most practical administrators in India, I had always preferred the Muslim to the Hindu … his charm was not put on if he liked you … he was naturally charming.
>
> In judging Jinnah, we must remember what he was up against. He had against him not only the wealth and brains of the Hindus, but also of nearly the whole of British officialdom and most of the Home politicians who made the great mistake of refusing to take Pakistan seriously. Never was his position really examined. There was no examination of what the Muslims were afraid of and of whether there was any way to remove their fears, other than the Partition. Instead there was nothing but politics and what looked ... like attempts to trap Jinnah into some difficult position or other ... When he did respond, as he did when the Cabinet Mission came to India, he was rebuffed and drew himself more into his shell ….

Lord Casey (then R.G. Casey[32]) writing of his experiences as Governor of Bengal during World War II remarked that he believed the principal motive behind the demand for Pakistan to be economic, the expression of an urge on the part of the Muslims to advance themselves and to get away from being the hewars of wood and drawers of water for the caste Hindus.

Among those vehemently opposed to Partition till the last was Khan Abdul Ghaffar Khan (1890–1988) of the Khudai Khidmatgar Movement in the NWFP, the Frontier Gandhi, the Mahatma's close friend and staunch ally. His parting words, to his erstwhile colleagues in the Congress, were: 'You have thrown us to the wolves'.

In August 1997, fifty years after the Partition, Felix Bernard (FB) Manley, a former officer of the Indian Police (IP) who was in the thick of the massacres in Lahore and Amritsar (as the Assistant Inspector General of the Punjab Railway Police), remembered:

> The pendulum of death and destruction swung, over a period of many months both before and after 15 August, 1947, across the whole of northern India from Calcutta to Kabul and back again. During those months, death was everywhere: in the towns and cities, in the thousands of villages, on the trains, on the roads. One of my duties in the railway police was to meet refugee trains, usually at Amritsar, coming in from newly created Pakistan.
>
> The carnage on these trains was beyond belief – to men, women and down to the smallest infants. The trains were packed with thousands upon thousands of dead bodies, and many more were strewn along the track sides. The same thing was happening in the opposite direction, where trains taking refugees out of India were, with the connivance of the railway staff, being deliberately derailed so that the passengers could easily be massacred. There was madness in the air that was almost tangible.
>
> In addition, nature took a hand that dreadful summer. During the monsoon there were flash floods in some places which swept away untold thousands of refugees along with their bullock carts and all their possessions.

---

32 Lord Casey (1890–1976), an Australian politician and diplomat, was the Governor of Bengal in 1944-46 and the Governor General of Australia in 1965-69.

> An old Indian Civil Service friend, who stayed on in Pakistan and I were discussing the question of the number of deaths, and he agreed with me that it must have been anything between one and two million, probably closer to two than to one.
>
> It will be many years yet, on both sides of the border, before the bitterness of Partition is forgotten.

Manley (IP, 1939), who passed away in London in January 2010, was one of two British officers who elected to serve in the East Punjab, India, post-1947. He quit in 1964 in protest against political interference and was, later, Bursar, Lawrence School, Sanawar, Himachal Pradesh. His eye-witness account of the Partition killings is poignant in content and accurate in detail.

At least one place in the Punjab, the princely state of Malerkotla, largely escaped the raging communal violence. The then Nawab, Muhammad Iftikhar Ali Khan (1904-82), had Hindu advisers and was respected and listened to by all the communities. Malerkotla had a long history and tradition of Sikh-Muslim amity and was merged with the Patiala and Eastern Punjab States Union (PEPSU) in August 1948.

From Pondicherry in what was then French India, Sri Aurobindo recorded a message for the All India Radio, Trichinopoly on August 15, 1947 saying: 'India today is free but she has not achieved unity ... which was necessary for the greatness of India's future ...' and expressing the hope that Partition would be a 'temporary expedient'.

That Pakistan might not last as a sovereign nation and could collapse under the weight of its own contradictions was an expectation harboured in several circles. To Leonard Mosley, biographer and novelist, Nehru confessed in 1960:

> The truth is that we were tired men, and we were getting on in years too. Few of us could stand the prospect of going to prison again – and if we had stood out for a united India as we wished it, prison obviously awaited us. We saw the fires burning in the Punjab and heard every day of the killings. The plan for partition offered a way out and we took it.
>
> But if Gandhi had told us not to, we would have gone on fighting, and waiting. But we accepted. We expected that partition would be temporary,

> that Pakistan was bound to come back to us. None of us guessed how much the killings and the crisis in Kashmir would embitter relations ....[33]

The uncertainty about Pakistan's future remained after the Quaid-i-Azam's passing in September 1948 and the assassination of Liaquat Ali Khan (the *Quaid-i-Millat*) in October 1951. It was the ninety odd ICS officers, opting for service in Pakistan, who provided an administrative machinery which kept things going in the early years. They were assisted by European civilians who stayed on in Pakistan in numbers higher than in India. Many of the Muslim ICS were from northern India or from the Bengal cadre and formed the core of a new central service called the Pakistan Administrative Service which was later rechristened as the Civil Service of Pakistan (CSP).

The movement of the Muslim ICS towards alignment with the Muslim League and the demand for Pakistan developed gradually. While very few of them had been pro-Congress, neither were they predominantly pro-Muslim League until 1945-46 when Indian politics polarized sharply. By the end of 1946, most ICS Indians in the Central Government were either pro-Congress or pro-Muslim League.

At Partition, three of the four provincial governors in Pakistan were ICS Europeans: Sir Francis Mudie (West Punjab), Sir Frederick Bourne (East Bengal) and Sir George Cunningham (NWFP). In 1950, seven of the top civil servants in Pakistan were still European.

Ironically enough, the Pakistan protagonists in the senior bureaucracy on the eve of the Transfer of Power were led by the Audit and Accounts Service, chiefly Chaudhri Muhammad Ali, a finance officer of exceptional merit and integrity who was appointed the first Secretary General of the Government of Pakistan. The first Finance Minister, Sir Ghulam Muhammad, had his origins in the Railway Accounts branch and served as the third Governor General (1951-55).

Jinnah had appealed to the government services generally and, particularly, to the Muslim ICS and IP to opt for Pakistan. Hailing from Mysore, the brothers, Agha Hilaly and Agha Shahi, had entered the ICS in 1936 and 1943 respectively and were connected with the family of Sir Mirza Ismail, the Diwan (Prime Minister) of the Princely State. Leaving behind considerable properties, they chose Pakistan, joined the Foreign Service and

33 Leonard Mosley: *The Last Days of the British Raj* (Weiderfeld and Nicolson, London, 1961) p. 248.

rose to positions of distinction. Agha Hilaly was the envoy at New Delhi and Washington D.C. and Agha Shahi became the Foreign Secretary in 1973.

Agha Hilaly's son, Zafar Hilaly, a former Pakistan diplomat and ambassador, recalls asking his father why he had not stayed on in India considering that he had twenty-eight houses to lose. His one word answer was 'Jinnah'. Agha Shahi's motivation was the same. Neither regretted the decision.

It was after the first decade or so of Partition, when the heat and dust had begun to settle and the programmes of rehabilitation and resettlement were well in hand, that discussion and debate commenced (and has continued) on the causes that contributed to this great human tragedy.

In later years, Chaudhri Muhammad Ali (1905–80) was to maintain that he had long believed in the idea of Pakistan but it was not until he met Jinnah in 1946 that he let Muslim League politics obtrude into his work as a civil servant. Influenced by Jinnah's personality, he soon became such a partial member of the Finance Department that his chief, Sir Archibald Rowlands, would welcome him with the greeting 'Pakistan Zindabad'.

Muhammad Ali thought that the Congress did not mind Muslims, what they were afraid of were intelligent or able Muslims. The big moment in his life came when the Muslim League had taken up its five places in the Interim Government and Jinnah had signified that while he would take no part in the Cabinet himself, he expected Liaquat Ali Khan to be allocated a portfolio of some consequence. The Viceroy, Lord Wavell, felt that Liaquat should be appointed Home Member. However, Sardar Patel was already the Home Member and he absolutely refused to give up the post; Congress suggested that Liaquat be given the portfolio of Finance Member (or Chancellor of the Exchequer in British parlance).

It was a monumental error for the Congress to have proposed this position for Liaquat. He had little idea of its tactical and strategic importance when he took it but then Chaudhri Muhammad Ali (as the Adviser, Military Finance) stepped in, pointing out that even though the Congress Party, through Nehru, proclaimed its sympathy for Socialism, its financial backing came almost entirely from Hindu millionaires who had made fortunes during the War. Muhammed Ali advised Liaquat that his Budget of 1946–47 should squeeze the rich bankers of the Congress Party. It did more than that. It profoundly changed the attitude of Nehru and Patel to questions of India's future.

Chaudhri Muhammad Ali admired Gandhi, saying that 'he had great subtlety of mind and a lawyer's wiliness behind all that simplicity'.

Sir Chimanlal Harilal Setalvad (recognized by Gandhi as an impartial advocate of great integrity) who served as a member of the Hunter

Commission of Inquiry following the Jallianwala Bagh massacre in 1919 and as Vice-Chancellor of Bombay University was strongly opposed to Partition; sadly, he lived to see its horrors before his death in December 1947. His son, M.C. Setalvad, was the first and longest-serving Attorney General for India (1950-63).

Another legal luminary, Hormasji Maneckji (H.M.) Seervai (1906-1996), a former Advocate General (of Bombay and Maharashtra) and a renowned constitutional expert has analysed[34], with exceptional, skill, the authoritative evidence in the twelve volumes of the Transfer of Power, 1942-47 documents (published by the British Government in the seventies and eighties) to expose and demolish 'the myths and untruths' about the Partition of India.

Seervai cites instances of anger against Gandhi for introducing religion into his politics, such as the resignation of Dr Annie Besant from the Home Rule League (HRL) for reasons of its having become 'intertwined with religion' and of Jinnah leaving the HRL on similar grounds.

In Seervai's view, the Partition became inevitable for, primarily, four reasons viz. (a) Jawaharlal Nehru's refusal in 1937 to honour the Lucknow Pact, which the Congress had signed with the Muslim League in 1916 accepting separate electorates for Muslims, (b) Gandhi's rejection of Jinnah's appeal following the 1937 elections to facilitate an 'honourable' Hindu-Muslim settlement saying that he (Gandhi) saw only an 'impenetrable darkness' on that front, (c) Congress' repudiation of the Desai-Liaquat Ali Pact of 1945 and (d) Congress' rejection of the Cabinet Mission Plan.

He writes that the idea of a separate State did not enter Jinnah's mind till Nehru's renunciation of the Lucknow Pact in 1937. What Jinnah was most apprehensive about was the Hinduisation of India.

The answer as to what made Jinnah, the 'Ambassador of Hindu-Muslim unity', resort to communal politics after 1940 can be read between the lines in Maulana Azad's *India Wins Freedom* where he quotes Jinnah as arguing; 'if the Congress could change so many times while the British were in the country and power had not come to its hands, what assurance would the minorities have that once the British left, the Congress would not again change and go back to the position taken up in Jawaharlal's statement [of 10th July, 1946 rejecting the Cabinet Mission Plan].'

It is Seervai's contention that 'Jinnah's policies must be judged as a reaction to the policies of the Congress and its leaders'.

34 H.M. Seervai: *Partition of India: Legend and Reality.*

The Jury is still out on the Partition of India.

Mountbatten was so piqued with Jinnah for being denied the Joint Governor Generalship of India and Pakistan that he took to settling scores with him on various sensitive issues. Seervai's book is a direct attack on Mountbatten; he lays the blame for the post-Pakistan mayhem, the massacres and the near total failure of the law enforcement machinery squarely at Mountbatten's door. According to Seervai, 'Mountbatten was preoccupied with his own self-image; he lacked the qualities of insight that Lord Wavell possessed'.

Mountbatten was known for his vanity and addiction to pomp and ceremony. Ian Stephens, Editor of the British-owned *The Statesman* between 1942–51, was present when, in July 1947, Mountbatten told journalists that Jinnah had decided to be the Governor General of Pakistan. Stephens recalled that 'his pride ... seemed hurt, though we thought needlessly; how could anyone, however able, function effectively as Governor General of both the new Dominions ...' Mountbatten could not conceal his displeasure. His dislike for Jinnah had commenced; he advised Stephens to abandon plans of publishing his paper from Karachi.

While there was a pro-Pakistan bias with Ian Stephens, he was otherwise wholly independent in outlook and in his analysis of the developments that were taking place. He had disagreed with Sardar Patel on many an issue but he respected the Deputy Prime Minister for being frank and cordial. After a meeting with the Sardar, he noted: 'Five minutes with him [Patel] was, in my experience, worth fifteen with Pandit Nehru'. When Stephens published an advertisement of the Pakistan-occupied-Kashmir (PoK) authorities in *The Statesman*, Patel advised him to return home for good.

Looking back, it may be said that Wavell made a mistake in raising with the British Cabinet, even before he had got out to India, the question of a political move. Sir Evan Jenkins, ICS (Wavell's Private Secretary) recalled R.A.(Rab) Butler's[35] view that the Viceroy-designate 'was wrong in seeking "guidance" from the Cabinet ... the right course was to go to India without settled ideas ...'.

At one stage, Wavell was inclined to Sir Maurice Hallettt's[36] view that for most Muslims, certainly in the U.P., the demand for 'Pakistan' was a 'forceful indication of the strength of Muslim opposition to a Hindu Raj' and that by

35 Rab Butler, later Master of Trinity College, Cambridge, has been called 'the best Prime Minister Britain never had'. In this memoirs, *The Art of the Possible* (1971), he wrote that his main regret was never having been Viceroy of India.

36 Sir Maurice Hallett, ICS, Governor of the United Provinces (1939-45).

screaming for Pakistan Muslims wanted to get 'coalition governments in the provinces and fifty/fifty representation at the Centre'.

Wavell's differences with Attlee's Labour Government were very damaging in their effects. In Churchill's cabinet, Attlee had seldom been helpful to Wavell over India but Wavell appears to have been unaware of this criticism and welcomed the more sympathetic attitude towards India's problems that was becoming apparent in Whitehall. However, the Labour Government through its India-expert, Stafford Cripps were already committed to the Congress point of view and this was the real source of the disharmony that developed.

During the Cabinet Mission, the sentiment in favour of the Congress was ill-concealed. Wavell tried to remain impartial and to hold the balance evenly between the two parties. The line, swallowed by Cripps, was that Wavell was in the hands of the ICS and so, by implication, of anti-Congress advisers. This led to the tactless suggestion that Wavell needed the legal assistance of someone like Sir Maurice Gwyer – a suggestion which Sir Maurice, who had a high opinion of Wavell – dismissed out of hand.

Then there was the antipathy that had developed between Cripps and Wavell; the former is said to have remarked: 'The trouble about Wavell is that he is no politician'.

If the report that Cripps was going to take Pethick-Lawrence's place as the Secretary of State for India had proved true, Wavell would probably have tendered his resignation and Cripps would have been glad to see him go. Wavell more than once told Pethick-Lawrence that if the Cabinet distrusted his judgment and were disinclined to accept his advice, they should replace him. It would have come to him as a shock to discover that Attlee had already approached Mountbatten to take over the Viceroyalty while he was still in London in December 1946.

Whatever the verdicts that history may yet pass on him, Wavell will rank as a leading figure on the British side in the period of World War II. In all the high posts that he filled, he invariably had to battle against heavy odds and without much support from His Majesty's Government. During his tenure as Viceroy, it was he who supplied the driving power in trying to break the deadlock between the Congress and the Muslim League and it was he who prevented a repetition of the Bengal famine.

He was the only soldier to hold the office of Viceroy after the Crown took over control of India from the East India Company in 1958 and he was also one of the few Viceroys to be drawn not from the aristocracy but from an upper middle-class family, the class of society that was the mainstay of the

British Raj and was largely responsible for its character. He typified the best qualities of this class through a deep sense of public duty and public service, complete integrity and the capacity for hard work.

If Wavell had a little luck or if he had been allowed to finish his task, he would have been acclaimed as a great Viceroy, not merely a good one.

Attlee's government rejected Wavell's demand for the fixing of a date for the British withdrawal and decided to replace him in the post of Viceroy, only to find that his successor, Mountbatten, was making the same demand and would not agree to take office unless it was accepted. So Attlee and his Cabinet capitulated, and for some time seemed quite happy to take credit for a decision that had, in fact, been forced upon them.

Wavell was influenced by the recollection that in 1942 when, as Commander-in-Chief, he was trying to secure India against Japanese invasion, Gandhi had unleashed the Quit India movement which had paralysed communications with the Eastern Front. Cripps and Pethick-Lawrence, by the time they left India, had begun to share this mistrust of Gandhi.

The Viceroy had a good opinion of Liaquat Ali Khan and a liking for him which was reciprocated. Although Nehru, without doubt, preferred Mountbatten to Wavell, he publicly stated that he held the latter in high regard. Wavell and Patel respected each other and got on well.

In the end, it was Azad who was left standing virtually alone. A multicultural India had been an article of faith with him. When he saw Nehru abandoning the idea of a united India (to be followed by the Mahatma himself), he was greatly shocked. He told Gandhi: 'If even you have now adopted these views, I see no hope of saving India from catastrophe'.

Azad and Rajaji were the only Congress leaders of the front rank to record appreciation of Wavell's contribution on the eve of his departure. Azad knew that Gandhi and Nehru were against the outgoing Viceroy; now a member of the Interim Government, he said:

> Mr Attlee's statement on India has evoked mixed feelings in my mind … I cannot help a feeling of regret that Lord Wavell, who was the initiator of a new chapter in the history of relations between India and England, is retiring from the scene.

> There was on all hands suspicion and distrust of British intentions at the time of the Simla Conference … but when I met Lord Wavell, I experienced a sudden change of mind. I found him a rugged, straight

> forward soldier ... direct both in approach and statement ... he came straight to the point and created ... an impression of great sincerity which touched my heart ...
>
> I do not know what communications passed between Lord Wavell and H.M.G. in the last two or three weeks. Obviously there were some differences which led to his resignation. We may differ from his appraisement of the situation. But we cannot doubt his sincerity or integrity of purpose. Nor can I forget that the credit for the changed atmosphere in Indo-British relations today must be traced back to the step which he so courageously took in June 1945. To Lord Wavell must belong the credit for opening the closed door. In spite of initial opposition from the Coalition Government, he was able to persuade them to agree to make a new offer to India. The result was the Simla Conference ....

Rajaji in a farewell letter ending 'Yours affectionately', paid tribute to the justice, firmness, patience and ability with which Wavell had worked for an honourable settlement.

Sir Henry (Chips) Channon (1897–1958), a sociable Member of the House of Commons and a Chamberlain supporter, was among Wavell's loyal friends in British political circles. Two days after the former Viceroy's death on May 24, 1950, 'Chips' wrote:

> What a curious man Lord Wavell was ... great in his way, full of humour, a touch deaf, with the power of shutting his mind, or almost all of it, to the assembled company .... He often gave the impression of being dull .... But if he liked somebody or was amused ... the problem was not how to make him talk, but how to stop him .... He was not a politician or a statesman ... as a writer, a friend and a general he was supreme .... His one eye had an uncanny way of seeing through one's weaknesses ... he remained in some ways a simple soldier .... He could do 'The Times' crossword in 20 minutes ... he cordially disliked Winston ... he should have protested against the folly of the Greek campaign ... he should have resigned in India ... he was anti-Munich and really quite silly when he discussed Neville Chamberlain .... I shall always remember him with much affection, and am proud and pleased that so great a man gave me his loving trust.[37]

---

37 *The Diaries of Sir Henry Channon* (Edited by Robert Rhodes James): Phoenix, 2003 (third impression).

The arrival of the Mountbattens in India in February 1947 was, overall, a complicating factor. The new Vicereine (perhaps, the most glamorous India had seen), Edwina Mountbatten, was soon to become – more than her husband – particularly fond of Jawaharlal Nehru and noticeably partial to his charming ways. Such closeness was, inevitably, to result in the Mountbattens being often in a position to influence Nehru's better judgement and, occasionally, cloud his perspective.

Be that as it may, Lady Mountbatten figured in two significant developments in the politics of the day, in 1947. First, her proximity to Nehru ensured that Jinnah decisively reject Lord Mountbatten's candidacy for the Joint Governor Generalship.

Another reason for Jinnah's refusal to accept Mountbatten as the Governor General of Pakistan was that the Quaid had found out about the Viceroy having shown Nehru the then Secret Plan at Simla on May 10, 1947 and that Nehru had been allowed to rewrite it. The Viceroy, it was obvious to all, liked Nehru and, correspondingly, disliked Jinnah.

Secondly, Lady Mountbatten's persuasive intervention with Nehru was instrumental in the Congress accepting a revised Plan for the Transfer of Power which, to begin with, gave only Dominion Status, even though the Congress had for long insisted on Purna Swaraj. She extracted a concession from Nehru that India accept an initial phase of Dominion Status.

Since the Congress was distrusted by the Princes, the acceptance of Dominion Status was of help with the accession of a few, like the Maharaj Rana of Dholpur, who were reassured by the knowledge that the King – Emperor would still remain the King of India.

The British cabinet had given Mountbatten until June 1948 to facilitate agreement between the Indian parties for working together within a single Federation, in other words, to implement the Cabinet Mission Plan. Mountbatten, however, proceeded in virtually the opposite direction and, in such terrific haste, that the actual lines of the Partition in the Punjab and Bengal were drawn, in a matter of five weeks, by a British jurist, Sir Cyril (later Viscount) Radcliffe who had never before set foot on the soil of either Province.

Sir Cyril (1899–1977) chaired the two Boundary Commissions for Punjab and Bengal respectively. The Punjab Boundary Commission had four other members who were judges of the Punjab High Court, namely, Justices Mehr Chand Mahajan and Teja Singh (nominees of the Congress) and Justices Muhammad Munir and Din Mohammed (nominees of the Muslim League). The Bengal Boundary Commission consisted of Justices C.C. Biswas (a later day Law Minister of India), B.K. Mukherji, Abu Saleh Mohammad Akram and S.A. Rahman.

The partition maps which Sir Cyril had managed, against the odds, to draw up were kept, in total secrecy, under lock and key, on Mountbatten's orders, at the Viceroy's House in New Delhi. Had the then British Governors of Punjab (Sir Evan Jenkins) and Bengal (Sir Frederick Burrows) known what to anticipate, they could, with that early knowledge, have saved countless lives by sending troops and trains to the worst-affected areas. But Mountbatten was having none of this; he consciously decided to wait until India's Independence Day festivities were over.

Immediately afterwards, all hell broke loose. The horrors of the tragic impact of the Partition were beginning to emerge with a vengeance.

After the announcement of the Boundary Awards, whose conclusions were welcomed by neither India nor Pakistan, Mountbatten faced criticism for interfering with the decision on Gurdaspur (in Punjab) most of which eventually went to India. The accusation was unfair. As early as in February 1946, Lord Wavell had been working on ideas about what might constitute Pakistan and was advised that Gurdaspur had to be kept with Amritsar. If it were not, Amritsar would be encircled to the east, west and north by Pakistan, rendering the Sikh position untenable. This would have proved a decisive factor in the allocation of Gurdaspur to India, regardless of the road link to Kashmir.

The case of Ferozepur was more contentious. Sir Cyril's Secretary in the Boundary Commission, Christopher Beaumont, believed that the Viceroy, who was under pressure from Nehru and the Maharaja of Bikaner over the question of control of the Ferozepur irrigation headworks, persuaded Radcliffe to redraw the line of Partition to award Ferozepur to India. Although it has been argued that there was a matching concession for Pakistan through the award of the Chittagong Hill Tracts in Bengal, the more credible view is that Chittagong was supposed to make up for Pakistan's loss of a far bigger prize, Calcutta.

Christopher Beaumont[38], who passed away in 2002 was a retired circuit judge and, like many old India hands, he retained a lifelong antipathy to the last Viceroy.

38 Christopher Beaumont joined the Indian Civil Service in 1936, serving as a district officer in the Punjab. Refused permission to join the Armed Forces during the War, he was appointed Radcliffe's private secretary, the day after Radcliffe's own appointment. After India's independence, Beaumont entered the Foreign Service and was posted to Vienna. However, he was soon keen to return home and decided to switch to the law. He was called to the Bar by the Inner Temple in 1951.

Beaumont thought a late-night visit by V.P. Menon was an attempt to ensure that the Ferozepur and Zira salient across the Sutlej would go to India in the Commission's recommendations – which they later did. He believed that the disputed border areas were discussed at a lunch between the Viceroy and Radcliffe from which he (Beaumont) had been deftly excluded. Beaumont was of the view that this brought grave discredit to both Radcliffe and Mountbatten, who was not supposed to have any knowledge of the Boundary Awards.

The Muslim League saw that the Partition of Bengal was meant to sabotage the future East Pakistan; the British (and Mountbatten), perhaps, thought, that if the plan presented to Jinnah was made patently unattractive, he might yet feel compelled to reconsider the whole idea of Pakistan. Jinnah surprised them by accepting Pakistan anyway.

When the authors of Freedom at Midnight[39], Larry Collins and Dominique Lapierre, were writing in the 1970s, the role of Lord Mountbatten as the last Viceroy was yet to be specifically identified as a subject of detailed scrutiny and assessment. On why August 15, 1947 became the date of Independence, Mountbatten, apparently, told them that: 'The date I chose came out of the blue. I was determined to show I was master of the whole event. When they (the press) asked about setting a date, I knew it had to be soon .... I thought it had to be about August or September and I then went to August 15. Why? Because it was the second anniversary of Japan's surrender ....

Briefly put, Mountbatten zeroed in on a date which was to be of vital and far-reaching importance not only for India and Pakistan but also for the British Commonwealth and, indeed, globally, just because it had, two years before, been his hour of glory in the South East Asia Command which had been victorious in a theatre of World War II.

In August 1943 Mountbatten made bold to tell Churchill: 'I have a congenital weakness for feeling certain I can do anything'. Churchill, unfortunately, held a similar view for, in consultation with President Roosevelt, he proposed Mountbatten for the new responsibility of Supreme Allied Commander, South East Asia. It was an appointment that invited derision in the top military circles, such as the opinion of the First Sea Lord, Admiral Cunningham; 'I think most people in the Service have just laughed' and of Field Marshal Alan Brooke, Chief of the Imperial General

39 Larry Collins and Dominique Lapierre: *Freedom at Midnight India: Vikas* (1975).

Staff (CIGS): 'Seldom has a Supreme Commander been more deficient of the main attributes of a Supreme Commander than Dickie Mountbatten'. General Bernard Montgomery agreed with these assessments.[40]

Mountbatten being a cousin of King George VI (who thought well of his abilities and drive) had connections with European royalty. Given his penchant for flamboyance and showmanship and Edwina Mountbatten's vast family inheritance, he made the most of his place in high society. As an Acting Vice Admiral of the Royal Navy (and a substantive Rear Admiral), he had neither the seniority nor the military standing to succeed a Field Marshal as Viceroy. The then Commander-in-Chief, India, Field Marshal Sir Claude Auchinleck, a legend in his lifetime, was made subordinate to him. He had been commissioned in the Punjab Regiment and had been promoted to full general in December 1940.

Auchinleck (1884–1981), one of the great men of World War II, held out against the division of the Indian Army for quite some time. The Indian Army was not divided until six weeks before Partition.

The fact of the matter is that Mountbatten's selection as Viceroy came far too early in the day and he was neither trained nor ready for such an appointment. After India, he next served as commander of the 1st Cruiser Squadron in the Mediterranean Fleet in Malta; having been granted the substantive rank of Vice Admiral in June 1949, he became the second-in-command of that Fleet, going on to be the Fourth Sea Lord at the Admiralty and, finally, the First Sea Lord (an appointment held by his father, Prince Louis of Battenberg during World War I) between 1955–59.

General Hastings Lionel (Pug) Ismay, later 1st Baron Ismay, was Chief of Staff to Viceroy Mountbatten for a few months (March – December, 1947. He was born in Nainital (now Uttarakhand) in 1887 and, after arriving in India soon came to the conclusion that the situation was heading for civil war and that 'India was a ship on fire in mid-ocean with ammunition in her hold'.

Ismay travelled to Kashmir to ask Maharaja Hari Singh to hold an immediate referendum about whether the State would join India or Pakistan. He was not successful; the Maharaja 'changed the subject' each time he tried to discuss the referendum.

In the days following Jammu and Kashmir's accession to India on October 26, 1947, Mountbatten had a volatile meeting with Jinnah about

40 Alex Von Tunzelmann: *Indian Summer, The Secret History of the End of an Empire* (Simon & Schuster, U.K. 2007) p. 128-129.

which he later wrote: 'Jinnah said that this accession had been brought about by violence. I countered this by saying that I entirely agreed that the accession had been brought about by violence; I knew the Maharaja was most anxious to remain independent and nothing, but the terror or violence could have made him accede to either Dominion … the violence had come from tribes for whom Pakistan was responsible …'.

A little earlier, the British High Commissioner in Pakistan, Sir Laurence Grafftey-Smith, had telegraphed to London that India should not accept Kashmir's accession without a plebiscite, but it was too late. Mountbatten and Nehru accepted the accession and Indian troops were flown out to Kashmir.

In late April 1947, Mountbatten sought Jinnah's reaction about Bengal, as a whole, becoming independent rather than joining Pakistan. Jinnah replied: 'I should be delighted. What is the use of Bengal without Calcutta; they had much better remain united and independent and I am sure they would remain on friendly terms with us'. The Muslim League in East Bengal being totally opposed to joining India, what was created, at Partition, was a province (soon to be East Pakistan and, afterwards, Bangladesh) that was incapable of supporting itself. In other words, one half of Pakistan was destined to fail.

Mountbatten was fortunate to have a few experienced 'India hands' on his staff, such as Sir Eric Mieville (1896–1971), a senior British civil servant who had been Assistant Private Secretary (1937–45) to King George VI and, earlier, Secretary to Lord Willingdon, Viceroy of India upto the latter's retirement in 1936. He was now on Mountbatten's staff.

In May, Mieville wired Mountbatten in London: "Jinnah … told me that he thought we were going too fast … I beg you to tell Lord Mountbatten once again that he will be making a grave mistake if he agrees to the partition of Bengal and the Punjab'.

Mountbatten did not respond but informed the India Committee of the Cabinet that he had received word from Governor Burrows of Bengal that Suhrawardy of the Muslim League and Kiran Sankar Roy of the Congress had reached an agreement that would allow them to unite in governing a Free State of Bengal 'which, the Governor felt, was' the only chance of averting grave disturbances. Mountbatten crushed the idea and negatively advised the India Committee that the establishment of a third Dominion would involve further complications and waste time.

A few days later, Mieville also met Nehru and 'I asked him how he viewed … an independent Bengal. He reacted strongly and said that there was no chance of the Hindus there agreeing to put themselves under permanent

Muslim domination, which was what the proposed agreement really amounted to. He did not, however, rule out the possibility of the whole of Bengal joining up with Hindustan'.

The generous praise and adulation that had surrounded the personality of Lord Mountbatten in the last days of the British Raj and the awe it inspired in the public mind had begun to dissipate by the time of his assassination at the hands of Irish terrorists in August 1979. It was more and more felt that he had not been able to deal effectively with the Partition riots and that, all things considered, his tenure had been a less than distinguished one.

Even in a liberal evaluation, Mountbatten's record in India is now seen as very mixed, mainly because, disregarding the counsel of his advisers, he hastened the course of events, unduly and recklessly, in 1947. He was also in a hurry to return to his promising naval career. John Kenneth Galbraith, the U.S. Ambassador to India (1961–63), a friend of Nehru, was harsh in his criticism of Mountbatten.

A part of the truth lies in acknowledging that Mountbatten was really out of his depth. He had the right connections but did not possess a political mind. He was more concerned with the pomp and splendour of the viceroyalty and should have had a better idea of what he was doing.

At a garden party at Anthony Eden's[41] home in London, after Mountbatten was back from India, he walked over to Churchill with arms outstretched. Churchill scowled, saying: 'Dickie, stand there … what you did to us in India was like whipping your riding crop across my face'.

In 1971, journalist Kuldip Nayar (then Resident Editor of The Statesman in New Delhi) interviewed Mountbatten at his English country estate at Broadlands and thought his self-righteousness annoying, as though he had made no mistakes while the others had. Mountbatten said that if he had gone to India when Lord Wavell (his predecessor) did '… I might have succeeded in keeping the country together'[42].

When Kuldip Nayar[43] had a conversation with Viscount Radcliffe, he found him 'very reluctant to talk about Partition and his responsibility …. Regret was written all over his face and he seemed like a person who felt

41 Robert Anthony Eden (1897-1977), 1st Earl of Avon, served three periods as Foreign Secretary in Conservative Party governments and as British Prime Minister from 1955 to 1957.

42 Kuldip Nayar: *Scoop!* (Harper Collins, 2006).

43 Born in 1923 in Sialkot, Punjab, British India; Journalist and Author, Indian High Commissioner in London (1990) and nominated Member of the Rajya Sabha (1997-2003).

that the killings during Partition were still on his conscience'. He told his visitor (Nayar) that the line he drew gave Lahore to India. Then he realized that by doing so, he would deprive Pakistan of any important city. Taking this into consideration, Lahore went to Pakistan. Viscount Radcliffe may have died unaware that the people of the then East Punjab never forgave him for the loss of this prize.

In pre-partition Punjab, the Sikhs were spread all across the provinces with concentrations of population in the western part. They had very important landed interests in the districts of Gujranwala, Sheikhupura, Lyallpur and Montgomery which now form part of Pakistan.

Lahore was then, and still is, the location of many of the religious and historical sites of the Sikhs and the Samadhi of Maharaja Ranjit Singh. The nearby town of Nankana Sahib has nine Gurdwaras and is the birthplace of Guru Nanak Dev. Each of the Gurdwaras are associated with different events in Guru Nanak Dev's life. This is one of the holiest places of pilgrimage for Sikhs worldwide. So is Gurdwara Panja Sahib which is situated at Hasan Abdal, about 50 kms from Rawalpindi in Pakistan.

In 1947, the area around Nankana Sahib was a tehsil of the Sheikhupura district in which there is another famous shrine, the Gurdwara of Sacha Sauda. The Sikhs were particularly attached to the western districts of the Punjab; their presence was a source of annoyance to the Muslims, and a hindrance to their economic supremacy. One need not wonder at the extent of resentment and the desire for revenge displayed by the Sikhs when they were uprooted from the lands they had developed and enriched, and were driven out of their houses.

The British Government had declared that the interests of the Sikh community would receive special consideration in determining the mode of Partition and demarcating the boundary line between India and Pakistan. The district of Sheikhupura was a Muslim majority area but the Sikhs formed a substantial minority comprising 18.85 per cent of the total population. The fears of the non-Muslims in the district were somewhat allayed by the expectation that the Boundary Commission would allot the district to India and they would be permitted to keep their homes and lands. For this reason, no large-scale exodus took place before August 17, 1947 on which date the Award of the Boundary Commission was announced. A stampede for safety then began. The non-Muslims were at a disadvantage, arrangements for evacuation could not be made by the civil administration and the military, no escape was possible and a ruthless campaign of murder, rape, arson and loot was unleashed upon them.

Sheikhupura became a by-word in the months that followed. In West Punjab, the hooligans used it to intimidate the non-Muslims, mainly the Sikhs, into handing over their property, accepting Islam or quitting their houses. 'If you do not do as you are told', they said, 'we shall enact another Sheikhupura here'.[44]

At this time, V.P. Menon offered a suggestion that Jinnah should be approached and persuaded to declare Nankana Sahib, 'a sort of Vatican'. It was a gesture that might have had a calming effect upon the highly emotional Sikhs and one which it would have cost Jinnah little to concede. The Viceroy and his Staff were well aware of what Nankana Sahib meant to the Sikhs.

There is no indication to show that Menon's suggestion was ever acted upon. The Sikhs suffered unspeakable horrors in the rioting in the Punjab.

Some years back, Raja Narendra Singh of Sarila (a small principality in Central India) took up a detailed study of the Partition. An ADC to Lord Mountbatten in 1948, he came across evidence to suggest that Partition may have been connected with the Great Game between Britain and the USSR – for acquiring influence in the area lying between Turkey and India and finding military bases and partners – which seemed likely to re-commence after World War II. Sarila thinks that Britain's Pakistan strategy succeeded brilliantly when the Baghdad Pact (and, later the CENTO) came into being to form a defence barrier against Soviet ambitions in the Middle East.

Sarila (1927–2011) quotes Edward Penderel (EP) Moon[45], a well-known civil servant and historian, who wrote: 'The determination of the Sikhs to preserve their cohesion was the root cause of the violent exchange of populations which took place; it would have operated with like effect even if the division of the Punjab had been put off another year'[46].

He was inducted into the Indian Foreign Service (retiring as the Ambassador to France) and was of the opinion that by the summer of 1947 Britain had neither the troops nor the administrative capacity to stay longer.

When, on the eve of the Transfer of Power, the moment of truth arrived for Princely India, the Rulers in the Chamber of Princes (the Narendra Mandal) – which had been established in 1920 – found themselves largely on

---

44 Justice G.D. Khosla, ICS: *Stern Reckoning, A Survey of the Events Leading Up To and Following the Partition of India*, Chapter Three (originally published in 1950).

45 E.P. Moon (later Sir) was in the ICS; he was serving in Bahawalpur State at Partition and wrote an eye-witness account in 'Divide and Quit'.

46 Narendra Singh Sarila: *The Shadow of the Great Game, The Untold Story Of India's Partition* (Harper Collins, India, 2005) p. 410.

their own. The British Government, having left the matter almost entirely with Viceroy Mountbatten (who was, by now, being advised by V.P. Menon) and with Lord Listowel, the Secretary of State for India, did not wish to intercede, not even for His Exalted Highness Mir Osman Ali Khan Asaf Jah VII, Nizam of Hyderabad and Faithful ally of the British Government. The Chancellor of the Chamber, Nawab Hamidullah Khan of Bhopal, had already resigned to chart his own course.

The best service done by Mountbatten was to arrange the accession of the States to India and to lay to rest the fears of a possible Balkanization of India. He was able to persuade Nehru and Patel of the reality of this lurking danger and successfully pushed for an early Transfer of Power.

In the words of Chaudhri Muhammad Ali, a former Prime Minister of Pakistan:

> ... In the new and tumultuous world of democratic politics and cataclysmic change, the princes felt lost and bewildered. They looked to the Viceroy for guidance and protection. To the traditional loyalty the princes owed to the representative of the British Crown was added the reverence due to a scion of royalty. The Congress leaders turned these sentiments to their advantage ... Mountbatten spoke to the princes as one who was keenly solicitous of their welfare and could perceive, with a superior wisdom, where there true interests lay ... By ceaseless persuasion and remorseless pressure, by friendly advice and viceregal admonition, he led them to accept what was the sure end of their power .... Perhaps, the princes were doomed to extinction anyhow, but that they should have been coaxed and driven to the slaughter house by the shepherd they trusted most is what adds poignancy to the scene ...'[47].

Mountbatten exerted his influence with his friend, the Nawab of Bhopal, to accede to India.

As the Viceroy and Crown Representative, Mountbatten could not, however, render much assistance in securing the accession of the major princely States of Hyderabad and Jammu and Kashmir to the Dominion of India. Even as the latter remains, in a manner of speaking, a continuing saga, the former was integrated with the Indian Union only in September 1948 through a Police Action (codenamed POLO) that was ordered two days after Jinnah's death in Karachi.

---

47 Chaudhri Muhammad Ali: *The Emergence of Pakistan* (Columbia University Press, 1967).

The Mountbattens had left India in June 1948.

The last Nizam of Hyderabad was seeking independence and had also been in contact with the Government of Pakistan. In a gracious move that is attributed to Sardar Patel, he was appointed the Rajpramukh after the merger of the State.

Two recalcitrant Princes, the Maharaja of Jodhpur and the Maharawal of Jaisalmer, were made to see reason by Patel and V.P. Menon.

Defying all logic, the last ruling Nawab of Junagadh (a 13-gun salute State in the Kathiawar Agency), Sir Muhammad Mahabat Khanji III Rasul Khanji (1900–1959) acceded, in September 1947, to the Dominion of Pakistan with whom there was no land border. The majority Hindu population protested and Junagadh was taken over by the Indian Army in November the same year. The Nawab, his family (and his dogs), as also the Prime Minister, Sir Shah Nawaz Bhutto (father of Zulfiqar Ali Bhutto) had already flown off to Karachi.

The Nawab's love of wildlife was instrumental in large tracts of the Gir forest being preserved to provide a stable habitat for the Asiatic lion.

In marked contrast to the spate of accessions to the Dominion of India, no princely State had acceded to Pakistan before August 15, 1947. Ten States, namely, Bahawalpur, Khairpur, Kalat, Las Bela, Kharan and Makran and the Frontier States of Dir, Swat, Amb and Chitral were contiguous to western Pakistan, had a Muslim majority in the population and were ruled by Muslim princes. Their accessions materialized in the succeeding months.

In 1943, at the Delhi Session of the Muslim League, Jinnah, the one-time Ambassador of Hindu-Muslim Unity had said about a possible Pakistan:

> It may come in my lifetime or not. You will remember these words of mine. I say this with no ill-will or offence … millions have killed millions of each other and yet an enemy of today is a friend of tomorrow. That is history ….

> The Partition of India became the final option because of the lack of realistic vision and an absence of imaginative leadership and of superior statesmanship on the part of the top political class in Britain and India alike. The blame can be assigned no more to Jinnah than to Nehru and Mountbatten. Had Churchill not been voted out in 1945, Indian freedom would have been delayed by at least a few years. One is, however, left

> wondering whether Clement Attlee realized, before he himself left office in 1951, what a dreadful mistake he had made in relying on Mountbatten's unsound judgment to bring forward the timetable for the British withdrawal.
>
> In the years to come, the Congress may continue to be accused for handing over Pakistan 'on a platter', as it were. That apart, it is indisputable that an undivided India, with all its early difficulties, would have been a much stronger global entity, on a par with China, and the interminable problems of Partition would not have had to be encountered.

Many Congress leaders liked to think that they chose the lesser evil and that the alternatives to Partition in 1947 were worse. Nor was Partition, in the judgment of these Congressmen, an unmixed evil. The unity of at least two-thirds of India had been preserved and the Congress had not compromised its ideals of secularism and democracy; in fact, it had ensured that these values would find freer play in the Indian Union of the future.

The All India Hindu Mahasabha and the Communist Party of India opposed the division but did not count for a great deal in the political discourse at that time. The entire purpose behind the parting of the ways, on grounds of faith and religion, would have been better served if it had been accompanied by a more complete exchange of populations from both sides. That did not happen and was, in fact, discouraged by the Congress.

When Dr S.A. Latif sent a proposal to Nehru in respect of an exchange of population between Hindu and Muslim 'territorial zones', Nehru described it as fantastic. In reply, Dr Latif wrote prophetically: 'You will have to move towards it, even as you move towards a fatality ... the spectre of Pakistan alone will stare you in the face tomorrow, if today you fail to use your opportunities to frame a constitution for the country agreeable to all.[48]

If Jinnah was working single-mindedly for Pakistan from 1940 onwards, why did he accept the Cabinet Mission Plan in 1946: a Plan which did not concede Pakistan? In April 1946 he had continued to state publicly that Pakistan must be a fully sovereign State, yet the League's own offer a month later to the Cabinet Mission and to the Congress was for a Federation in which the six Muslim provinces were to be grouped together and were to deal with all subjects, except the vital ones of Foreign Affairs, Defence and Communications. According to M.A.H. Ispahani, a member of the League's

48 S.A. Latif: *The Pakistan Issue* (1943).

Working Committee and a prominent Bengal politician, Jinnah welcomed the opportunity afforded to him by what was termed 'Congress deviousness' over the Cabinet Mission Plan to withdraw his own acceptance of the Plan and to reassert the demand for Pakistan.

Gandhi may have felt powerless in the last months of the Raj but he might have attempted to restrain Nehru from pushing Jinnah to a point of no return after the departure of the Cabinet Mission from India.

In 1956, Nehru told Michael Brecher, one of his early biographers:

> ... I suppose it was the compulsion of events and the feeling that we could not get out of that deadlock or morass ... It became worse and worse. Further, a feeling that even if we got freedom for India with that background, it would be a very weak India, that is a federal India with far too much power in the federating units ... Also the fact that we saw no other way of getting our freedom – in the near future ... And so we accepted it and said, let us build up a strong India ... if others do not want to be in it, well how can we and why should we force them to be in it?

The Congress got what it wanted and then complained, for years, that they had been deprived of their goal of a United India. At the end, they did not fight for it, but for exclusive power, giving up the ideal of an undivided India, for Congress Raj.

This was reflected in Mountbatten's appointment as the Dominion of India's first Governor General who delivered a chaotic Independence. He had expected to be the Governor General of both Dominions but Jinnah himself became the Governor General of Pakistan.

From neighbouring Burma (now Myanmar) came an ominous warning: 'A divided India', remarked Aung San, 'augurs ill not only for the Indian people but also for all Asia and world peace'.

The late Aung San was prescient. The calamitous path that India-Pakistan relations have traversed, over the years, has spelt doom for regional security and for the economic and social well-being of the people of the sub-continent. With the Uri attack and the continuing cross-border violence, these relations have hit a new low.

For the present generation, the ties with their across-the-border families are loose. It is more about being part of a network, than a feeling of being family. Says the veteran journalist, Saeed Naqvi: 'In a large measure, the generation who grew up together, or played together, and for whom Partition was a wrench, are gone, or dying'.

About their country's Founder, most scholars of modern history in Pakistan subscribe (or seem inclined) to the view that 'had there been no Mahatma Gandhi, there would still have been Indian Independence; had there been no Lenin or Mao Zedong, the Russian and Chinese revolutions would still have happened, though differently. But had there been no Jinnah there would have been no Pakistan, certainly not in 1947 …'[49].

In a final analysis, the Congress leadership – Nehru and Patel, only weakly resisted by Gandhi, whose overriding authority was becoming a thing of the past – brought the Partition upon themselves. They comprehensively failed to recognize the imperative, or desirability, of a course-correction, even after Pakistan had emerged as a distinct possibility, ahead of the Congress – League negotiations in the final months which Mountbatten should have mediated more patiently and ably.

In post-partition India, the Punjabis have some of their Punjab, the Bengalis still have some Bengal, their languages are spoken and continue to flourish. The Hindu Sindhis, however, have no Sindhi; no part of their ancestral lands exist on this side of the border. That, perhaps, is why Sindhi is not growing as a language.

When C.S.Venkatachar (ICS, UP, 1922)[50] visited Pakistan in November-December 1966, several leaders of that country, including Sir Firoze Khan Noon, a former Prime Minister, Mian Mumtaz Daultana[51] and Choudhry Khaliquzamman did not agree with him (Venkatachar) that a United India would have been a better place to live in for all the communities in the country. All of them talked of Hindi and the threat faced by the Muslim culture in India before 1947.[52]

The state of India-Pakistan relations, past and present, ranks high among the major failures of the foreign policies of both countries.

---

49 Pakistan, Stacey International, London (1977).

50 Venkatachar, a distinguished civil servant, was Secretary to the Ministry of States (after V.P. Menon), Secretary to the President of India and High Commissioner in Canada.

51 Mian Mumtaz Daultana, a close friend of the Quaid-e-Azam and Chief Minister, Punjab (1951-53).

52 Geoffrey Tyson in *Nehru: Years of Power* (1966) quotes Liaquat Ali Khan as saying that the Muslims in the United Provinces feared that Hindi would be imposed on them; that was one of the factors in the creation of Pakistan.

In August 2017 was the 70th Anniversary of the Partition. This could have been an occasion to remember how two Gujaratis – Gandhi and Jinnah – once made history by striving together for Indian Independence. A United India eluded Gandhi. Opposing each other, both witnessed the birth of Pakistan.

The present Prime Minister, Narendra Modi, is not the first Gujarati to be making history.

❖

NEHRU SHOULD HAVE ADDRESSED THE ISSUES OF ADMINISTRATION AND GOVERNANCE IN INDIA

In the mid-thirties, Jawaharlal Nehru was quite sure that 'no new order can be built in India so long as the spirit of the Indian Civil Service pervades our administration and our public services', it being, therefore, essential for the ICS and similar services to disappear completely.

Yet, when the British left and the new government took over, ICS Indians were invited to stay on. As a senior journalist later remarked: 'this would be unbelievable were it not true'.

The ICS tradition not only survived, it prospered. A few weeks before his death in May 1964, Nehru was asked what he considered to be his biggest failure as India's first Prime Minister. He reportedly replied: 'I could not change the administration, it is still a colonial administration'. Nehru then went on to elaborate his belief that the continuation of that colonial administration 'was one of the main causes of India's inability to solve the problem of poverty'. Later, his daughter, Indira Gandhi, had occasion to regret that 'her father had not seized the opportunity to overhaul the administration'.

DAVID C. POTTER: INDIA'S POLITICAL ADMINISTRATORS, 1919–1983
(OXFORD UNIVERSITY PRESS, 1986)

PART II

Prime Ministers of the First Seven Decades (1947-2017)

After making history at Tashkent, Lal Bahadur himself has taken a sudden journey towards the Valley of the Immortal.

C.N. ANNADURAI, DRAVIDA MUNNETRA KAZHAGAM, MADRAS (JANUARY, 1966)

Recalling Shastri's decision for the Indian Army to launch a counter attack and march towards Lahore on September 6, 1965, Lt. General Harbaksh Singh, the then GOC-in-C, Western Command observed: 'The tallest decision was made by the shortest man'.

❖

I BEGIN ON A PERSONAL NOTE.

As a young boy, caught a glimpse of Jawaharlal Nehru when he was on a visit to Bhopal. I was spending my school holidays there. Bhagwan Sahay (ICS, UP, 1928) was the Chief Commissioner and Dr Shankar Dayal Sharma (later President of India, 1992–97), the Chief Minister of the then Part 'C' State of Bhopal. Nehru slowly drove past in an open car and waved to the children.

I saw him at closer quarters on November 14, 1953 at a time when he was, without doubt, the darling of the Indian masses. Accompanying my grandfather[1], a well-known scientist, who was close to Nehru and who was that morning at Teen Murti House to greet Panditji on his birthday, I was then

1 Sir Shanti Swarup Bhatnagar, FRS.

nine years old and was bowled over by the surroundings. What I remember best is that, in my reverie, I succeeded in stepping on the toes of Indira Gandhi who was incharge of all the arrangements. She uttered a fairly audible 'ouch'; but my grandfather, looking back, did not quite fathom as to what exactly had happened. She gave me a forgiving smile.

Nehru took office as the Member for External Affairs and Commonwealth Relations in the Executive Council of the Viceroy, Lord Wavell, in early September 1946. The British Raj was still there. The Viceroy appointed Nehru as Vice President of the new Council, expecting him 'to act when I was absent' and designated it an 'Interim Government'. Before the end of October, Liaquat Ali Khan was sworn in as the Finance Member and four more of Jinnah's nominees took other portfolios in the Interim Government. A few days later, Nehru could not keep an appointment with Wavell. He wrote that he had been under mental strain which had been compounded by the difficulty he felt in daily dealings with 'our new colleagues'. While he also informed the Viceroy that he might decide to resign, a few days later he resolved to stay on.

One of the early difficulties which arose was that Liaquat Ali Khan would not acquiesce in Nehru's position as Vice President of the Council, taking umbrage, for instance, at being invited for a meeting by an official (Tarlok Singh, ICS, Punjab, 1936 who was the Private Secretary) on behalf of Nehru. At no stage could the Interim Government function as a cohesive team; it folded up to become another stepping-stone to the eventual Partition.

Speaking to the students of the Islamia College in Lahore in October 1946, Raja Ghazanfar Ali Khan[2], a Muslim League nominee in the Interim Government, said: 'We are going into the Interim Government to get a foothold to fight for our cherished goal of Pakistan and I assure you that we shall achieve Pakistan'. Perhaps, the point was also being made that once inside the Interim Government, the Muslim Leaguers would try to convince the Congress that no Indian government could function without the cooperation of the League.

In the Muslim League, Jinnah was more powerful than was Nehru in the Congress. His unquestioned authority was on display in the nominations of five League representatives in the Interim Government in 1946 which did not include Nawab Mohammad Ismail Khan of Meerut, a pillar of the Muslim League, or Khwaja Nazimuddin (1894–1964), a former Premier of Bengal.

2 Raja Ghazanfar Ali Khan, also a later-day Pakistan High Commissioner to India (1954-56).

Nawab Ismail Khan (1884–1958)[3] was the grandson of Nawab Mustafa Khan 'Shefta', an accomplished Persian and Urdu poet who was one of Mirza Ghalib's closest friends and associates. He had been in the forefront of the Khilafat Movement and was one of Jinnah's closest advisers. The Nawab presented his cap (which became known as the Jinnah Cap) to the Quaid at Lucknow in 1937. After graduating from St. John's College, Cambridge, and being called to the Bar from the Inner Temple, he was told by his father to train with Pandit Motilal Nehru for a few years and stay in Anand Bhawan, Allahabad.

A politician of independent disposition, he did not hesitate to disagree with Jinnah and once sent in his resignation from the League Working Committee when Jinnah took exception to his correspondence with Jawaharlal Nehru. The matter was settled through the good offices of Liaquat Ali Khan.

After the Partition, Nawab Ismail Khan accepted to become the Vice Chancellor, AMU, for the second time and invited Nehru and Mrs Sarojini Naidu to the Convocations of the University. However, when he sensed that the AMU's interests might suffer on account of his presence, he resigned and returned to Meerut in 1948.

A founding figure of Pakistan, Nawab Ismail Khan lies buried, alongside his preceding generations, in an area earmarked for the family graveyard at the shrine of Hazrat Nizamuddin Aulia in New Delhi.

Unlike his U.P. colleague, Choudhry Khaliquzzaman, Nawab Ismail Khan did not migrate to Pakistan. Two of his sons, G.A. Madani (ICS, UP, 1937) and I.A. Khan (ICS, Bengal, 1939) opted for Pakistan. The older son built a formidable reputation in the eastern wing where an avenue in the Gulshan area of Dhaka was named after him. The younger son was the District Magistrate, Murshidabad, in 1947 and is well-remembered for his involvement with hockey and cricket in Pakistan.

Choudhry Khaliquzzaman's brother, Dr Salimuzzaman Siddiqui, FRS, a well-known scientist who specialized in natural product chemistry, left in 1951 to set up the Pakistan Council of Scientific & Industrial Research.

Khwaja Sir Nazimuddin (1894–1964) of the Dacca Nawab family did not make it to the Interim Government in 1946 but became, after Jinnah, the second Governor-General and, after Liaquat Ali Khan, the second Prime Minister of Pakistan. On the issue of state religion, he said: 'I do not agree that

3 Nawab Ismail Khan's ancestral home, Mustafa Castle, in Meerut was the headquarters of the U.P. Muslim League and a centre of political activity for over four decades.

religion is a private affair of the individual nor do I agree that in an Islamic State every citizen has identical rights, no matter what his caste, creed or faith may be'.

His dismissal as Prime Minister in 1953 by the then Governor General, Ghulam Muhammed, signalled the beginning of a suicidal trend in Pakistan's early political history.

Jinnah named Jogendra Nath (J.N.) Mandal, a Scheduled Caste Hindu, for the Interim Government (he became the Law Member) which upset the Congress who saw this as a challenge to their claim of being the sole representatives of the 'deprived classes'. A Congressman, Jagjivan Ram, was already in the Government and became a particularly long-serving minister at the Centre, whether under Nehru, Shastri, Indira Gandhi or Morarji Desai.

Mandal was the Minister of Law and Labour in Pakistan. He was asked by Jinnah to preside over the Session of the Constituent Assembly when the Quaid was sworn is as the Governor General of Pakistan.

About Mandal, the following is on record:

> On 15th October, Wavell sent the five nominations of the League to London for the King's approval. Pethick-Lawrence[4] replied to him, 'I truly believe that the royal consent cannot be granted unless you declare these names to Nehru. There is a possibility that Congress will take issue with the nomination of an Untouchable, and withdraw from the government. At this stage, the King should not be dragged into this issue ....
>
> After the 3rd June 1947 announcement, Sylhet District was to vote in a plebiscite to join either Pakistan or remain in Assam [the State that was to become part of India]. The Hindus and the Muslims of the district equalled each other in terms of population. However, there were a large number of Untouchables, whose vote could sway the poll to either side.
>
> Following Jinnah's instructions, Mandal arrived in Sylhet to influence the opinion of the Untouchables; when he departed from Sylhet it had voted to join Pakistan.

Mandal (1904–68) had a short stint in the Pakistan government and migrated to India after submitting his resignation on grounds of an anti-Hindu bias in the administration.

---

4 Raja Ghazanfar Ali Khan, also a later-day Pakistan High Commissioner to India (1954-56).

Jinnah made no effort to conceal his disdain for Nehru. Every time a reference was made to the Interim Government, Jinnah would set the record straight by telling Mountbatten: 'You mean the Viceroy's Executive Council? A spade should be called a spade'[5].

After the Partition Plan was formally endorsed by the Congress in early June 1947, Sarat Bose, Kiran Sankar Roy and H.S. Suhrawardy still continued to pursue the possibility of an independent Bengal but encountered the suspicions of Nehru and Patel that Suhrawardy might eventually succeed in getting a United Bengal to join Pakistan.

Jawaharlal Nehru became Prime Minister not because there were no other aspirants or because he enjoyed majority support within the party but because Gandhi declared him his heir.

Patel's loyalty to Gandhi was unquestioned and he accepted Gandhi's appointment of Nehru as the next leader. One of Nehru's biographers, Dr S. Gopal, notes that what forestalled a rupture between Nehru and Patel was mutual regard and Patel's stoic decency.

When a few (muslim) members demanded separate electorates, ostensibly to protect the interests of the minorities, Patel forcefully made his stand clear in the Constituent Assembly, as early as on August 27, 1947:

> The agitation was that 'we are a separate nation, we cannot have either separate electorates or weightage or any other concessions or consideration sufficient for our protection. Therefore, give us a separate State'. We said, "All right, take your separate State". But in the rest of India, in the 80 per cent of India, do you agree that there shall be one nation? Or do you still want the two nations talk to be brought here also? I am against separate electorates. Can you show me one free country where there are separate electorates? If so, I shall be prepared to accept it. But in this unfortunate country if this separate electorate is going to be persisted in, even after the division of the country, woe betide the country; it is not worth living in. If the process that was adopted, which resulted in the separation of the country, is to be repeated, then I say: Those who want that kind of thing have a place in Pakistan, not here. Here, we are building a nation and we are laying the foundations of One Nation, and those who choose to divide again and sow the seeds of disruption will have no place, no quarter, here, and I must say that plainly enough.[6]

5 *Transfer of Power*, Vol.XI (p. 76).

6 Constituent Assembly Report on Debate, August 27, 1947, vide, vol. 5.

In the immediate aftermath of Partition, Nehru wrote to Rajendra Prasad: 'I must confess to you that recent happenings in Punjab and in Delhi have shaken me greatly … shaking my faith in my own people. I could not conceive of the gross brutality and sadistic cruelty that people have indulged in …'.

Gandhi visited the refugee camps around Delhi every day. He felt ashamed, unable to understand how things could go so wrong in Delhi, 'in spite of our Government …'. In September 1947, Nehru was assuring millworkers in Delhi: 'As long as I am at the helm of affairs, India will not become a Hindu State … The very idea of a theocratic State is not only medieval but also stupid …. One can either follow the lead given by Mahatma Gandhi or oppose it. There is no third way open …. India is getting a bad name in countries abroad …'.

It was to take months for a return to any semblance of normalcy in several parts of the country.

Gandhi was devastated by the turn of events. He said to Louis Fischer[7]: 'I am a spent bullet' and to G.D. Birla: 'My voice carries no weight in the Working Committee. I do not like the shape the things are taking, and I cannot speak out'[8].

As C.N. Patel, Deputy Director of the CWMG told the India-born American writer, Ved Mehta: 'Although he imparted to his countrymen, humiliated by their British enslavement, a certain self-confidence and energy, he felt toward the end of his life that he had failed in everything and in a sense he had. Yet, at the same time, he went a long way toward attaining knowledge of God'.

On August 9, 1947, the *Times of India* wrote: 'Mr Gandhi today is a very disappointed man indeed. He has lived to see his followers transgress his dearest doctrines; his countrymen have indulged in a bloody and inhuman fratricidal war; non-violence, khadi and many another of his principles have been swept away by the swift current of politics …'.

The erstwhile princely states of Alwar and Bharatpur in the then Rajputana (bordering Delhi) were the scene of violent attacks on the Muslim Meos, a cultivating class, who fled their homes; an estimated 30,000 Meos are believed to have been killed in the widespread rioting. On the request of a Meo leader, Chaudhary Yasin Khan, who was a member of the Punjab

---

7 Louis Fischer (1896–1970), Jewish – American journalist and author of *The Life of Mahatma Gandhi* (1950).

8 *The Collected Works of Mahatma Gandhi* (CWMG) 84/125.

Legislative Assembly, Gandhi visited the village of Ghasera (since known as Gandhi Gram Ghasera) to convince the Meo refugees on their way to Pakistan not to migrate. About half of them listened and stayed back.

Some eyewitnesses (now in their nineties) still recall the Mahatma's speech in which he said that his word was not as powerful as it used to be;'… if it had been so powerful, not a single Muslim should have found it necessary to migrate to Pakistan … and not a single Hindu or Sikh to leave their homes in Pakistan …'. An academician, Siddique Ahmad 'Meo', author of several books on Mewat, thinks that the Congress leaders, like Sardar Patel, were warned by the Hindu Mahasabha of the dangers of having a large Muslim population close to the national capital. Today, Ghasera (45 kilometers from Gurgaon or Gurugram) is home to about 25,000 inhabitants, mostly Muslim Meos, who are agriculturists, cattle-grazers and vehicle mechanics.

Gandhi and, later, Jawaharlal Nehru, were expected to receive the Nobel Peace Prize. The omission is the more glaring in regard to Gandhi whom the renowned Romain Rolland (himself a Nobel Laureate for Literature in 1915) called 'the greatest Indian after Buddha and the greatest human being after Christ'.

Gandhi was very much in contention for the Award in 1937, but the Nobel Committee (NC) rejected the nomination on the ground that his actions in politics were 'tactical with sly calculations'. He was recommended again in 1938, 1939 and 1947; the NC wanted to award a posthumous Prize when a technical difficulty came up: where would the prize money be sent? Gandhi had left no estate and no testament.

Nehru missed the Peace Prize, rather narrowly, in 1950 (Ralph Bunche, an African American was selected for his late 1940s mediation in Israel) and he was nominated again between 1954-61. The NC documents suggest that, considering the desire of the Norwegian government to award Nehru, the matter would have gone through but for the Kashmir issue, the military action in Goa and the deteriorating Sino-Indian relations.

The Mahatma had been gone nearly two years when, in 1949, Nehru and Patel had a major disagreement over the selection of the first Head of State – the President – of the new Republic which was to come into being within a few weeks. Nehru was clearly of the view that when the governor generalship became a presidency, the incumbent, C. Rajagopalachari (Rajaji), with whom the prime minister had an excellent equation, should stay on. Patel, however, preferred Rajendra Prasad (then chairing the Constituent Assembly) who was close to him and also had wider support within the Congress Party.

Nehru seems to have assured Rajaji that he would be President and was taken aback when Patel put forward Prasad's name instead. Patel's nomination prevailed.

Rajaji did not take the outcome to heart. On the aircraft that flew him to Madras (now Chennai), he wrote to Rajendra Prasad: 'I go out with joy in my heart at the beautiful way in which the little changeover has taken place, God bless you all'. He also complimented Nehru and Patel: 'The Prime Minister and his first colleague, the Deputy Prime Minister, together make a possession which makes India rich in every sense of the term. The former commands universal love, the latter universal confidence …'.

This, however, was not to be the end of Rajaji's political journey. He was soon back as Minister without Portfolio in the Nehru cabinet, eventually becoming the Minister of Home Affairs for about ten months in December 1950 upon Sardar Patel's death. Differences with Nehru persisted after his return to Madras where he served as the Chief Minister between 1952-54; he had not contested the 1952 elections and had been nominated to the Madras Legislative Council by the Governor, Sri Prakasa, a close friend of Nehru from his Cambridge days. Having resigned from the Congress, Rajaji founded the Swatantra Party in 1959, as a right-wing alternative, with significant support from the former princely order, that won 45 Lok Sabha seats in the 1967 general elections and emerged as the single largest opposition party.

A second setback was in store for Nehru when Purushottam Das (P.D.) Tandon was elected the Congress President with Patel's backing. Like Nehru, Tandon hailed from Allahabad and was a personal friend but he was also an orthodox Hindu whose ideas and cultural values did not coincide with those of the prime minister. Much annoyed, Nehru wrote to Rajaji '… all my instincts tell me that I have completely exhausted my utility both in the Congress and Government …. I do not think I can function with any satisfaction to myself in future …'.[9]

Tandon, like Seth Govind Das of Jabalpur, was an unswerving votary of Hindi. After the Sardar's demise, it was only a matter of time before Tandon, under intense pressure, tendered his resignation.

The Patel-loyalist Chief Ministers were no less vulnerable. Hira Lal Shastri of Rajasthan was the first to be axed. Gopi Chand Bhargava of East Punjab was the next to go under presidential rule. Although Ravi Shankar Shukla in Madhya Pradesh, K. Hanumanthaiah in Mysore and Sinha in Bihar

9 Ramachandra Guha: *India after* Gandhi (Picador, 2007) p. 129.

were Patel's men, they were able to survive because they were not, necessarily, anti-Nehru. So steadfast was Hanumanthaiah in his loyalty to the Sardar that he wrote to Tandon: 'So far as Mysore votes are concerned almost to a man they will stand by you .... I also had a discussion with Sardar Patel. I expect you and the Sardar to work unitedly ... to lead us out of the chaos and confusion that Pandit Nehru's leadership has landed us in'[10].

An outcome of Sardar Patel's death in December 1950 was that Nehru was left unchallenged in the Government and the Congress Party transformed, more and more, into a sort of personal fiefdom. In course of time, with the perpetuation of the Nehru-Gandhi family as the leaders of the Party, the Congress became their vehicle to gain political power in successive elections.

Of the last days of his illness in Bombay, the Sardar's devoted Private Secretary, V. Shankar (ICS, Bombay, 1932) records:

> Sardar had received a letter from Pandit Nehru expressing concern about his health and hoping that the change [in Bombay] would do him good. In the letter he also conveyed to Sardar that he would not have to deal with his departmental affairs but that the States Ministry would be looked after by Gopalaswamy Ayyangar and the Home Ministry by himself. Knowing full well that the arrangements would hurt Sardar in the current state of his health with a weakening heart and progressive failure of the kidneys, I decided, in consultation with Maniben[11], not to take the risk of showing him the letter. I am convinced that thereby I prevented Sardar from harbouring the last feelings of anguish and distress at Pandit Nehru's attitude with the possibility of an aggravation of his condition.[12]

Writing on the Sardar's contribution in May 1959, President Rajendra Prasad, observed:

> ... No attempt has been made in Delhi to erect a memorial. Even the portrait in the Parliament House is the gift of a ruling Prince (Gwalior). Let us not, therefore, run away with the thought that his services are any the less valuable because we choose not to recognize them.

10 S.S. Gill: *The Dynasty* (Harper Collins, India, 1996) p. 46.

11 Maniben Patel: *Sardar Patel's daughter.*

12 V. Shankar, *My Reminiscences of Sardar Patel* (Vol.1, Macmillan & Co., 1974).

The President disregarded Nehru's advice when he accepted the invitation to inaugurate the re-constructed Somnath Temple in Saurashtra, the first among the twelve Jyotirlingas.

Some years after the Paul Appleby Reports, an initiative was taken by Prime Minister Lal Bahadur Shastri (1964–66) to review the Indian public administration system and an Administrative Reforms Commission (initially headed by Morarji Desai) was constituted. The Commission recommended the setting up of Lokpal as early as in 1966. Sardar Patel had, much earlier, ensured that the loyalty and commitment of the civil services to the new India remained intact. On the eve of the Transfer of Power, he addressed the first IAS probationers:

> The days of the ICS of the old style are going to be over ... The IAS marks the inauguration of an all-India Service officered entirely by Indians and subject completely to Indian control ... Your predecessors had to serve as agents of an alien rule, and even against their better judgment, had sometimes to execute the biddings of their foreign employers .... A Civil Servant cannot afford to, and must not, take part in politics. Nor must he involve himself in communal wrangles. To depart from the path of rectitude in either of these respects is to debase public service and to lower its dignity.

Many among the Indians in the ICS – the elite service that Nehru and Patel inherited in 1947 – were models of mediocrity with a chip on their shoulder. When Rajaji was asked about his view of the ICS, he replied: '... my experience was that the Englishmen were, on the whole, better than brown people who suffered from an inferiority complex and overdid their arrogance'.

Uptil 1937, Burma (now Myanmar) was a province of British India and had its own share of ICS officers to run the administration. Thereafter, it was a separate Crown Colony.

After Independence in 1948, the government headed by U Nu adopted a novel procedure to utilize the services of the 'ICS remnants' in Burma (about 50 officers or so) which was entirely different from what had been done in India. The Burmese Government retired all ICS officers with proportionate pensionary benefits and re-employed those whom they considered suitable on new pay-scales. In India, the magnitude of the issue was much bigger; the Indian members of the ICS had been assured by Sardar Patel that their conditions of service would be protected.

Nehru was instrumental in the setting up of the States Reorganization Commission (SRC) in 1953 to recommend the redrawing of State boundaries. This step was taken also to determine whether the States should be formed only on a linguistic basis. Earlier, in 1920, the Indian National Congress had agreed on linguistic reorganization as one of the party's political goals. The Provincial Congress Committees were established accordingly. The Congress reaffirmed its stand from time to time, including in the Election Manifesto of 1945-46.

By 1952, the demand for a separate Telugu-majority State had become powerful. The Andhra State was formed in 1953 after a prominent activist supporting the demand had died during a fast-unto-death. The SRC, which comprised Justice Sir Fazl Ali, Sardar Panikkar and Pt. H.N. Kunzru, reported in September 1955 and stated that 'it is neither possible nor desirable to reorganize States on the basis of the single test of either language or culture, but that a balanced approach to the whole problem is necessary in the interest of our national unity'.

Nehru (unlike Indira Gandhi) had an uninterrupted innings as Prime Minister, Some chroniclers have opined that his best years as the 'first servant of the Indian people' were coming to an end around 1955 when the Bandung Conference was held. Over the years, he signified his desire to quit more than once, to begin with, in the lifetime of Deputy Prime Minister Patel with whom the partnership remained uneasy but was also of unique value in the first years of freedom.

In April 1958, Nehru made an attempt to resign as Prime Minister. He said he felt exhausted. Following a long conversation with her father, Indira Gandhi wrote a letter urging him to act on his desire to exit. She advised that since Nehru had publicly raised the issue of resignation 'is it wise to go back to the status quo? … Let them try to manage by themselves, otherwise they will drag you down with their own rottenness. If you are outside, it may at least reassure the general public that you were not responsible for all the wrongdoing …'.

Indira Gandhi did not want her father to be tainted by the corruption that was increasingly in evidence. She might even have felt that he needed to be protected from it. Here, she underestimated him because, while Nehru was occasionally a poor judge of men and character, he was politically very astute.

Nehru's image was tarnished by the single act of dismissal of the Kerala government in 1959; it was a blot on his prime ministership.

On the eve of Indira Gandhi's birth anniversary on November 17, 2016, a biography of her estranged husband, authored by a Swedish journalist:

Feroze: The Forgotten Gandhi revealed Feroze's outburst in 1959 after the Nehru administration had dismissed the Communist Government led by E.M.S. Namboodiripad in Kerala. Indira Gandhi was the Congress President that year and had, apparently, forced Nehru's hand.

The author of the biography, Birtil Falk, records that the subject came up at breakfast in Teen Murti House, the Prime Minister's residence, when Feroze Gandhi said: 'It is just not right. You are bullying people. You are a fascist'. Nehru looked distressed, but an angry Indira retorted: 'You are calling me a fascist? I can't take that', and stormed out of the room.

According to Falk, Indira thought Nehru *weak and indecisive* which he may well have been by the close of the fifties. Falk quotes from a letter Indira Gandhi wrote her American friend, Dorothy Norman: 'He (Nehru) has given a very good lead from the beginning but he is incapable of ... rough shodding over the views of his senior colleagues'.

When the time seemed more than ripe for Nehru to step down, following the disaster of the India-China war and when his health was in steady decline, he preferred to sally forth, like any other politician, to introduce the Kamaraj Plan, his continuance at the apex being, apparently, of great importance to him. As Stanley Wolpert, one of Nehru's more sympathetic biographers records:[13]

> The original plan was for Kamaraj (Chief Minister of Madras) and a few other chief ministers, primarily Biju Patnaik of Orissa, to announce their resignations to return to their grass roots to revitalize enthusiasm and support for Congress among the common people and help lift the sagging morale of the nation. But if that would work in the provinces, why not try the same thing at the center? So Nehru called his senior cabinet ministers to meet with Kamaraj and announced that he considered this so good an idea that he was inspired by Kamaraj's example to submit his own resignation, in order to go back to private work at his Allahabad roots.

'When he said this', Morarji recalled, 'Kamaraj and two or three other colleagues said that that was an impossible proposition .... Jawaharlalji did not need much persuasion to give up his suggestion.' Home Minister Lal Bahadur Shastri, who was famed for his loyalty to Nehru and may well have been his decoy elephant, then offered his resignation, and immediately told Morarji about it. 'I suspected that some game was being played behind the scenes',

13 Stanley Wolpert: *Nehru, A Tryst with Destiny* (OUP, 1996).

Morarji reflected, but by then he had been a minister for two decades and submitted his letter of resignation, which Nehru quickly accepted. Morarji later charged that there had been an understanding between Nehru and Shastri to bring the latter back into the Cabinet after a few months. Shastri was, indeed, appointed Minister without Portfolio early in 1964, shortly before Nehru died.

It is interesting to note that the second Prime Minister of Jammu and Kashmir, post-1947, Bakshi Ghulam Mohammad, was persuaded, after eleven years in office, to offer a token resignation under the Kamaraj Plan to strengthen Nehru's hand even though he did not belong to the Congress. In a move that typified the strange relationship between New Delhi and J&K, Bakshi's resignation was accepted alongwith those of six Union Ministers and five Chief Ministers.

With the exception of Subhas Bose, Nehru was ahead of his contemporaries in perceiving the necessity of planning for the economic and social reconstruction of India. In his picture of the future, he gave the first place to industry, science and technology. He thought that these together would have decisive influence in changing social structure and social attitudes; perhaps, he under-estimated the extent to which scientific and technological progress itself depended upon social and structural changes. He looked to the processes of democracy to create pressures for social change and was confident that, through planning under democracy, it would become possible to counter the pulls in favour of an acquisitive society.

More than fifty years after his passing, through all the changes that have since occurred, there are many within the country and abroad who are struck by the deep impact he made on his times and the sense of continuity which marks the evolution and growth of India's economy and polity.

History is replete with instances where faults are discovered in personalities of a previous era with the benefit of hindsight. Nehru is no exception. It is a pity that the Congress of today is unable to remember him (or project his achievements) in a correct perspective.

When Rajendra Prasad and Rajaji were in the Central Cabinet they, alongside Patel and Maulana Abul Kalam Azad, counted as Nehru's equals, more or less. There were others like Gobind Ballabh Pant and Rafi Ahmed Kidwai in the U.P. and Bidhan Chandra Roy in West Bengal who enjoyed Nehru's trust in a special measure. Kidwai died in October 1954 and Azad four years later.

Ironically enough, it was Azad who might have found himself left out in the musical chairs for the first Cabinet, despite his known proximity to Nehru. In a letter of July 24, 1947, Gandhi wrote to Nehru:

> … I did not say anything yesterday about the Maulana Saheb. But my objection stands. His retiring from the cabinet should not affect our connection with him. There are many positions which he can occupy in public life without any harm to any cause. Sardar is decidedly against his membership in the cabinet and so is Rajkumari[14]. Your cabinet must be strong and effective at the present juncture. It should not be difficult to name another Muslim for the cabinet …

Strange, but true. From all accounts, Gandhi had shown respect for the Maulana, even accepting him as a guide from time to time. But Nehru stood by his friend whom he had succeeded as Congress President on the eve of Independence and Azad became the first Education Minister of free India.

Gandhi probably had someone like Zakir Husain, an active proponent of his ideas on Basic Education (*Nai Talim*) in mind, to replace Azad as the Congress' Muslim face. Azad and Zakir Husain shared an uneasy relationship and the latter (the AMU Vice Chancellor) could only come into his own after Azad's exit from the scene in 1958, serving, successively, as the Governor of Bihar, the Vice President and the third President of India (1967-69). In Azad's lifetime, he was outpaced in the race to become the second Chairman of the University Grants Commission when C.D. Deshmukh was selected by Azad to succeed S.S. Bhatnagar.

Even though colleagues of considerable experience were at hand within the Congress, Nehru thought it fit to bring in talent from outside. The first three Finance Ministers of Independent India, Sir Shanmukham Chetty, a former Diwan of Cochin State, Dr John Mathai and Sir C.D. Deshmukh (of the ICS) did not have their origins in the Congress Party. Others of the eminence of Dr B.R. Ambedkar and Dr Syama Prasad Mookerjee enjoyed a standing in public life and could work with Nehru on their own terms. Both did not last in the Cabinet for very long.

Nehru had some of the best ICS men in the Foreign Office and in various Ministries of the Government India at his disposal. One of his biggest failures, amazingly, was in the field of foreign affairs, the area of his prime

14 Rajkumari Amrit Kaur, Union Health Minister (1947-57).

expertise, because of his heavily flawed China policy. The prevailing doctrine at the time being 'Panditji knows best', very few, if any, of his close advisers questioned him.

His handling of the Kashmir issue subjected him to wide-ranging criticism in India and abroad. The criticism continues.

In the conflict in Kashmir in 1947-48, Maj. Genl. Akbar Khan led what has been called the 'Pakistan Army on leave'. Mountbatten, now a constitutional Governor General, placed more faith in the United Nations Organization (UNO) than Nehru.

According to Vincent Sheean[15], a leading American journalist, a technical error, on the part of the team headed by Sir Girija Shankar Bajpai, led to India's appeal to the United Nations on Kashmir being considered a dispute rather than an act of aggression by Pakistan. The appeal should have been made under Chapter 7 of the UN Charter rather than Chapter 6.

The actual reference got off to an unpromising start. By early February 1948 Nehru was telling Mountbatten that it had been a grave mistake to pin any faith in the United Nations and that the world body had been a great disillusionment to him for it was clearly an American racket. Mountbatten's biographer, Philip Ziegler, notes that 'the inept presentation of the Indian case, as opposed to the skilled professionalism, both legal and oratorical, of the Pakistan representative, Sir Zafrullah Khan, was a factor in India's lack of success ...'[16].

By that time, the damage had been done, Nonetheless, Mountbatten continued to press the British Government to be more supportive towards the Indian position. In March 1948, Nehru seemed reasonably satisfied with the way things were going at the Union Nations. While the possibility of fresh hostilities had receded, that of a final solution was remote. The rest, as they say, is history.

In his last days, Nehru reached out to his old friend, Sheikh Abdullah; it was their first meeting at Teen Murti House, New Delhi, after the Sheikh's arrest way back in 1953. It was by then too late for Nehru to have undertaken any decisive intervention on Kashmir.

It has been argued that had Patel (and V.P. Menon) fielded the responsibility for Kashmir rather than Nehru (and Mountbatten), an extremely difficult

15 Vincent Sheean: *Nehru, The Years of Power* (1960).

16 Philip Ziegler: *Mountbatten, The Official Biography* (Collins, London, 1985).

situation would not have been inherited by the Indian Prime Ministers who followed, Lal Bahadur Shastri to begin with.

Jawaharlal Nehru – unlike Sardar Patel – shied away from building up the armed forces. However, when cornered, he was not averse to employing the military, as in the case of Kashmir in 1947–48 and, again, in Goa in 1961. He preferred, instead, to wax eloquent on disarmament and non-alignment. When the first Commander-in-Chief of the Indian Army, General Sir Robert Lockhart (a British officer who had, earlier, served as the GOC-in-C, Southern Command) went to Nehru with a formal defence paper that sought a policy directive from the Prime Minister, Nehru exclaimed to this effect: 'Rubbish .... We don't need a defence policy. Our policy is ahimsa (non-violence). We foresee no military threats. As far as I am concerned, you can scrap the army – the police are good enough to meet our security needs ...'

Not long afterwards, Nehru had to eat his words when faced by the invasion of Kashmir by the tribal hordes in October 1947. Lockhart left his post two months later.

Nehru kept the portfolio of External Affairs for himself, thus adding to his heavy burden as head of the whole Government of India. It was a disadvantage also for the Indian Foreign Service (IFS) at a formative stage of its growth. Notwithstanding the availability of some very able men, such as Sir Girija Shankar Bajpai, K.P.S. Menon (Sr), Subimal Dutt, B.N. Chakravarty, Rajeshwar Dayal, B.F.H.B. Tyabji and Arthur Lall (a Krishna Menon loyalist) – all of the ICS – it was not, overall, a good service, certainly not good enough for a country of India's emerging importance. There was not enough training or professional competence and too much eagerness to please the boss, made worse by an excessive habit of publicity and propaganda, Nehru was usually far too busy to go into the details or to get to know the officers, except for the very senior ones or a few favourites. This, in turn, encouraged sycophancy, ad hoc approaches, amateurishness and subjectivity. On occasion, the Indian Missions abroad sent back to New Delhi the kind of reports which they thought would be congenial to their superiors in South Block. Matters stood further complicated by the ambiguous position allowed to Krishna Menon who, in some fields, was virtually a second Foreign Minister for the five years or so prior to his fall in 1962.

During the prime ministerships of Nehru and Indira Gandhi (and, to an extent, Rajiv Gandhi), a few diplomats, both ICS and IFS, came to enjoy appreciably more prominence than their other colleagues. Ratan Kumar (R.K.) Nehru (ICS, CP and Berar, later Madhya Pradesh, 1924), the third and last-but-one Secretary General of the Ministry of External Affairs) was of the extended Nehru clan and related to Jawaharlal. So also was Braj Kumar (B.K.) Nehru (ICS, Punjab, later UP, 1933) who, although not seconded to the Foreign Service, was envoy to the USA and, subsequently, the U.K.

It was B.K. (Bijju) Nehru who was, as the Ambassador in Washington D.C. in 1962, required to deliver the Indian Prime Minister's communications to President Kennedy seeking immediate U.S. assistance against the Chinese. Ambassador Nehru was so stunned by the contents of the messages that he did not show them to any of his staff and kept the only copies with himself. Many years later, he told an American journalist that Nehru must have been exhausted and psychologically devastated by the news of India's defeats. Similar letters went to the then British Prime Minister, Harold Macmillan.

Why B.K. Nehru, despite a spectacular innings in the government (and residence in the Raj Bhawans) should have titled his 1997 memoirs: *Nice Guys Finish Second* seems an enigma until one learns that he was seriously considered for the post of U.N. Secretary General (on the death of Dag Hammarskjold in 1961) and that Krishna Menon scotched the idea by misleading Adlai Stevenson (the then U.S. Ambassador to the U.N.) that the proposal was not acceptable to the Government of India. U Thant got the job of the 'top diplomat in the world'. Perhaps, it is this setback that accounts for the title of the book.[17]

In his memoirs, B.K. Nehru writes '... Krishna Menon had ... a Rasputin – like effect .... What continues to be an unresolved mystery is the extraordinary hold Krishna Menon had on Jawaharlal Nehru .... Nobody has an answer. The only explanation that has appealed to me is the one given by Mrs Pandit who said that the influence came from the fact that Krishna Menon was the only person among his colleagues to whom Nehru could relate. Both were 'Englishmen', though of very different classes, both were very much more comfortable in the values and mores of the West than in their own Indian environment .... To this view I would subscribe and would add that Jawaharlal's real passion was international affairs, and once again the only person he could turn to as one having knowledge of these affairs was Krishna Menon ...'

There were others at the Foreign Office like T.N. (Tikki) Kaul (ICS, UP, 1936) and J.K. (Makkhi) Atal (ICS, CP & Berar, later Madhya Pradesh, 1936), a grandson of Sir Tej Bahadur Sapru, who could claim access to the

17 B.K. Nehru: *Nice Guys Finish Second* (Penguin, 1997).

top echelons. Still others, such as the late Romesh Bhandari (IFS, 1950), K. Natwar Singh (IFS, 1953) and Mani Shankar Aiyar (IFS, 1963) were at pains to stress their connections and pursued successful careers with the blessings of the First Family.

As early as in February 1959, T.N. Kaul, then the envoy at Teheran, was advising the new Congress President, Indira Gandhi, on a range of issues. Amongst other matters, he wrote to her to say that '... we must guard against certain national dangers like (i) the possible splitting up of India (ii) domination by a military or other dictatorship and (iii) aligning India with one or the other power blocs in the world. For this purpose, only people with hundred per cent loyalty to India and India's ideals should be appointed to key positions, where policy is formulated and executed, in the Congress Party and the Government. At present, enough consideration does not seem to be given to this matter, either in Government or in the Party.'

The advice could, perhaps, be interpreted as a precursor to the emergence of 'one family rule' and the desire to establish a 'committed and subservient bureaucracy'.

When Kaul was named the new Indian Ambassador to the U.S.A. by Prime Minister Indira Gandhi in 1973, the then U.S. Ambassador to India, Daniel Patrick Moynihan, wrote an unflattering assessment about him. In a cable sent on March 17, 1973, Moynihan said:

> Kaul, like the Nehru family, is a Kashmiri Brahmin, self-assured to the point of arrogance by birth. His career, most notably as ambassador to Moscow and more recently as foreign secretary, has been marked by pro-Soviet bias ... However, Kaul is also a sensitive weathervane of Indian foreign policy ... he will seek to improve relations with the United States, if that is GOI policy, and will criticize our actions, if so instructed ... I have not yet met him but all here agree he is inclined toward 'slyness', especially in his dealings with westerners. ... As the British say, he is 'too clever by half', a characteristic which many western chiefs of mission in New Delhi have found distasteful and trying.

M.K. Rasgotra (IFS, 1949) who served as Foreign Secretary in the mid-eighties and, briefly, as India's High Commissioner in the United Kingdom was also close to Indira Gandhi. According to Rasgotra, the then U.S. President, John F. Kennedy, had offered to help India detonate a nuclear device considerably before China did in 1964. Jawaharlal Nehru refused the offer. If India had gone ahead in this field, the entire nature of the relationship with China would have acquired a different complexion and the military confrontation of 1962 may not have occurred.

Nehru committed another blunder when he declined, in favour of China, a proposal of the major powers for India's permanent membership of the United Nations Security Council.

Crucial documents are stowed away in the papers of Mrs Vijayalakshmi Pandit (1900–1990) at the NMML, New Delhi. The importance of the Pandit papers lies in her relationship to her brother, Jawaharlal Nehru, and her high-profile diplomatic posts, which included the Soviet Union, the United States and the United Kingdom. While the published Nehru papers contained in his voluminous *Selected Works and Letters to Chief Ministers* are a rich resource for studying the Nehru period, they are only a partial record. The status of Nehru's personal collections amplifies the significance of the Pandit papers for understanding Nehru's thinking on foreign affairs in the 1940s and 1950s. The Pandit papers have been used before for general histories of Independent India and broad examinations of Indian foreign policy, but they have not been much deployed in studies focussed on India's relationship with China.

In August 1950, Pandit wrote to her brother from Washington, DC, where she was then posted as India's Ambassador to the United States:

> One matter that is being cooked up in the State Department should be known to you. This is the unseating of China as a Permanent Member in the Security Council and of India being put in her place.... Last week, I had interviews with [John Foster] Dulles[18] and [Philip] Jessup, reports of which I have sent to Bajpai[19]. Both brought up this question and Dulles seemed particularly anxious that a move in this direction should be started. Last night I heard from Marquis Childs, an influential columnist of Washington, that Dulles has asked him on behalf of the State Department to build up public opinion along these lines. I told him our attitude and advised him to go slow in the matter as it would not be received with any warmth in India.

18 John Foster Dulles (1888–1959) served as U.S. Secretary of State under Republican President, Dwight D. Eisenhower from 1953 to 1959 and was a significant figure in the early Cold War era.

19 Sir Girija Shankar Bajpai (1891–1954) was an eminent member of the ICS. He was appointed the first Secretary General of the Ministry of External Affairs by Prime Minister Nehru whom he is believed to have warned about the potential of a Chinese invasion more than a decade before it happened.

Nehru's response was unequivocal:

> In your letter you mention that the State Department is trying to unseat China as a Permanent Member of the Security Council and to put India in her place. So far as we are concerned, we are not going to countenance it. That would be bad from every point of view. It would be a clear affront to China and it would mean some kind of a break between us and China.... We shall go on pressing for China's admission in the UN and the Security Council. I suppose that a crisis will come during the next sessions of the General Assembly of the UN on this issue. The Peoples' Government of China is sending a full delegation there. If they fail to get in, there will be trouble which might even result in the USSR and some other countries finally quitting the UN. That may please the State Department, but it would mean the end of the UN as we have known it .... India, because of many factors, is certainly entitled to a Permanent Seat in the Security Council. But we are not going in at the cost of China.

But for these miscalculations, India would have not only been spared its desperate bid for NSG membership, her influence in world affairs would have been much more effective and Pakistan may well have felt compelled to abandon its efforts to seize Kashmir.

The reverses in the India-China war changed all that. On the conflict itself, there are analysts who believe that when Zhou Enlai was in New Delhi as Mao Zedong's emissary in April 1960, a hint was dropped in respect of a possible east-west swap, which (subject to negotiation) meant that if India recognized the Chinese claim over Aksai Chin, China would concede the Indian claims in the eastern Himalayas. The tension underlying the discussions was palpable at that stage. Nehru hesitated in responding to Zhou Enlai's approach and a chance to pragmatically resolve the vexed boundary issue was allowed to slip. In this case also, the 1962 confrontation could have been forestalled.

Aksai Chin was lost to China as a consequence of the humiliating military defeat.

Nehru was lucky in having the advice and assistance of scientists and organizers of science of the calibre of S.S. Bhatnagar, Homi Bhabha, P.C. Mahalanobis and K.S. Krishnan, all Fellows of the Royal Society, Jnan Chandra Ghosh, D.S. Kothari and S. Bhagavantam; their devotion was invaluable to the scientific progress made since Independence, on the foundations of which the country has celebrated such successes as the Mission to Mars.

In the S&T sector, Nehru's greatest contribution was the setting up of the National Laboratories which Sir C.V. Raman termed the 'Nehru-Bhatnagar Effect'.

In the early fifties, Nehru explained how scientists had to be treated differently from others, 'because they are different'. In a letter to C.D. Deshmukh, the Finance Minister, in 1952, he wrote:

> ... The work of scientific workers is rather peculiar. It is not routine work. A bright individual with initiative and vision might go far and do extraordinarily useful work. Another person might simply plod on. Hence it is necessary not to follow the normal rules of promotion etc. but to judge by sheer merit and work done ... [20].

The top scientists working with Nehru had direct access to him, sometimes more than members of the cabinet; they were as powerful as ministers.

A British scientist whom Nehru regarded highly was Patrick (PMS) Blackett (1887–1974) who won the Nobel Prize in Physics in 1948. Blackett, a friend of both Bhatnagar and Bhabha, met Nehru in early 1947 and became one of his military and scientific advisers. He spoke about Nehru in 1967:

> He was a superb leader. But he did not know how to get things done very well. He believed in science in a rather naïve way. We all did at the time ... It was enormously valuable that he should put science first in making Indians scientifically minded. But science is only part of a game and the real effect of science comes from producing wealth ... Now India is finding out that the problem of turning science into wealth ... is much more difficult than just doing science. It is not his fault that he did not fully understand this ...

Patrick Blackett (later, as Lord Blackett, to become President of the Royal Society) spoke out publicly against the development of nuclear weapons. Nehru had read his book, *Military and Political Consequences of Atomic Energy* which was published a year before the Soviets declared to the world in 1949 that they too knew how to make an atomic bomb.

---

20 Robert S. Anderson: *Nucleus and Nation, Scientists, International Networks and Power in India* (The University of Chicago Press, 2011) p. 260

As a school-boy, in my grandfather's time, I had opportunities to seek autographs from such leading scientists as Meghnad Saha (1893-1956), K.S. Krishnan (1898-1961), Homi Bhabha (1909-66) and D.N. Wadia (1883-1969). I could do the same with personalities like Sir Shri Ram of the DCM group and the Roerichs – Svetoslav (son of the famed Russian philosopher, painter, explorer and archaeologist, Nicholas Roerich) whose portraits of Nehru and Indira Gandhi adorn the Central Hall of Parliament and his wife, Devika Rani, a relative of the Tagores and widely acknowledged as the first lady of Indian cinema.

Saha had been active in the National Planning Committee set up in 1938 when Subhas Bose headed the Congress. While he did not enjoy the same proximity to Nehru as he did with Bose, he received Nehru's consideration and respect. Saha successfully contested the first Lok Sabha election in 1952 and opposed Nehru, in Parliament, on Science Policy.

His scientific reputation was formidable. He had formulated the ionization equation that opened the door to stellar astrophysics but he did not join the Atomic Energy Commission (AEC) and was often at odds with its Chairman, Bhabha. When direct communication was difficult between them, each wrote about the other to Bhatnagar, who then mediated. Bhatnagar's CSIR was the source of funds for the work of both Saha and Bhabha.

Science in India was on a high, an important landmark having been the 1944 Report of Archibald Vivian (A.V.) Hill, a Nobel Laureate in Physiology, who toured Indian scientific institutions as a representative of the Royal Society, London. Post-independence, Nobel Laureates Arthur Holly Compton (1892–1962), Irene Joliot – Curie (1897-1956), Alexander Todd (1907–97) and a host of outstanding foreign scientists were in India for the Annual Science Congress and for inaugurations of the National Laboratories when Nehru was always present; he attended dinners at my grandfather's place, especially when scientists were invited.

Nehru also came to a party in 1953 when Chaudhri Muhammad Ali, the then Finance Minister of Pakistan was in New Delhi en route to Dhaka. Ali had been a student of my grandfather at Lahore and one in whom his chemistry teacher took special pride. Ali's papers in the Audit & Accounts Service examination were Chemistry and Persian. He suffered a heart attack in Dhaka and, while still recovering, sent a hand-written note to him.

Like (or unlike) his mentor and the person to whom he owed everything, the Father of the Nation, Nehru did not always stand behind his colleagues. For instance, he did not join the Congress Socialist Party (CSP) which was founded in 1934 as a socialist grouping within the Indian National Congress to transcend communal divisions through class solidarity and to advocate decentralized systems in which cooperatives, trade unions and local authorities would wield economic power.

Not altogether homogeneous in its composition, the CSP's prominent members, from different streams, included Acharya Narendra Deva and Jayaprakash Narayan (JP), Minoo Masani, Asoka Mehta and Ram Manohar Lohia. The CSP was active in the Quit India movement of August 1942 but Nehru's lukewarm support seems to have caused disappointment among its members who felt let down and saw him as unwilling to put his socialist slogans into action.

Nehru, later, had occasion to express admiration for his friends in the CSP. In an emotional obituary in the Rajya Sabha when Acharya Narendra Deva passed away in 1956, he said:

> The death of Acharya Narendra Deva is something much bigger for many of us and, I think, for the country than just the passing away of an important person. He was a man of rare distinction – distinction in many fields – rare in spirit, rare in mind and intellect, rare in integrity of mind ... Only his body failed him. I do not know if there is any person present in this House who was associated with him for a longer period than I was. Over 40 years ago, we came together and we shared innumerable experiences together in the dust and heat of the struggle for independence ... and inevitably got to know each other intimately .... There is the public sense of loss and there is the private sense of loss and a feeling that somebody of rare distinction has gone and it will be very difficult to find his like again.

The tribute is the more generous when it is recalled that Narendra Deva had this to say in 1949:

> Jawaharlal derives strength from the people. He likes vast crowds. Personal popularity leads him to believe that the people are satisfied with his administration: this conclusion, however, is not always justified.

Much has been recorded about the bonds of affection subsisting between JP and his wife, Prabhavati (who predeceased him) and the Nehrus: Kamala and Jawaharlal, even Indira. This seems more true of the Kamala-Prabhavati relationship. In November 1974, in a poignant gesture, JP handed over to Indira Gandhi the letters written by her late mother to his late wife.

JP, a figure of great moral authority, lives in public memory as a hero of the Quit India movement, his role especially acknowledged by Gandhi himself. He joined the Congress Working Committee at Nehru's insistence but did not accept a ministership on which also Nehru appears to have been keen. At the same time, Nehru was not pleased to hear any talk of JP being a possible successor to him as head of government. The story is reliably told that at a dinner arranged in connection with the Indian Science Congress (over which Nehru presided in January 1947), he overheard Field Marshal Sir Claude Auchinleck, then Commander-in-Chief, India, introducing JP to another guest as a future prime minister. Nehru did not so much as exchange a word with JP (who had accompanied Rajendra Prasad) at this event.

When Sardar Patel – of whom JP had been a vocal critic – initiated an amendment to the Constitution of the Congress that members of other political parties could not remain within the Congress organization, no option was left to those in the CSP but to sever relations with the Congress and leave.

In 1948, JP was in the forefront of forming a new Socialist Party as a left-wing alternative to the Congress. After the 1952 elections, Nehru reached out to JP to explore the possibility of the socialists rejoining the Congress. The talks were inconclusive; by now, JP had begun to lose interest in active politics altogether and was becoming increasingly attracted to the *Bhoodan* and *Gramdan* movements started by Acharya Vinoba Bhave. As such, on the eve of the 1957 general elections, he was not associated with any political party.

During the campaigning for the elections, JP advised Nehru that the prime minister function as a 'national rather than a party leader … and encourage the growth of an Opposition … to soundly lay the foundations of parliamentary democracy in India …'. Nehru was critical of JP for 'playing hide-and-seek' between politics and social service and for claiming to have given up politics but continuing to dabble in it. On his part, JP was quick to point out that, whatever the outcome of the elections, 'the verdict is inescapable that the present political system has proved a failure. Therefore, the need after the elections is for the leaders of the country to get together in order to find out if there is a better alternative. I think there is and, in the larger interest of the country, we must seek it out. It is here that your leadership is most needed, because without you this cannot be done'.

Nehru's position in the Congress would have been strengthened if the socialists had not drifted apart. In their support, he would have found a sturdier ideological platform from which to function. This possibility receded when the CSP broke away from the Congress.

In one of the most quoted instances of probity in public life, Lal Bahadur Shastri resigned as the Minister of Railways in November 1956, taking moral responsibility for the Ariyalur train accident in the then Madras State. Prime Minister Nehru described him as a man of the highest integrity after the resignation. Shastri's popularity surged and he succeeded Nehru in the top job.

There still remained a few voices of dissent such as D.P. Mishra in Madhya Pradesh, a Patelite, who left the Congress after a showdown, only to return (via the Indira Gandhi route) in 1963 in Nehru's twilight months. Indira Gandhi was chairing the high-powered National Citizens Council after the Chinese aggression and secured Mishra's rehabilitation; he was a politician of the old school, a high caste Brahmin and he became a beneficiary of the Kamaraj Plan when the resignation of the Chief Minister, Bhagwantrao Mandloi, was accepted.

It was during Mishra's term as Chief Minister that the titular Maharaja of Bastar, Pravir Chandra Bhanj Deo, was killed in the police firing in the precincts of his palace in March 1966 – a blot on the State administration that still survives in public memory. Mishra was, later, a key planner and strategist for Nehru's daughter in the 1969 presidential election which V.V. Giri won with her backing, against the official Congress nominee, N. Sanjiva Reddy.

When his writ ran unhindered in both government and party, Nehru could still not get S. Radhakrishnan, the Vice President, to succeed Rajendra Prasad in 1957 because of the opposition of Maulana Azad. Later, in 1962, while Nehru made sure that Radhakrishnan became the second President of the Republic, their relationship experienced a noticeable downslide after the government's unbelievingly inept handling of the conflict with China.

It was Azad again who, for months, stood out against Nehru's wish to induct Krishna Menon (1896–1974) as a minister. It was with some difficulty that Nehru persuaded Azad not to resign when Menon was introduced into the Cabinet. Neither Patel nor Azad liked the influence Menon exercized on Nehru. Azad later wrote: '... I felt Krishna Menon often gave Jawaharlal wrong advice. Sardar Patel and I did not always see eye to eye but we were agreed in our judgment about Krishna Menon'.

Having been out of India for nearly thirty years, Menon, when he returned in 1954, was less known amongst his compatriots than he was in London or New York. When he became Prime Minister, Nehru chose Menon to be India's High Commissioner to the United Kingdom. His involvement was suspected in what became known as the jeep scandal but he emerged unscathed, first becoming Minister without Portfolio in the Nehru cabinet and, later, the Defence Minister in 1957.

Few then knew that the relationship between Nehru and Menon was an old one. Menon had some big faults like self-assertiveness, rudeness, strong dislikes (such as, surprisingly enough, of Homi Bhabha, a Nehru favourite) and an incapacity for team work. Menon also had differences with Nehru's sister – Mrs Vijayalakshmi Pandit – at the United Nations in 1952–53. She was the chief Indian delegate when Menon, who was the deputy chief, denied her access to the reports he was sending Nehru. She protested to her brother but Nehru paid no heed.

Menon's virtues were of a kind which put him on a plane reached by no more than a handful in the Nehru dispensation.

By the late 1950's, several ministers (and party functionaries) were provincial mediocrities who held office because this or that State or language or caste had to be represented. About Krishna Menon, it can be said that he was one of a shrinking group that counted in the government and was a particularly close associate of the prime minister. He was, from time to time, at loggerheads with such senior colleagues as Morarji Desai and S.K. Patil, among others.

The action by the Indian Armed Forces that brought the Portuguese rule in Goa, Daman and Diu to an end in December 1961 was publicized as a feather in Menon's cap as the Defence Minister.

Jamsheed Marker[21], a veteran diplomat, claimed in a recent interview to the *Herald* of Pakistan that Nehru, under the influence of Defence Minister, Krishna Menon, would have destroyed Pakistan. Marker said: 'India would have attacked Pakistan if Krishna Menon would have been successful in bringing around Nehru' and added '… he (Menon) was completely Nehru's man … a rare, evil genius and a Rasputin …'.

Nehru left his old friend of the freedom struggle days, Acharya Kripalani, in the lurch and campaigned vigorously for Menon in the North Bombay constituency during the general elections of 1962. He took the challenge to Menon as a challenge to himself.

More than once, Nehru lost patience with the Defence Minister, especially with the atmosphere of tension Menon would generate. But Nehru

21 Jamsheed Marker (born 1922) belongs to a well-known Parsi family of Quetta. He served as Ambassador of Pakistan between 1965-95 and is listed in the Guinness Book of Records as having been 'ambassador to more countries than any other person'. His recollections entitled 'Quiet Diplomacy: Memoirs of an Ambassador of Pakistan' appeared in 2010.

utterly failed to check, indeed admonish, Menon when this was most needed, that is, when General Thimayya, arguably independent India's most illustrious Chief of the Army Staff (COAS) to date, sent in his resignation to the Prime Minister; he had been driven to the wall by Menon's discourtesy, unwarranted interference in the Army's functioning and his pronounced disinclination to appreciate or discuss the seriousness of the Chinese challenge across the borders with its manifold implications.

The COAS was the first and only Indian officer to command a fighting brigade in the Arakan during World War II and had been awarded the Distinguished Service Order (DSO). Publicly, while Nehru seemed to like him, he also saw Thimayya as a rival who could challenge his position as Prime Minister.

Thimayya had entered into an argument with Nehru when he told him, point blank, that the arbitrary decision of making the Indian Army responsible for the North East Frontier Agency (NEFA, now Arunachal Pradesh) as announced in Parliament, was completely against the country's interests, the more so without providing the additional resources required. He urged the Prime Minister to 'undo the mistake'. Rather than consider anything of the kind, Nehru and Menon decided to neutralize Thimayya.

Thimayya had made no bones about being greatly disturbed at the continuing neglect of the Army and Menon's growing hostility whenever the lack of preparedness to meet the Chinese threat was raised with him. It was now that the tact and guile of a much-adored Nehru came into play in August-September 1959. The Prime Minister turned on his charm to persuade Thimayya to withdraw the resignation, he succeeded in isolating the COAS from the Naval and Air Chiefs, namely Vice Admiral Katari and Air Marshal Mukerjee (to prevent a collective stand) and he then proceeded to criticize and castigate Thimayya in Parliament.

At a time when Thimayya's professional advice should necessarily have prevailed, Nehru chose to side with Menon whom he thought 'simply brilliant'. It was yet another nail in the coffin of galvanizing the armed forces to better face the Chinese when the moment of reckoning arrived.

A clear warning of the Chinese intentions had come in a 1960 assessment of Lt. General S.P.P. Thorat, then GOC-in-C, Eastern Command which invited Menon's ire. The Defence Minister also sent off an outstanding IAF Commander, P.C. Lal, into early retirement with the rank of Air Vice Marshal; in the wake of the Chinese aggression, Lal was recalled to active service and was Chief of the Air Staff between 1969-73.

Thimayya was hopelessly disillusioned with Nehru and Menon when he hung up his boots in May 1961. Of him, the late Lt. General P.S. Bhagat, VC, said:

> A General Thimayya is not born in every generation. The like of him there will seldom be, a soldier, a general, a man's man; the Army, his soul, his soul, the Army.

Menon made sure that Thimayya was succeeded not by Thorat but by a more pliable COAS who was at the helm during the India-China war and resigned in November 1962 in the face of the debacle.

Lt. General Bhagat, a Victoria Cross winner of World War II, was himself to be overlooked for appointment as COAS during the Indira Gandhi regime.

Lt. General Depinder Singh[22] in his book on Manekshaw records: 'In the first week of January 1973, the Government decided that Lt. General G.G. Bewoor[23], PVSM, the Southern Army Commander would be the next Army Chief in succession to the Field Marshal ... the Chief's choice, which he could only convey to the Prime Minister verbally, was Lt. General P.S. Bhagat, VC. Mrs. Gandhi was, however, under tremendous pressure from Mr. Y.B. Chavan to grant Lt. General Bewoor an extension beyond his retirement date and appoint him as COAS. During one discussion between the Chief and the Prime Minister, she mentioned that one reason why Bewoor was preferred over Bhagat was that the latter was pro-Sikh. On the Chief's asking how this conclusion was reached, she remarked that there were numerous photographs of Bhagat with Sikh troops. The Chief's explanation that Bhagat, being a Colonel of the Sikh Light Infantry, naturally appeared in these photographs, evidently was not accepted.'

Another, perhaps more important reason, was that soon after the Chinese aggression, Bhagat (at that time a Brigadier) had co-authored the Report of the Henderson Brooks Committee which squarely blamed the then political leadership headed by Nehru for the defeat of the Indian Army.

Nehru had a host of admirers in Britain. Malcolm Muggeridge (1903–90), author, journalist and media personality who, among others, brought Mother Teresa to popular attention in the West and is credited with stimulating the

---

22 Lt. General Depinder Singh: *Field Marshal Sam Manekshaw, Soldiering with Dignity* (Natraj Publishers, 2013), p. 203.

23 General G.G. Bewoor was the younger son of Sir Gurunath Venkatesh Bewoor (1888–1950), a very senior member of the ICS in the British Raj.

debate about Catholic theology, was not one of them. Nor was *Hugh Gaitskell* (1906–63) who succeeded Clement Attlee as Leader of the Labour Party and seemed on the verge of becoming Prime Minister when he died suddenly.

Muggeridge thought Nehru 'rather a conceited second-rate person'. Gaitskell said, 'He is a very arrogant man; I think that is one reason he makes such long speeches. He really thinks everyone wants to listen to him'.

By the end of the 1950s, Nehru was worried enough about the growing wealth and income inequality to set up the Mahalanobis Committee to inquire into it.

One of Nehru's favourites among the Chief Ministers of the day – Sardar Pratap Singh Kairon in Punjab – exhibited extraordinary vision and drive. He firmly put post-partition Punjab on the developmental path; he also faced charges serious enough to force a reluctant Nehru to appoint a Commission of Inquiry which concluded that '... there is no getting away from the fact that S. Pratap Singh Kairon knew or had more than ample reason to think or suspect that his sons and relatives were allegedly exploiting his influence and powers'. Kairon seemed inclined to ignore the Report of Justice S.R. Das, a former Chief Justice of India, but had to resign eventually during the Shastri prime ministership.

The final phase was sad for Nehru who had long been loved by his people. His visit to the U.S.A. in November 1961 turned out to be a disaster. President Kennedy's aide (and 'court historian') Arthur Schlesinger, recalled: 'by 1961, Nehru, alas, was no longer the man he had once been'[24]. However, the then U.S. Ambassador to India, John Kenneth Galbraith, portrayed the visit as more successful than it had actually been.

Nehru's first serious illness in forty years occurred in the spring of 1962, a kidney affliction known as pyelonephritis, from which he recovered, albeit with a slight stoop. The following year, soon after the Kamaraj Plan was operationalized, the question arose as to who would be the next Congress President to assume office at the beginning of 1964.

The process of consultations began in early October, 1963 in the temple-town of Tirupathi in Andhra Pradesh, with Kamaraj, the West Bengal party boss, Atulya Ghosh, the host State's Chief Minister, N. Sanjiva Reddy and S. Nijalingappa, Chief Minister of Mysore (now Karnataka) participating.

---

24 JFK's *Forgotten Crisis* (Tibet, the CIA and the Sino-Indian War): Bruce Riedel (Harper Collins, India, 2016) p. 70.

S.K. Patil kept in touch by telephone. This was when the 'Syndicate' took birth, a powerful grouping of Congress leaders, which was to play a vital role in the management of the succession to Nehru in May 1964 and to Shastri in January 1966. A major aim was to keep Morarji Desai from the Congress Presidency and thereby isolate him further from the centre of political power.

Around this time, a leading journalist observed that if Nehru's illness had led to his withdrawal in August 1963, the Kamaraj Plan would not have been launched and Morarji would have been much closer to an Acting Head of Government.

In November 1963, Kamaraj was unanimously elected as the party president.

The significance of Shastri's return to the Cabinet, shortly after Nehru took ill at Bhubaneswar in January 1964 was not lost on commentators, foreign and Indian. The Guardian, London welcomed Shastri's return 'for two reasons: first that the problem of succession is at last being tackled, and secondly, that Mr Shastri is the man in view'.

A special function was also being carried out by his daughter, Indira Gandhi; the Prime Minister's schedule, his appointments, the papers to be shown him – all came within the purview of her scrutiny and control. While she may not have played a substantive role in respect of governmental working, she was an important element in the power structure, by virtue of her unique access to her father, still the seat of ultimate decision.

The India-China war shattered Nehru, politically and personally. He had only himself to blame and he was never the same man again. The faults and failures that can be attributed to his term as prime minister have had a long-term impact, impeding growth and development.

The (late) T.N. Kaul[25] wrote that in the early 1950s '…Nehru was not sure of China's attitude …. China was not yet a super power and, like India, needed peace to rebuild its social and economic structure. This was the best time to make a rapprochement with China. It might still be possible to reach a tacit understanding on our border and other problems peacefully …'.

These are Kaul's words not Nehru's but, if they accurately reflect Nehru's assessment, then it was a very costly error of judgment indeed and one that has bedevilled India's advancement for decades.

That said, it should be acknowledged that Nehru was a statesman of international stature and a popularly – elected leader who strove to keep a newly-partitioned country united. While he could have been less of a

25 T.N. Kaul: *Diplomacy in Peace and War, Recollections and Reflections.*

democrat and more of a dictator, he nurtured parliamentary democracy and brought about a spirit of togetherness in India. For this achievement alone, he will rank among India's great Prime Ministers.

It was a case of a man who had done so much for his country staying around for too long.

When Nehru died in May 1964, Indira Gandhi was determined that her father would be the first and last Indian occupant of Teen Murti House, earlier the residence of the British Commander-in-Chief. Shortly after the mourning period was over, it was officially announced that Nehru's home would become a memorial to him. In the vicinity was another house, owned by the billionaires of the Birla family, that became a memorial to the Mahatma, now known as Gandhi Smriti.

Shastri, as prime minister, continued to live at Motilal Nehru Place.

The late Mrs Pandit – Nehru's sister – was known to assert that her brother did not regard, let alone designate Shastri as his successor. Dynastically inclined herself, she was never in the race, having long shared an uneasy, even strained, relationship with her niece whose name, however, was very much in contention. The influential Jagjivan Ram tried to pitch for Indira Gandhi seeking, thereby, to block Shastri who seemed accommodating: 'If she is the unanimous choice of the Party, I will be the first to nominate her'. But a key member of the Syndicate, Atulya Ghosh, was very blunt: 'Why should Shastri stand down; what sins has he committed?'

From his side, Morarji Desai expressed doubts about Indira Gandhi being able to run the country, noting her lack of administrative experience.

In the end, with the Syndicate's backing and on the basis of his own standing and popularity, Lal Bahadur Shastri emerged as the most acceptable choice to succeed Nehru. He was installed as Prime Minister on June 9, 1964. Two days later, in his first broadcast, he said:

> There comes a time in the life of every nation when it stands at the cross-roads of history and must choose which way to go. But for us there need be no difficulty or hesitation, no looking to right or left. Our way is straight and clear – the building up of a socialist democracy at home with freedom and prosperity for all, and maintenance of world peace and friendship with all nations.

In forming his Cabinet, Shastri revealed his political style; the process was cautious and undramatic. All thirteen senior ministers of the Nehru cabinet were retained, the notable changes being only in the addition of three members – Indira Gandhi, S.K. Patil and Sanjiva Reddy.

Indira Gandhi agreed to join the government after a display of reluctance and was said to have opted for the relatively light charge of Minister of Information and Broadcasting. She appeared to still be in a somewhat unsettled frame of mind. As a section of the media observed at the time, she was really the replacement for the father. However, she had never been as trusting of Shastri as her father; indeed, she seemed to harbour a certain dislike of him.

What exactly could have been the reasons for Indira Gandhi's annoyance? According to (Sir) C.P. Srivastava, an IAS aide of Shastri, the view, generally, has been that during the last years of Nehru's prime ministership, Indira Gandhi had come to regard herself as the heir-apparent and successor to her father as India's prime minister and was, therefore, unhappy that Shastri had, as she thought, 'usurped' that position; her unhappiness had been aggravated by the success of Shastri's prime ministership. Whatever her reasons, it is clear that Indira Gandhi did not have a favourable opinion of Lal Bahadur Shastri.[26]

The Prime Minister subtly denied the External Affairs portfolio to Indira Gandhi; he took the portfolio himself and when the medical advice was for him to lighten his burden, he did not offer the post to her and chose Swaran Singh instead.

Two eminent physicists, Homi Bhabha and D.S. Kothari, were believed to have declined cabinet positions in Shastri's government in June 1964. They were of sterner stuff than two others, coming after them, in the scientific leadership – M.G.K. Menon and Raja Ramanna – who accepted junior ministerships in the short-lived dispensation of V.P. Singh in 1989-90.

An important change was effected by Shastri when Sachindra (Sachin) Chaudhuri, a well-known Calcutta barrister, replaced T.T. Krishnamachari (TTK) as the Finance Minister. TTK had joined the Nehru government in 1952 as the Minister of Commerce and Industry and, later, was twice responsible for the Finance Ministry; there is reason to believe that Nehru preferred him over Morarji Desai for the Finance portfolio.

While TTK had shown himself to be one of Shastri's supporters in the succession; he was closer to Indira Gandhi. Rumour had it that he was now meeting her ever so often, possibly 'belittling' the Prime Minister. Shastri had never thought highly of TTK and the reports reaching him could have proved to be the last straw. Shastri had also received a memorandum signed by

26 C.P. Srivastava: A Life of Truth in Politics (OUP, 1995).

eleven Members of Parliament making specific allegations of corruption and nepotism against TTK. His exit carried the stamp of Shastri's authority.

Jawaharlal Nehru had kept a compact personal secretariat (PMS) headed by a Principal Private Secretary (of the level of Joint Secretary in the Government of India) to assist him with routine papers. An early incumbent was Dharma Vira (ICS, UP, 1929) and Kesho Ram (ICS, UP, 1938) was the last.

M.O. (Mac) Mathai was Nehru's chief aide; his functioning was not confined to the formal organization that existed for the Prime Minister to whom he had direct access. He was born in Kerala and had started working as a secretarial assistant for Nehru as early as in 1946. Over the years, he began handling important matters and tended to become overtly powerful and controversial; he was eased out in 1959 when an enquiry conducted by the then Cabinet Secretary, Vishnu Sahay (ICS, UP, 1924) did not clear him of charges. He went on to write books of even more controversial content.

Mathai should be regarded as the first in a line of men of humble beginnings – Yashpal Kapoor, R.K. Dhawan, Vincent George, among others – who came into the enjoyment of disproportionate power and prominence, thanks to the styles of working of their political masters to whom the *erosion* of administrative norms did not really matter. These men were often in the know of ultra-sensitive matters. Dhawan (and M.L. Fotedar) became Union Ministers in Congress governments.

Shastri soon took steps to form a full-fledged Secretariat for the Prime Minister. A highly regarded ICS man, L.K. Jha (Bihar, 1936) who had served as an Additional Secretary with Shastri when he was the Minister of Commerce and Industry in the early sixties was selected for the crucial position of Secretary to the Prime Minister, along with two IAS Joint Secretaries, both kayasthas, like Shastri, from Uttar Pradesh.

Jha drafted Shastri's key policy statements; there is ample evidence to suggest that the Prime Minister's Secretariat, through his forceful personality, fast became a major power centre. It exerted pressure on many issues, especially in the vital spheres of economic affairs and foreign relations.

In the succeeding Indira Gandhi regime (1966–77), L.K. Jha carried on for over a year as Secretary to the new Prime Minister, before handing over the baton in 1967 to P.N. Haksar who had been the Indian Ambassador to Austria. Jha can be said to have created a structure at the very top which progressively curtailed the importance of the Cabinet Secretary and which, after the Indira Gandhi years, was again an effective instrument during the prime ministership of P.V. Narasimha Rao (1991–96).

Although Lal Bahadur Shastri had a very short innings, he proved his mettle in several ways. He directed a revision of the planning strategy and initiated a series of Annual Plans. Agriculture began to receive greater focus and the Indian Council of Agricultural Research was reorganized. The Green Revolution followed. In 1965, Verghese Kurien (1921–2012) was asked to head the National Dairy Development Board and replicate Amul's 'Anand model' nationwide, bringing millions out of poverty.

Shastri came out as one rooted to the ground realities when he said:

> No doubt we have to have bigger projects, bigger industries, basic industries, but it is a matter of the highest importance that we look to the common man, the weakest element of the society. When we think in terms of the common man, we have to think of his food, his clothing, his shelter, medical facilities, recreation for the children. These are some of the basic necessities of life which everyone needs, and more so in the rural areas. We cannot ignore this fact in whatever we may plan, and however big our plan might be. We cannot go on doing things which do not touch the common man, which do not touch the weaker element in our society. [The present Prime Minister has had occasion to voice similar views]

Shastri was the first of Nehru's successors to have to militarily confront the bitter legacy of Partition and the perennially hostile attitude of Pakistan.

Indian and Pakistani troops clashed in the Rann of Kutch in March, 1965. Air Marshal Arjan Singh of India and Air Marshal Asghar Khan of Pakistan who had served together in British India agreed not to commit their aircraft to the conflict. In June that year, a Ceasefire Agreement – mediated by the British – was signed in New Delhi by M. Azim Hussain, ICS, Secretary in India's Ministry of External Affairs (a son of Sir Fazle Hussain, he had opted for India) and his cousin, Arshad Hussain, a son of Mian Afzal Hussain, (noted agricultural scientist) who was then Pakistan's High Commissioner to India.

The significance of the Rann of Kutch encounter was the false sense of optimism and superiority engendered with the Pakistan military establishment concerning its capacity to take on the Indian army. The immediate fallout of the 'perceived' success in the Rann was that the elements in Pakistan's ruling circles that stood for an active policy on Kashmir were greatly encouraged to challenge India. The mood had turned jingoistic and militaristic. Thus was born a plan, Operation Gibraltar, to send infiltrators into Kashmir; the plan was shown to President Ayub Khan who directed that the main objective should be to capture Akhnoor which had great strategic value.

In the event, Akhnoor did not fall into Pakistani hands. One version is that Ayub Khan lost his nerve just when Pakistani forces were poised to capture Akhnoor and decided to call off the operation because he did not want to provoke a full-scale war with India.

A full-scale war did, more or less, ensue and on September 6, 1965 the Indian Army crossed the international border in Punjab, the orders having come from the Prime Minister whose political leadership, alongside the military leadership of Lt. Genl. Harbaksh Singh, GOC-in-C, Western Command, carried the day for India. The defeat of the Pakistan Army in the tank battle of Asal Uttar was one of the great setbacks suffered by their forces.

There were those in Pakistan who believed at the time that Ayub Khan was not fully aware (or made aware) of the reasons for the 1965 war and his close advisers like Aziz Ahmed and Nazir Ahmed (former ICS men) and A.B. Awan (ex-Indian Police), as also Z.A. Bhutto prevailed on him and convinced him that the operations initiated in Kashmir were only a small programme and would not lead to a war with India. It is possible that the advisers, particularly Bhutto, also sought to weaken Ayub's hold on the government. Foreign Secretary Aziz Ahmed, a long-time hawk, put in his papers after the Tashkent Declaration only to return to the government under Bhutto after Bangladesh had come into being.

Ayub Khan and Bhutto paid a closely guarded visit to China on September 19-20, 1965 to meet Zhou Enlai in Beijing. The Chinese, apparently, urged Pakistan to fight on, but neither Ayub Khan nor Bhutto was prepared for a long-drawn conflict.

For the Pakistan military, the 1965 war was an exercise in image-building, even though the operations were, essentially, a failure. The influential Information Secretary, Altaf Gauhar (ghost-writer of Ayub Khan's political autobiography, *Friends not Masters*, which appeared in 1967) played a key role in recording failure, as success, in the public mind.

India's stand, under Shastri's prime ministership, was fully vindicated when, in September 2005 on the fortieth anniversary of the war, Air Marshal Malik Nur Khan who was heading the Pakistan Air Force (PAF) in 1965 had this to say:

> The performance of the Army did not match that of the PAF mainly because the leadership was not as professional. They had planned

> 'Operation Gibraltar' for self-glory rather than in the national interest. It was a wrong war. And they misled the nation with a big lie that India rather than Pakistan had provoked the war and that we were the victims of Indian aggression … the Army came to believe its own fiction … and, therefore, has continued to fight unwanted wars – the 1971 war and the Kargil fiasco in 1999 …. In each of the subsequent wars we have committed the same mistakes that we committed in 1965 ….

For several years, Shastri was almost wiped out from the pages of history by his own party; only P.V. Narasimha Rao can be said to have suffered a worse fate. Both men were 'agents of change' whose substantial contributions have, lately, been highlighted by the BJP.

Had Shastri lived longer, he may have charted Congress' path away from a dynastic course, keeping it a normal, democratically – run party. Equally importantly, the shift in emphasis from heavy industry to agriculture which he introduced would have continued. He had a sound grasp of fundamental issues, as was evident when he spoke in the Lok Sabha in September 1964:

> To my mind, socialism in India must mean a better deal for the great mass of our people who are engaged in the various factories and the middle classes who have suffered much during the period of rising prices.

By 1991, when Prime Minister Narasimha Rao resumed on the path Shastri had begun to traverse, considerable damage had been done.

The mystery surrounding Shastri's very sudden death in Tashkent on January 11, 1966 has not been satisfactorily resolved, if one were only to go by the views expressed, with a degree of conviction, by some of the family members from time to time. After the lapse of over half a century, the truth may never be known.

The public posture of restraint until after Shastri's funeral was scrupulously respected by the Congress elite. In this second succession, the Acting Prime Minister, Gulzarilal Nanda, made a bid for interim continuity – until the 1967 polls – but Kamaraj had already decided, from the outset, that Indira Gandhi was the most suitable candidate. This time, however, Morarji Desai stood his ground against the Syndicate and forced a contest in the Congress Parliamentary Party which Indira Gandhi won convincingly.

After the general elections of 1967 which saw the Congress secure only a slender majority in the Lok Sabha, Morarji Desai again made clear his desire to become prime minister. A compromise mediated by two former Chief Ministers – D.P. Mishra of Madhya Pradesh on behalf of Indira Gandhi and C.B. Gupta of Uttar Pradesh for Desai – was worked out under which Desai was appointed Deputy Prime Minister and Finance Minister.

The 1967 election saw a few 'shock' defeats, such as of Kamaraj, the Congress President, from the Virudhunagar State Assembly seat in Madras (Tamil Nadu) and of S.K. Patil to the Lok Sabha from the Bombay South constituency. Good fortune was beginning to shine for Indira Gandhi as the process commenced of the dismantling of the Syndicate which had catapulted her to power in the first place.

His loyalty, trustworthiness and integrity never in doubt, the stage was now set for her Principal Secretary, P.N. Haksar's intellectual calibre and political acumen to be put to the test.

P.N. (Babboo) Haksar has been described as 'an intellectual powerhouse and one of India's most successful strategists who astutely established the political omnipotence of a weak prime minister, Indira Gandhi' through path-breaking measures like the Nationalization of the 14 largest Commercial Banks in 1969 which, in turn, saw the exit of Morarji Desai from the cabinet. Haksar had earlier advised her that 'the best way to vanquish the Syndicate would be to convert the struggle for personal power into an ideological one'.

From 1967 to 1973, Haksar was arguably the most powerful person in the government. He shared his influence with four others – Kashmiri Brahmins, like him – namely, D.P. Dhar, a politician turned diplomat who had served as a deputy minister under Sheikh Abdullah in the early fifties in J&K, T.N. Kaul, a career diplomat who rose to be the Foreign Secretary, P.N. Dhar, an economist turned bureaucrat and R.N. Kao (IP, 1940), a police officer turned super spy and security specialist. Their caste links were strong and they were collectively known as the *Panch Harkare* (Five Messengers) who were part and parcel of Indira Gandhi's innermost coterie.

Haksar played a key role in negotiating the 1972 Simla Agreement with Pakistan and may have been the only one on the Indian side who was privy to the secret negotiations that took place between Indira Gandhi and Zulfiqar Ali Bhutto over the Kashmir issue; to this day, the state remains an extremely volatile flashpoint where armed militants have been waging a civil war since 1989 which has claimed thousands of lives, young and old.

One of the actions for which Haksar has, with justification, come in for criticism relates to the advice he, apparently, proffered to Indira Gandhi to let Bhutto 'off the hook' at Simla (now Shimla) and not to *insist* on the

Cease Fire Line being recognized as the International Boundary between Pakistan and India. The outcome of this misjudgement continues to haunt the present NDA II government in a crisis of unprecedented proportions in the Valley.

India did not take advantage of the defeat inflicted on Pakistan in December 1971. The Simla Agreement is perceived as a colossal political failure because of Indira Gandhi's inability to obtain a final settlement on Kashmir. Inspired by the likes of P.N. Haksar and T.N. Kaul, the Agreement was a weak expression of the Nehruvian foreign policy establishment. Zulfiqar Ali Bhutto had agreed to formalize the Line of Control (LoC) but requested time, in order to consolidate his position at home. Years later, when General Musharraf proposed a peace formula, Vajpayee probably lost the opportunity to have the LoC recognized as an international border. The rest is history.

It was a measure of Haksar's overriding importance at Simla that he (and not T.N. Kaul, technically his senior in the Foreign Service) led the delegation of Indian officials for the discussions with their Pakistan opposite numbers. Haksar, according to A.G. Noorani, always tried hard to conceal his poor opinion of T.N. Kaul.

Haksar's leftist leanings served the Prime Minister well in projecting a '*Garibi Hatao*' image that was further reinforced (before the 1971 general elections that were called a year ahead of schedule) through the abolition of the privy purses and privileges of the erstwhile Princes; with so many Indians so poor, these privileges were, in the words of P.N. Haksar, 'out of place and out of time'. Land reform policies were also introduced.

As is widely known, it was through the unremitting efforts of Sardar Patel and V.P. Menon that the Princes were brought around to integrating their States with the Dominion of India in consideration of which they were to be paid a Privy Purse. In October, 1949, Sardar Patel persuaded the Constituent Assembly to include Articles 291 and 362 in the Constitution to guarantee the payment of Privy Purses and safeguard the Personal Rights and privileges of the erstwhile Rulers. He also informed the Constituent Assembly that if the monies received from the Rulers of Madhya Bharat alone were invested, the interest would cover the payment of Privy Purses to all the Princes.

After the Sardar's passing, demands began to be raised for the abolition of the Privy Purses but Nehru refused to budge. V.P. Menon was so appalled by these demands that he remarked: 'As an honourable party to an agreement, we cannot take the stand that we shall accept only that part of the settlement which confers rights on us, and repudiate or whittle down that part which defines our obligations. As a nation aspiring to give a moral lead to the world, let it not be said of us that we know the 'price of everything, and the value of nothing'.

In the 1967 elections, several former Rulers entered the fray on the ticket of the Swatantra Party headed by Rajaji and some of them defeated the Congress candidates. Indira Gandhi was now determined to abolish the Privy Purses; the Constitution Twenty Fourth Amendment Bill, 1970 was introduced and passed in the Lok Sabha but defeated in the Rajya Sabha. She then advised President V.V. Giri to derecognize the Rulers. The derecognition was successfully challenged in the Supreme Court of India by none other than Nani Palkhivala in the celebrated Privy Purses case. Months later, Indira Gandhi's landslide win in the 1971 elections enabled her to amend the Constitution stating, in Parliament, that the concept of Privy Purses and Special Privileges was incompatible with an 'egalitarian social order'.

Thus, in just about two decades, the Congress Party of which Sardar Patel was a towering figure, betrayed the solemn guarantees given to the Rulers by the Constituent Assembly. It was primarily on Patel's assurance that the Rulers had signed the Instruments of Accession that created a united India.

Lord Mountbatten was among those still alive in the seventies who had been on the scene in India when the princely States were being integrated with the Indian Union in 1947-48. He expressed great disappointment over the abolition of the Privy Purses. As Viceroy and Governor General, he had been of considerable assistance in bringing the Princes around to signing the Instruments of Accession, in a sense, their own death warrants.

The Indira Gandhi – led Congress won a two-thirds majority in the Lok Sabha, decimating the opponents in the fight against whom the first split of the Grand Old Party (GOP) had occurred in 1969.

Indira Gandhi adhered to the basic elements of her father's foreign and domestic policies, a continuing commitment to the Non-Aligned Movement (NAM) whose Seventh Summit was held in New Delhi in March 1983, an emphatic support for socialistic measures and a performing public sector and last, but not the least, a strong belief in the crucial role that Science and Technology had to play in the country's development and in the emancipation of its poor.

After Homi Bhabha's death in a plane crash in January 1966, her first choice for his successor as Chairman, Atomic Energy Commission was S. Chandrasekhar, FRS, the Chicago-based, internationally acclaimed astrophysicist who was to go on to win the Nobel Prize in Physics in 1983;

when Chandrasekhar declined, she appointed Vikram Sarabhai (1919-71) of the Physical Research Laboratory (PRL), Ahmedabad. Sarabhai also headed the Space Commission which was established by the Indira Gandhi government in 1972 and in which he was succeeded by Satish Dhawan.

S. Chandrasekhar and his wife, Lalitha, had their last meeting with Indira Gandhi at her home in 1, Safdarjung Road, New Delhi in February 1982.

Chandrasekhar recalled:

> She was gracious enough to give me an appointment for the asking of it and for no particular reason. I began by asking her whether I was wrong in thinking that the pride and the hope which characterized India of the twenties and thirties were no longer the characteristics of the India of 1982. She responded with a certain grimness, 'I am afraid that is so. National pride is no longer a national commodity, instead criticism and distrust seem to be the present national pastimes.
>
> My last question to Mrs. Gandhi was: 'Are you optimistic about the future of India?' Her instant reply was, 'I cannot afford not to be optimistic.'
>
> At that, her face which had till then been grave, broadened into a most charming smile .... She was a great lady if ever there was one."[27]

In her political career, the issues pertaining to *Poverty and Environment* were always among the most important on her agenda. At the U.N. Conference on Human Environment in Stockholm in 1972 – when a global focus was first directed to the concept of environmental security – she famously asked: 'Are not poverty and greed the greatest polluters?' ... and added that 'it would be ironic if the fight against pollution were to be converted into another business, out of which a few companies, corporations or nations would make profits at the cost of the many'.

The Stockholm Conference is the genesis of many of the environmental measures that have since been brought into force in India.

In 1973, her government launched Project Tiger, a major Tiger Conservation Programme, of which she was the main inspiration. Her passion for the preservation of wild life (a concern her father does not seem to have

---

27 Kameshwar C. Wali: *Chandra, a Biography of S. Chandrasekhar*, University of Chicago Press, 1992 (p. 289).

shared in his day) and the unbending support she extended for a clean and healthy environment guarantee, by themselves, a high pedestal for her in public life.

Indira Gandhi played her hand brilliantly in the liberation of Bangladesh. Following the surrender of the Pakistani forces, she announced:

> 'Dacca is now the free capital of a free country'.

India was in the right on the legal and moral plane and had internationalized the tragedy of the Bangla refugees. It allowed space to the government-in-exile and offered tactical and technical support to the liberation army. The intervention broke up Pakistan and tilted the balance of power in India's favour. The year 1971, therefore, had huge consequences for the sub-continent.

There were many who subscribed to the view that Sheikh Mujib was not keen on Independence, that he wanted to be Prime Minister of the whole of Pakistan and that it was because of the obdurate attitude of the Yahya military regime and Zulfiqar Ali Bhutto that Mujib had to declare Independence. He was still willing to negotiate but the Awami League's Youth Wing remained firm.

Contrary to expectations, Dacca proved to be 'no puppet'. Within four years of the liberation, the army had taken over and Sheikh Mujibur Rahman had been assassinated with many of his family members, on an anniversary of India's Independence Day, August 15, 1975, which shook Indira Gandhi very badly. The Islamic – rather than the Bengali – identity of the new nation was being emphasized and India's role was left much diminished, even in Indira Gandhi's lifetime.

While India today has a friendly government in Bangladesh, the politics remains fluid and uncertain. The radicalization has been spearheaded by the Jamaat – which opposed liberation in the first place – even as the Bangladesh Awami League tries to defend the founding values of Bangladesh.

An important effect of the Bangladesh war was that Indira Gandhi's delusions of omnipotence increased. She was now very popular and began to establish a combative style of leadership which was highly personalized. Unlike Nehru around whom there was never a coterie, his daughter began to concentrate all power in herself, both within the Congress and with her Cabinet. The result was that both the Party and the Cabinet ceased to function democratically. The ministers were, by and large, not colleagues any more but sycophants and hangers-on. Several individuals of leftist disposition became part of a kitchen cabinet; Mohan Kumaramangalam, once a member of the Communist Party, was very influential.

Corruption became second nature to the Congress leadership. It was now entrenched and institutionalized and bolstered the party coffers.

Chief Ministers were appointed and removed at will. One such, Hemwati Nandan (H.N.) Bahuguna (1919–89) who hailed from Pauri Garhwal (UP), was well-liked and was known for his administrative and organizational capabilities, was forced to resign in 1975 after a spell as Chief Minister. His anguish was expressed in an Urdu complet:

Hum baa-wafaa they, isliye nazron se gir gaye,
Shayad tumhein talaash kisi be-wafaa ki thi
(I paid the price of loyalty and fell from grace,
The search was, perhaps, for someone disloyal)

Her dynastic successor, Rajiv Gandhi, did not abandon the practice.

In early 1973, the Supreme Court was hearing a petition challenging a new law which gave Parliament greater powers to amend the Constitution. A full Bench heard the matter. Seven judges, including Justices Shelat, Hegde and Grover, were in favour of restricting Parliament's power while the other judges, including Justice A.N. Ray, were on the government's side.

In a sharply divided verdict, by a margin of 7-6, the Supreme Court held that while the Parliament has wide powers, it did not have the power to destroy or emasculate the basic elements and the fundamental features of the Constitution.

Weeks later, in breach of the established practice of appointing the senior-most judge as the Chief Justice of India (CJI), the government chose Justice A.N. Ray for this top constitutional appointment, even though three judges, Justices Shelat, Hegde and Grover were ahead of him. The appointment was widely attacked, among others, by JP, as being politically motivated and an indication of government's increasing desire to control the judiciary.

The three senior judges were left with no option by the Indira Gandhi government but to resign. Justice Hegde was later elected to the Lok Sabha and was the Speaker (1977–80).

Justice Ray's elevation was linked to the case in which he had, lately, sided with the government, as also to a view held by Haksar, still the Principal Secretary, that judges as well as civil servants should be 'committed' to the politics and ideology of the government in power. Justice Ray was also the judge whose sole dissent in the eleven-judge Bench decision in the Bank Nationalization case had pleased the government.

A former CJI, Justice M. Hidayatullah summed up the 'First Supersession' (as it came to be to known) as 'an attempt of not creating forward looking judges but the judges looking forward to the plumes of the office of Chief Justice'.

A former Attorney General for India, C.K. Daphtary (then a nominated Member of Parliament) said in the Rajya Sabha that 'the boy who wrote the best essay has now got the first prize'.

The process continued with the controversial appointment of Justice M.H. Beg superseding Justice H.R. Khanna in 1977.

Indira Gandhi was known to discard her closest advisers at the drop of a hat, one such case being that of the wily D.P. Mishra, a key adviser between 1963–72. Haksar's turn to leave coincided, broadly, with the rise of Sanjay Gandhi who was increasingly jealous of the Principal Secretary's influence over his mother. Haksar was shifted to the Planning Commission where he made a sterling contribution. The Emergency was not long in coming; in the elections which were held in 1977, the Congress was wiped out and Indira and Sanjay themselves lost their seats. There were many who felt that if Haksar had been at Indira Gandhi's side, the situation would not have spiralled out of control.

When questions began to be asked in Parliament about Sanjay Gandhi's 'small car' project, Haksar advised the Prime Minister to abandon the Maruti project and extricate herself from her younger son's doings. The advice was disregarded.

In later months, such was the atmosphere of animosity obtaining under the Emergency that Haksar's relatives in Connaught Place, New Delhi were raided by the sales tax authorities on flimsy grounds.

To those who knew him, Haksar was kind and generous. He intervened to arrange an alternative posting at the Centre for the outgoing Home Secretary, N.K. Mukarji (ICS, Punjab, 1943) who was being reverted to the parent cadre in June 1975.

In January 1973, Haksar declined the Padma Vibhushan and wrote to the then Union Home Secretary to say that he would be grateful '... if you will kindly convey to PM my deep and abiding gratitude for the privilege I had to serve under her.' Obviously, this man was unique.

Sanjay Gandhi's rise also coincided with the beginning of trouble in Gujarat – the home ground of the present Prime Minister – where student protests, demanding the dismissal of an extremely corrupt Congress government turned violent. The movement called itself Nav Nirman and inspired students in Bihar to launch a struggle against misgovernance in their State. While left-wing groupings were the first in the fray, these were soon overtaken by the Akhil Bharatiya Vidyarthi Parishad (ABVP) – the student union linked to the Jana Sangh and, later, to the BJP – which forged a united front with other non-communist groups that became known as the Chhatra Sangharsh Samiti (CSS).

The CSS approached JP, a revered and respected figure with an impeccable and unassailable reputation, to lead their movement. One of the conditions JP imposed was that the movement should not be confined to Bihar. Shortly afterwards, clashes occurred in Patna prompting JP to say that he would no longer remain a silent spectator '... it is not for this that I had fought for freedom ...' and would combat corruption and misgovernment in all parts of the country; he also demanded an overhaul of the educational system.

From now on, it was the 'JP movement' that took wing in India. A series of acrimonious exchanges took place between Indira Gandhi and JP who spoke of 'total revolution'. A nuclear device was successfully exploded at Pokhran in Rajasthan and the process initiated of the integration of the quasi-independent State of Sikkim with the Indian Union. But the real magic lay with the JP movement whom some even hailed as a 'second freedom struggle'.

It was the Allahabad High Court verdict of June 12, 1975 declaring her election to Parliament as null and void that transformed the whole scenario for Indira Gandhi. A fortnight later, to the day, a rubberstamp President declared a 'state of emergency'.

Shanti Bhushan, a much respected member of the legal profession in India, was the senior counsel for the socialist leader, Raj Narain, in the case filed to challenge Indira Gandhi's election to the Lok Sabha in 1971. The judgment pronounced by Justice Jagmohanlal (JML) Sinha of the Allahabad High Court convicted her of electoral malpractices, disqualified her from Parliament and barred her for six years from holding any elected office.

Years later, when Shanti Bhushan[28] was asked if Justice Sinha's verdict had changed the course of the country's history, he said: '... The Emergency

28 Shanti Bhushan (born 1925 at Allahabad) was the Law Minister in the Morarji Desai government from 1977 to 1979.

as well as Indira Gandhi losing the 1977 election was the direct result of Justice Sinha's judgment .... Justice Sinha was a very able, honest and god-fearing judge. Before the judgment, an attempt was made to influence him by the then Chief Justice of the Allahabad High Court, Justice D.S. Mathur, ICS who visited him at his residence, alongwith his wife, for the first and only one time to convey that he had been informed by Dr K.P. Mathur, who was related to him and was the personal physician of Mrs Gandhi, that she had decided to elevate Justice Sinha to the Supreme Court after he had decided the case. However, Justice Sinha's strong conscience did not permit him to take the bait. This was conveyed to me long after the judgment by Justice Sinha himself ...'.

Indira Gandhi's tendency to identify and reward her favourites in the civil service unsettled the bureaucracy by enhancing factional splits and disputes. At the same time, she depended on the bureaucracy when imposing repressive policies. During the Emergency, the IAS stood forth as the ruling elite, taking orders directly from the Prime Minister's men. The IAS mechanism was positioned to coordinate the Emergency throughout the country.

As Prime Minister, Rajiv Gandhi continued his mother's approach in respect of the relationship of the PMO with the bureaucracy. His initial moves suggested that he might relax the hold of his trusted bureaucrats like Gopi Arora (IAS, UP, 1957) over the government but he soon gave that up. The partisan promotions and transfers of senior bureaucrats caused much rancour and resentment. He went so far as to sack, on the spot as it were, a serving Foreign Secretary of known ability and merit.

Gopalaswami Parthasarathi (or GP, as he was commonly known), son of Sir N. Gopalaswami Ayyangar, was a trusted confidant of Indira Gandhi. A tried and tested diplomat, he was an adviser and trouble-shooter in more than one area of policy making. He discouraged Rajiv Gandhi from intervention in the civil war in Sri Lanka by sending in the Indian Peace Keeping Force (IPKF). His recommendations went unheeded.

Unlike her father, Indira Gandhi tried to influence and interfere with the functioning of institutions of proven worth and value like the Judiciary and to curtail the freedom of the Press. In the process, she succeeded in inflicting damage of a fairly permanent nature.

Jawaharlal Nehru was quite the opposite in his attitude and approach to the judiciary. In November 1948, Sir Harilal Kania (1890–1951), the then Chief Justice of the Federal Court, informed Nehru of the Bihar government's failure to release detainees even after the Patna High Court had directed that they be set free. Nehru wrote to the Chief Minister, Sri Krishna Sinha (Sri Babu):

> This is a serious matter for it will bring the High Court into disrepute. It is essential that our High Courts should have the reputation of full independence and integrity and that Governments should not interfere in any way with the work of the Judiciary.[29]

The military action in Amritsar in June 1984 and the unspeakable atrocities suffered by the Sikhs after Indira Gandhi's assassination were truly disastrous in their consequences. The Emergency, with all its brutalities, remains the biggest blot of all. The sterilization programme undermined her credibility among her strongest supporters, the Muslims, Dalits and the Backward Classes.

Under the malevolent influence of her younger son, Indira Gandhi took India into an abyss of authoritarianism and a rejection of the democratic principles and ideals her father so cherished. It was the persistent criticism of old British friends such as Horace Alexander, Fenner Brockway and Mountbatten, among others, that weighed with her when, in January 1977, she announced fresh elections and brought India back to democracy. She could not have missed what John Grigg, historian and politician, wrote in August 1976: 'Nehru's tryst with destiny seems to have been turned into a tryst with despotism – and by his own daughter'. He implored Indira Gandhi to free herself of her son's dominating role and return to the values of Jawaharlal Nehru's generation. To do so, he observed, 'would be the hardest act of her career, but it would also be the bravest and best.'

When the Rajmatas of the former royal houses of Gwalior and Jaipur were arrested during the Emergency, Lord Mountbatten was distressed and missed no opportunity in the United Kingdom to be publicly critical:

> You have locked up so many decent people, including our friends. The reaction here to your Emergency should not surprise you. It should worry you. It comes from your friends.[30]

In her Birth Centenary Year, 2016–17, Indira Gandhi is prone to be recalled more for the Emergency and Operation Blue Star than for her

29 S. Gopal (ed), *Selected Works of Jawaharlal Nehru,* 2nd series (Delhi, 1989) p. 199.

30 K. Natwar Singh: *Profiles and Letters* (Rupa, 1997).

achievements. And yet, in a country where 5 or 6 out of every 10 people have been born after her assassination thirty-two years ago, she is still part of the national discourse.

It is to be hoped that the Centenary Year will do greater justice to Indira Gandhi who was the moving spirit behind 'Smiling Buddha' or Pokharan-I, India's first successful nuclear bomb test in May, 1974.

After the decisive defeat of the Congress in March 1977, Morarji Desai was sworn in as the first non-Congress Prime Minister of India. His political roots had always been in the Congress, as was the case with many of his new Janata Party colleagues like Jagjivan Ram, Chaudhary Charan Singh, Hemwati Nandan Bahuguna and Biju Patnaik. Desai had waited several years for his place in the sun, having come close to fulfilling his ambition in 1966 and 1967. At 80 years, while he was fairly old for the high office, he was remarkably fit and mentally agile.

In some respects, the Desai cabinet had better talent than the outgoing regime. Desai's selection as Prime Minister from within the ranks of a disparate political outfit, which was now called the Janata Party, was made by JP, the man who had made an alternative government feasible in the first instance, and the ageing Acharya Kripalani, a former Congress President who had shared a 'fluctuating' relationship with Nehru. Desai commanded respect and his Principal Secretary, V. Shankar, ICS (of the Sardar Patel era) who had been brought out of retirement, ran quite a tight ship at the PMO. There were a few colleagues from outside the Congress, such as Atal Bihari Vajpayee and L.K. Advani of the Jana Sangh and the socialists, Raj Narain and George Fernandes. Madhu Dandavate made a mark as an able and pragmatic minister in Railways.

The Janata Party had far too many factions and prospective prime ministers to function properly. Men as diverse as Desai, Jagjivan Ram, Charan Singh, George Fernandes and Vajpayee could only agree on the need to bring Indira Gandhi to justice; Vajpayee who had hailed her as a Durga of the modern age, after India's military victory in the erstwhile East Pakistan, now said that the Janata government would 'consign Indira Gandhi to the dustbin of history'.

Beyond the fighting and the factionalism, the Janata government made a notable contribution by repairing the Constitution from the Emergency's depredations, by reviving open parliamentary practice through its consultative style and by restoring the independence of the Judiciary.

On the eve of the 1977 elections, Morarji Desai had assured that, if the Janata Party won, they would 'work for the removal of fear which has enveloped the people' and that 'we will ensure that an Emergency like this can never be imposed. No Government should be able to do so'. In pursuance of this promise, several amendments enacted during the previous two years were repealed under the supervision of the hard working Law Minister, Shanti Bhushan.

Around this time, the Shah Commission was very much in the news and a string of books on the excesses of the Emergency were being published.

Apart from showing that Congress could be defeated, the Janata government, inspired by the JP movement, was seen to contribute to championing the rights of the Dalits and the landless workers which, in turn, intensified caste wars, more so in the U.P. and Bihar. A Commission headed by B.P. Mandal (1918–82), then a Lok Sabha member and, earlier, a thirty-day Chief Minister of Bihar in 1968, was appointed. When the Report was ready, the Janata Party was no longer in office; it was not to be implemented till the Congress had been defeated a second time and been replaced by the V.P. Singh – led dispensation.

Morarji Desai came to office after a distinguished career in politics. He was convinced of the importance of Parliament as a representative institution, to the point of being dogmatic and inflexible over the need for wider consultation.

He remains the only Indian national to be decorated with Pakistan's highest Civilian Award, the Nishan-e-Pakistan, which was conferred on him by the then President, Ghulam Ishaq Khan, in 1990. Nelson Mandela was another foreign recipient of the Award in 1992.

The Janata period (1977–79) left an important legacy in that it ensured the growth of the Jana Sangh which had joined the coalition. After some time, voices both from within and outside were raised in respect of the Jana Sangh's dual allegiance – to the Janata Party and to its ideological parent, the RSS. The Jana Sangh leadership refused to sever the relationship with the RSS and left the Janata Party which was now in disarray. The BJP became the new vehicle for Hindu nationalism.

In 1978, Indira Gandhi successfully contested a by-election for the Lok Sabha from the Chikmagalur constituency in Karnataka. A slogan *Ek sherni, sau langoor, Chikmagalur, Chikmagalur* (one tigress, hundred monkeys, Chikmagalur, Chikmagalur) was coined by the then Chief Minister, Devaraj URS, for this election which helped set the stage for Congress' recapturing power at the Centre and in U.P.

It was more the fragmented nature of the opposing parties rather than the popularity of the Congress that brought Indira Gandhi back. The Janata government had floundered because of the vaulting ambitions of the likes of Chaudhary Charan Singh and was divided when the elections were held. The Congress, despite polling only about 36 per cent of the vote, regained its old 350 plus seats, one more than in 1971.

Chaudhary did not once face Parliament during his six months in the prime ministerial chair following the resignation of Morarji Desai; he is better remembered for being a pioneer, as Revenue Minister in the U.P., of the path-breaking land reforms of the 1950s.

Indira Gandhi was a chastened person in her last years in power (1980–84). Within months, her personal world lay in ruins in the wake of Sanjay's passing in June 1980. She turned to spiritualism and to the higher powers, as advised by Dhirendra Brahmachari, who himself continued to prosper materially. It is fair to say that she never quite regained her balance. As Sonia Gandhi was to put it later, after the 'disaster' of Sanjay's death, Indira Gandhi 'for all her courage and composure was broken in spirit'.[31]

She knew that Sanjay's persona aroused strong feelings. He was either worshipped or demonized. Despite his failings and his many enemies, he could have inherited power from his mother who made no secret of the fact that this was what she wished. He had already shown his electoral mettle in engineering Indira Gandhi's return as Prime Minister.

In the backdrop of the Janata Government's dismal performance and the political uncertainties that had come to the fore, the Indira Gandhi – led Congress was perceived to be on a 'comeback trail' in the 1979–80 Lok Sabha elections. With Sanjay Gandhi's encouragement, several members of the erstwhile feudal order, including ex-royals, quickly boarded the Congress' bandwagon. Among others, the titular Maharaja of Gwalior, Madhavrao Scindia (1945–2001) was elected from Guna (Madhya Pradesh) on the Congress ticket.

Sanjay Gandhi left a very dangerous legacy in Punjab, having been a central figure behind the government's covert backing of Jarnail Singh Bhindranwale and his fast growing band of Sikh militants, with the short-sighted objective of weakening the Akali Dal. This secret aiding and abetting of Bhindranwale was to culminate in Operation Bluestar and the storming of the Golden Temple at Amritsar in June 1984; the assassination of the Prime Minister by her own bodyguards followed after four months.

Her final period as Prime Minister saw the meteoric rise of Pranab

31 Sonia Gandhi: Rajiv (p. 6).

Mukherjee (later to be the President of the Republic) on the political firmament. As the Finance Minister, he presented the Budget for 1982-83 and signed the letter appointing Manmohan Singh as the Governor of the Reserve Bank of India.

Indira Gandhi kept the Congress in power till 1989, as much by her death as by her life.

Of the Presidents who served in Indira Gandhi's time, two (Fakhruddin Ali Ahmed and Giani Zail Singh) were selected for their pliability. Neelam Sanjiva Reddy (1977–82) was installed by the post-Emergency Janata Government and did not owe his position to her. Reddy made vigorous criticisms in private and muted comments in public. Her last choice of a President – Zail Singh in 1982 – was intended to give her still greater leverage. By raising him to the exalted office, she could ensure his gratitude. He was duly elected President and was later to fall out with her son.

Indira Gandhi, albeit to a lesser extent than her father, liked to have a few brilliant minds around her, one such being the late Sukhamoy Chakraborty (1934-90) who was brought into the Planning Commission after the abrupt dismissal of the entire body in early 1970 which saw the departure of the Deputy Chairman, D.R. Gadgil; he had disagreed with her decision to nationalize the commercial banking system.

The Prime Minister was quick to perceive that, in Chakraborty, she had by her side a formidable scholar who, in turn, was steadfastly loyal to her till the end.

Arjun Sengupta (1937-2010), also an economist, worked closely with her, including as Special Secretary in the PMO between 1981-84. A veteran journalist wrote that Sengupta's critical stance towards 'the neo-liberal school of economic thought' and his unwillingness to 'cultivate political godfathers' meant that he would be 'one Finance Minister India never had'.

The next three decades, 1984–2014, saw a procession of prime ministers of whom as many as four completed their full terms; the last, a Congress nominee, who was in the job more in theory than in practice, actually carried on for two terms.

The short-lived tenures of H.D. Deve Gowda and Inder Kumar Gujral (1919–2012) were a reason for the impact of their administrations, such as it was, to simply fade away in public memory.

When Rajiv Gandhi became Prime Minister on October 31, 1984 – which put a final seal on dynastic succession in the Congress – he gave, in the beginning, an impression of being more like his grandfather, that is, a consensus

– builder in a federal polity. This impression disappeared quite quickly when his own credibility (and that of his government) began to sink on account, chiefly, of the Bofors matter. Between 1985–89, he changed a number of Congress Chief Ministers.

Like those who were to succeed him in South Block, barring Narasimha Rao, the new Prime Minister was almost immediately surrounded by a set of special favourites. The Doon School boys, the ubiquitous Arun Nehru (a distant cousin and a grandson of Uma Nehru, a former parliamentarian) and some others seemed to be all over the place. This was Rajiv Gandhi's first coterie and it survived for nearly two years till the storm broke over Bofors. He was supremely confident in their company. This was the computer generation now unexpectedly finding itself at the top.

Within months, the new government was rocked by a serious spy scandal with links to the Prime Minister's Office. A conman of an Indian firm who had established close connections with foreign missions was found to have been passing on photocopies of classified documents to his clients. The then Principal Secretary, P.C. Alexander, a retired IAS man (not of the ilk of L.K. Jha or P.N. Haksar but who was later to display lofty political ambitions) resigned owning moral responsibility for the lapse.

Arun Nehru and, to a considerable extent, Arun Singh, exerted immense influence across the length and breadth of the government. As a Joint Secretary, I saw the former in action as the Minister of State for Power (1985–86) when he all but sidelined the senior minister, B. Shankaranand, himself no political lightweight; the latter, more a man of principle, made his exit over the differences that had, apparently, surfaced in regard to Bofors.

Nehru left the government about a year after his appointment as the Minister for Internal Security. It seemed a sudden development about which there was no dearth of speculation at the time. In August 1986, the tenure was also cut short of a capable civilian, incidentally, a Kashmiri brahmin, P.K. Kaul (IAS, UP, 1951), a hand-picked Cabinet Secretary; his replacement was the then Maharashtra Chief Secretary, a CKP. However, Kaul was accommodated as the next Indian Ambassador in Washington D.C.

Arun Nehru stayed out of favour and, in due course, joined the Jan Morcha, an outfit floated, in 1988, by Rajiv Gandhi's one-time Finance Minister, Vishwanath Pratap (V.P.) Singh. Alongwith Mufti Mohammed Sayeed of Jammu & Kashmir, Nehru (and his ally, Arif Mohammed Khan, who had parted company with the Congress over the Shah Bano case) emerged among the leading lights of the Morcha.

On October 11, 1988, J.P's birthday, V.P. Singh founded the Janata Dal by the merger of the Jan Morcha, the Janata Party, the Lok Dal and the Congress (S). He was elected President of the Janata Dal. A coalition formed by the Janata Dal with three regional parties (in Tamil Nadu, Andhra Pradesh and Assam) called the National Front next came into being with N.T. Rama Rao as president and Singh as convener.

The National Front did well enough in the 1989 elections to catapult V.P. Singh (1931–2008) to the prime ministership with the backing of the BJP, the CPM and the CPI.

With a huge victory in the December 1984 elections behind him (his Party won 401 seats in the Lok Sabha, more than his mother or his grandfather), Rajiv Gandhi (1944–91) had the space for manoeuvre. He took initiatives in Punjab and the North East and introduced a change of vision for the Indian economy by pursuing an explicit programme of deregulation and relaxing the constraints imposed decades earlier. The visit to China in December 1988 was hailed as a 'leap forward' in the direction of improving Sino-Indian relations.

While the electoral win was more a sympathy vote for Indira Gandhi's assassination than a positive vote for her son, Rajiv Gandhi could still have consolidated his position but for the charges of corruption brought against him by opponents like V.P. Singh who was known for his integrity. The media had a field day with the Bofors and Rajiv Gandhi's standing suffered an irreparable blow.

Before Rajiv Gandhi lost power in 1989, his government had, two years earlier, signalled a change in the Sri Lanka policy. There had been a history of discrimination against the Tamils in that country and a Simhala – only policy had been brought in way back in 1956. The non-Simhalese speaking people found themselves second-class citizens. When a Tamil party fighting on the plank of secession did well in the 1977 elections, the inter-community relations deteriorated further and anti-Tamil rioting broke out, the most serious in 1983.

India now began arming the Tamil rebels – a decision motivated partly by an aspiring regional power's desire to flex its muscles and partly as a response to the outrage expressed by South India's own Tamil population. A definite thrust came under Rajiv Gandhi so that when the Sri Lanka government blockaded Jaffna, India unilaterally airdropped food supplies to the peninsula. These operations had the effect of moderating President J.R. Jayawardene who agreed to the Thirteenth Amendment that would guarantee a degree of devolution to the North and the East. Sri Lanka and India signed an Accord and New Delhi sent in the Indian Peace Keeping Force (IPKF) to enforce the same during one of the phases of the civil war. The Liberation Tigers of Tamil Eelam (LTTE) resisted this action.

The operation failed and the IPKF returned to Indian shores. The defect probably lay in the nature of the Accord which may have had a better run had it been concluded between Colombo and the Tamil parties, with India guaranteeing its implementation. The consultations with the Tamil parties were done in haste and, in the end, the mediator became the key actor and the villain. The arch rivals, the Simhalese regime and the Tamils, stood united in their opposition to the IPKF.

The Sri Lanka enterprise scarred India and cost Rajiv Gandhi his life. The LTTE was determined to prevent his second installation as Prime Minister and extracted revenge through a fatal bomb attack in May 1991 when the electioneering for the mid-term polls was in full swing.

It is a moot question whether Rajiv Gandhi ought to have been advised with more judicious circumspection, not only by the generals and the intelligence agencies but also by the key diplomats, including J.N. Dixit, the then High Commissioner in Colombo and his senior colleagues in the Indian High Commission. An ill-advised and misguided intervention should have been avoided. At any rate, the ultimate consequences for India could hardly have been worse.

According to lately declassified documents, President J.R. Jayawardene had told a U.S. diplomat, Peter Galbraith, that Sri Lanka was forced into making a deal with India as its own armed forces had refused to 'take Jaffna'. In 1986, Jayawardene, apparently, had a very negative view of India, given that New Delhi was reported to be training Tamil insurgents. He seems to have told a visiting U.S. Senator, Charles Percy; 'I am a very peaceful man. But India's role in this [ethnic] matter is reprehensible and the Indians have to be held responsible for their actions'.

Rajiv Gandhi undertook, with a measure of success, an ambitious exercise to push forward the concept of 'Responsive Administration' and establish the Panchayati Raj Institutions.

His regime was generally free of communal bias but witnessed at least two riots of frightening proportions – the Meerut carnage of 1987 and the anti-Muslim outrage in Bhagalpur in Bihar when the 1989 election campaign was in progress. The thoughtless handling of the Babri Masjid – Ramjanmabhoomi dispute, in which Arun Nehru and the then U.P. Chief Minister, Vir Bahadur Singh, were involved, eventually led to the destruction of the Babri Masjid in December 1992.

The reversal in Rajiv Gandhi's political fortunes was, in part, self-inflicted. His record in economic policy was good and his rise to national leadership symbolized a generational change. He had the potential to do much more to modernize India. He was in office for only five years and would not be prime minister again. Had he lived, the country would likely have seen the re-emergence of a mature and energetic figure who was still in his forties.

A younger Morarji Desai in the 1960s or an older Rajiv Gandhi in 1991 might have steered Indian politics on quite a different course and changed things for the better. They could, each in his own way, have hastened the transformation of India towards the goal of a progressive society.

Twenty two years after the first Janata experiment, a second one started with the rise to power of the Janata Dal (JD) in 1989. Once again, its success was due to the North Indian voters since 101 of the 143 seats won by the JD were from the four largest States of the Hindi belt. It was a significant achievement for a party that had been founded only a year earlier, yet it had not started from scratch.

Between themselves, the two Thakurs of divergent backgrounds, one the 1931-born Raja of Manda near Allahabad, Vishwanath Pratap (V.P.) Singh, and his successor, Chandra Shekhar (1927-2007) of an agriculturist family hailing from Ballia in eastern U.P, an avowed disciple of Acharya Narendra Deva, brought to an end, over a period of just eighteen months, another opportunity to provide a stable non-Congress government at the Centre. That chance was to come yet again, this time to the Hindu Right, under Atal Bihari Vajpayee.

In his first address to the Nation after being sworn in, JP and Ram Manohar Lohia were the names V.P. Singh mentioned as his mentors.

He identified senior civil servants and effected a number of transfers to bring them into key positions, as had happened with changes in the government since the mid-sixties. The power of the PMO was reduced and there was a noticeable shift to allow more autonomy to the ministers and their departments, with the Cabinet Office coming again into the picture, for purposes of coordination. Also, the days of the PMO calling up the district officers had gone, suggesting that the administrative over-centralization, nationally, was being relaxed. In another way, however, administrative centralization was set to increase due to the development of an extensive computer network.

Singh faced his first crisis within days of taking office when Rubaiya Sayeed, a daughter of Mufti Mohammad Sayeed, the then Union Home Minister was kidnapped; the government accepted the demand of releasing militants in exchange and set the stage for unrest on a widespread scale from

1990 onwards. The Atal Bihari Vajpayee government, under the amazingly inept handling of the then Principal Secretary-cum-NSA, a long retired diplomat, and the then Cabinet Secretary, took forward this train of horrifying lapses and administrative failure in December 1999 when the terrorists who had hijacked an Indian Airlines Airbus had to be released at Kandahar, in the presence of Jaswant Singh, a senior minister.

V.P. Singh favoured, like Morarji Desai, a wider role for Parliament, having earlier criticized the Rajiv Gandhi government for indifference to the legislature. During his short tenure, he regularly attended debates and evolved a system of interacting with parliamentary group over proposed legislation. However, given his limited parliamentary support, he had little choice but to keep consulting the 'crutches' of the National Front Government – the right wing BJP, the Left parties and, at times, even the Congress.

In announcing the implementation of the Mandal Commission he declared that '... no section can be uplifted merely by money. They can develop only if they have a share in power and we are prepared to provide this share. In this year of justice, in memory of Dr Bhimrao Ambedkar [whose birth centenary was then to be celebrated soon in 1991] the Government has ... taken a decision to give reservation to the backward classes in jobs in government and public sector. Bureaucracy is an important organ of the power structure. It has a decisive role in decision-making ...'.

V.P. Singh and Chandra Shekhar, despite their roots in the Congress, could not have been more disparate, politically. The latter was, by far, the more senior but if he imagined that he should have been elected to become the Prime Minister in 1989, he had clearly mis-read the signs. The flow of public opinion was then so much tilting towards the Raja of Manda that an alternative leader was not a possibility, regardless of the shifting positions of Chaudhary Devi Lal.

V.P. Singh's integrity was unquestionable and he was one of the very few in the Congress who was free of caste bias. Unlike Chandra Shekhar, he did not look out for favourites of Rajput lineage; there are several instances of this being the case during the seven months of Chandra Shekhar's prime ministership.

He was also virtually alone in standing against corporate pressures and extraneous influence.

In May 1985, as Finance Minister, Singh stopped the import of Purified Terephthalic Acid (PTA) from the Open General Licence Category which, as a raw material, was very important to manufacture polyester filament yarn.

This, in turn, made it difficult for Reliance to carry on operations, even though they were able to secure, from financial institutions, Letters of Credit that would allow import of almost an year's requirement of PTA. In 1990, the government controlled financial institutions like the LIC and the GIC stonewalled attempts by the Reliance Group to acquire managerial control over Larsen and Toubro (*L&T*). Sensing defeat, the Ambani family patriarch preferred to quit as L&T's Chairman and made way for D.N. Ghosh, IA&AS, a former Chairman of the State Bank of India.

V.P. Singh did not waiver in his commitment to the Mandal cause. His credibility among the Muslims was high. When the BJP withdrew support in the wake of Advani's arrest in Bihar during the *rath yatra*, the Prime Minister expected, for some time, that the Congress might stand behind him. A different reason put across for the government's collapse was that if V.P. Singh had not implemented the Mandal Commission recommendations, the BJP would have continued its support.

He found it difficult to run a minority government, particularly because he had powerful detractors within his own party. The chief among these, Chandra Shekhar, seized the moment and, with Congress support, became the prime minister, his lifelong ambition. He appears to have seriously believed that he missed the post in 1977 and, again, in 1990. The fact of the matter is that on the first occasion, the choice was between Morarji Desai and Jagjivan Ram; Chandra Shekhar was then not in the picture, it was not without some difficulty that he was even selected to head the Janata Party. If there was, at all, a third candidate for the prime ministership it was Chaudhary Charan Singh. On the second occasion, Chandra Shekhar could not have become prime minister because the loyalty of members of the Janata Dal was split between V.P. Singh and Devi Lal.

The term of the Chandra Shekhar government saw corruption thrive once again. It was also a time of financial stress and strain. The five years of the Rajiv Gandhi dispensation had led to a crisis which, according to the (late) Dr I.G. Patel, was created because 'we lived in an era when money did not matter'. The seeds of the crisis had been sown during the tenure, as Finance Secretary, of S. Venkitaramanan (IAS, Tamil Nadu, 1953), a Reliance-backed appointee who, for that reason, went on to become the RBI governor.

As the Finance Minister, Yashwant Sinha, formerly of the IAS (Bihar, 1960) steered the country through the difficult months of the 'balance of payments' crisis. Writing in July 2016, he had this to say:

> Reforms are a continuous process. In the wake of the 1991 crisis ... reforms took place in capital markets, banking and industrial policy. This was very impressive, but then did we continue down the path of reforms? The dynamics of the Congress ensured that reforms were given up the moment the crisis abated. I don't agree with Dr Manmohan Singh that we only act in crises .... We have done nothing on administrative, judicial, police or municipal reforms .... In India, the history of reforms has been stop-go, stop-go, and the pace has been very slow ...

After I.K. Gujral declined the offer, Chandra Shekhar chose Vidya Charan (V.C.) Shukla for the External Affairs portfolio. Shukla had been called the Goebbels of the Emergency which Chandra Shekhar had fought tooth and nail. However, he had no compunction in including Shukla in the cabinet for the few votes that the latter may have had at his command.

The *Indian Express* carried a series of interviews last year to mark the 25th year of the beginning of Economic Reforms. Deepak Nayyar, a former Chief Economic Adviser, who was closely associated with the process, said:

> ... any government that came to power in mid – 1991 would have done roughly the same. The blueprints existed. There was little choice. The room for manoeuvre was negligible. However, it was possible only for an elected government with a mandate from the people. And it happened because Prime Minister Narasimha Rao was most decisive in this incarnation .... The reforms were crisis-driven rather than strategy-based. Even so, Narasimha Rao deserves much credit for the deft political management ...

Rakesh Mohan, also a former Chief Economic Adviser opined: '... the biggest role in the 1991 to 1996 reforms was played by A.N. Varma (Principal Secretary to Prime Minister Narasimha Rao); he is the most unsung hero ...'.

Another hero of that period is Naresh Chandra (IAS, Rajasthan, 1956), an exceptionally able and assertive bureaucrat on whom Narasimha Rao relied a great deal. Chandra, a few places below Varma in the IAS list, was appointed Cabinet Secretary by Prime Minister Chandra Shekhar and Varma was sent packing as Member-Secretary in the Planning Commission. After Narasimha Rao took charge, Varma was selected as Principal Secretary, some believe on the advice of Rao's friend and confidant, P.C. Alexander, himself a one-time Principal Secretary in the regimes of Indira Gandhi (1980–84) and Rajiv Gandhi (1984–85).

While Varma and Naresh Chandra did not see eye-to-eye on many an issue, Narasimha Rao had the political and administrative sagacity to engage them both as key advisers and to derive the best from their capabilities.

When Rajiv Gandhi was assassinated in May 1991, the Lok Sabha elections forced by Congress' withdrawal of support to Chandra Shekhar were in progress. The expected sympathy factor worked in favour of the Grand Old Party (GOP) but not quite enough. Winning 244 seats, the Congress was the largest single party but still fell nearly thirty seats short of a majority.

It was obvious that whoever succeeded Rajiv Gandhi as the Congress President was likely to be the next Prime Minister.

In writing about Narasimha Rao's ascension to the party presidency, it is appropriate to recall that a day or so after Rajiv's funeral, Natwar Singh seems to have suggested to Sonia Gandhi that she obtain advice about a possible successor from an old war-horse, P.N. Haksar, Indira Gandhi's capable Principal Secretary who, later, had a tempestuous relationship with the First Family.

Haksar bright-eyed, all over again, in his new-found but short-lived importance (he was now 77 years, no less) first suggested the name of Dr Shankar Dayal Sharma, an earlier Congress Chief, the then incumbent Vice President of India, and a Brahmin of Bhopal origins who had been appointed by Nehru and Azad as the Chief Minister of the erstwhile Part 'C' State (comprising the two districts of Sehore and Raisen of the former princely State) as early as in 1952. He was then teaching in the Law Faculty in Lucknow University when Acharya Narendra Deva was the Vice Chancellor.

Sharma was well-liked and respected, a virtue that, Haksar felt, was the need of the hour. Aruna Asaf Ali and Natwar Singh were asked by Sonia Gandhi to meet with Sharma.

He surprised everyone by declining the offer on grounds of age and health. When Haksar was summoned again, he proposed Pamulaparti Venkata (PV) Narasimha Rao (1921-2004). That recommendation of Haksar went through; Rao's known confidant, PC Alexander, was not very much in the picture at this stage. His proximity to Rao was a reason behind Sonia Gandhi's subsequent distrust of him.

It is a measure of Rao's astute Brahmin intuitions that he kept Sharma waiting for a few weeks before confirming his nomination as the Congress

Party's candidate to succeed R.Venkataraman (1910-2009). Not that Rao had a complete say in the matter, when Sonia Gandhi's support for Sharma was already assured. But Rao was still not ready to play ball.

Even if Rao was tempted to offer the presidency to someone else, he seems to have weighed the alternatives and realized that he could not refuse the man who had turned down the chance to be the country's prime minister before him.

Nonetheless, there was a serious trust-deficit between Sharma and Rao. It is possible that the problem travelled back to 1973 when Prime Minister Indira Gandhi decided to remove Rao as the Chief Minister of Andhra Pradesh when he failed to judge that the Prime Minister wanted someone both powerful and powerless. In mid-January, 1973, he was asked to come to New Delhi and told by Shankar Dayal Sharma, the then Congress President, that the High Command would be imposing President's Rule for some time. Rao disagreed, but did not rebel.

This compliant attitude stood him in good stead in the years to come.

During Sharma's occupancy of Rashtrapati Bhawan, whenever Sonia Gandhi attended the State Banquets or official functions, the protocol accorded to her was on a par with that for Prime Minister Narasimha Rao; the President himself made sure of this.

Rao's equation with the then Vice President, K.R. Narayanan, was less frosty.

Narasimha Rao was only the second Congressman from outside the Gandhi-Nehru fold to become Prime Minister. To my mind, he is also the last, till date, to have established a credibly functioning PMO. His record in the sphere of economic reforms is well-documented but recognition came late in the day, thanks to the attitudes obtaining at the very top in his own party. It is a crying shame that he was denied, even in death, the dignity and respect which he very much deserved.

About whether he strove to function independently and disfavoured interference from the First Family, there should be no two opinions. In his Cabinet, he brought in men like Vidya Charan (V.C.) Shukla (partly as a counterweight to Arjun Singh) who had little loyalty left to the Gandhis, having actively opposed Rajiv, especially in the confrontation with President Zail Singh. As if this were not enough, Rao went ahead to rehabilitate Pranab Mukherjee as Deputy Chairman of the Planning Commission which too could hardly have been music to the ears of 10, Janpath. Another old-timer, Raja Dinesh Singh, was the Minister of External Affairs between 1993-95.

In a lately published account: *The Turbulent Years, 1980-1996*, Pranab Mukherjee addresses a range of events and developments and touches upon the issue which led to speculation that he wanted to edge out Rajiv Gandhi for the top post saying '... Many stories have been circulated that I aspired to be the interim Prime Minister .... These stories are completely false and spiteful ...'. At the same time, it is no secret that Mukherjee had to fight for every inch of the ground to regain a position at the centrestage of Indian politics. It is here that the support of well-wishers, like Narasimha Rao, proved invaluable to him.

In January 2017, Mukherjee cautiously commenced amending his stance on demonetization, acknowledging a possible economic slowdown and the miseries of the poor as some of its 'temporary' outcomes and going on to say:

> 'While I appreciate the thrust on transition from entitlement approach to an entrepreneurial one for poverty alleviation, I am not too sure that the poor can wait that long. They need to get succour here and now, so that they can also participate actively in the national march towards a future devoid of hunger, unemployment and exploitation ....'

The comments marked a subtle shift from the position he had taken when the note withdrawal was announced on November 8, 2016.

Mukherjee was an integral part of the Congress leadership that crafted rights-based welfare schemes like the Rural Employment Guarantee Programme and the Food Security Act. In 2013, he became the first Indian President to allow the Rashtrapati Bhavan to be a venue for a business celebration – the NDTV's twenty-fifth anniversary as an independent Channel.

Narasimha Rao could not persuade his first choice, the noted economist, I.G. Patel, to join as Finance Minister; the second choice, Manmohan Singh, was able to cope with the challenges of an emerging era of change and policy reorientation. Having had to prevail upon Singh not to quit midstream as the Finance Minister, Rao may have felt unsure about him jumping ship, as and when things got really tough; he seems, at one stage, to have toyed with the idea of inducting another economist into the government (perhaps, by again approaching I.G. Patel) when P. Chidambaram resigned as the Commerce Minister in July 1992.

Narasimha Rao's tenure witnessed its share of bribery and corruption but the worst had already happened, early on, with the demolition of the Babri Masjid in Ayodhya, the U.P. township near Faizabad associated with the hallowed memories of Lord Rama.

The Governor of the state, when the Masjid was brought down in December 1992, was B. Satyanarayan Reddy (1927–2012) who served in this position between 1989–93. He was appointed by the V.P. Singh government and had participated in the Hyderabad Peoples' Movement. He was close to the socialist leadership and did not join the Congress.

Reddy was in his mid-sixties when the demolition occurred and was in touch with the then President, Shankar Dayal Sharma. The President entertained serious reservations about the ability or the reliability, or both, of the Kalyan Singh government to protect the structure.

Eventually, the worst came to pass on December 6, 1992. I can say that the President would rarely have been so distressed and distraught as on that day.

Sonia Gandhi, not yet the party president, issued a statement which condemned the razing of the Masjid but did not directly blame Rao. However, the mother-son duo of the Congress had other grievances against him with Rahul Gandhi going so far as to say: 'That man is not a Congressman, because of him we have lost U.P. forever'[32].

Makhan Lal (M.L.) Fotedar[33], (born March 1931), a diehard Gandhi-Nehru family adherent who was Indira Gandhi's Political Secretary from 1980 to 1984 and of Rajiv Gandhi (when he became Prime Minister) for about three years, before himself joining the Union Cabinet, later recorded his own version of the Babri Masjid episode, as it unfolded, on December 6, 1992. He wrote:

> I sought an appointment with President Shankar Dayal Sharma ... when I met Dr Sharma he started weeping .... He looked up at me and said, 'What has P.V. done?'. I shared with him all that had transpired between me and the Prime Minister during the day .... The President told me that he had spoken to the U.P. Governor, B. Satyanarayan Reddy and had got the impression that he had been advised against the imposition of President's Rule by the Prime Minister. I was devastated .... Just before I

32 Vinay Sitapati: *Half Lion; How P.V. Narasimha Rao Transformed India* (Penguin Random House, 2016), P. 297.

33 M.L. Fotedar: *The Chinar Leaves, A Political Memoir* (Harper Collins Publishers, India, 2015). Fotedar, a Pandit from Mattan in the Kashmir Valley, is believed to have played a role in ensuring that Rajiv Gandhi succeeded his mother after her assassination. He was also among those responsible for inducting Sonia Gandhi into active politics, but later lost favour with her.

> was to leave, Reddy called and informed the President that Kalyan Singh[34] had tendered his resignation and had recommended the imposition of President's Rule … .

Rao was attacked by his opponents in the Congress for entering into an electoral alliance with Mayawati's BSP in 1996 which, they contended, had badly affected the Congress in northern India.

The Prime Minister's desperation to protect his minority government – with the tenuous support of the Jharkhand Mukti Morcha (JMM) – clouded his instincts. The decisions on the economy were possibly easier to reach than on the Babri Masjid in respect of which all the options carried political risks. In the end, he placed his faith on protecting the Masjid in the various Hindutva groups with whom he had been in secret negotiations. He was badly let down.

In his remaining years, Narasimha Rao was often at pains to defend his role in the Masjid episode. He could never live down the 'stigma'. Manmohan Singh remained loyal and was one of the few Congressmen to attend his birth anniversary functions. He once spoke of Rao as 'a saint in politics'.

In the 1996 elections, the BJP was the dominant party with 161 seats; the Congress won 140. The BJP claimed that it would be able to muster the numbers to demonstrate its majority. President Sharma (who liked Vajpayee) decided to give the BJP an opportunity to do so on the Floor of the House since it was the largest Party in the Lok Sabha. Vajpayee went ahead to form a full-fledged Cabinet, more or less, with Murli Manohar Joshi, Pramod Mahajan and Sushma Swaraj, (amongst others) as the Ministers of Home Affairs, Defence and Information & Broadcasting respectively. The appointment of the foster son-in-law, as an Officer on Special Duty (OSD) in the PMO, caused consternation, not least in the RSS. A former Indira Gandhi acolyte, B.N. Tandon (IAS, UP, 1951) served as the Principal Secretary for less than two weeks.

On the thirteenth day, Prime Minister Vajpayee submitted the resignation of his government because no support had been forthcoming.

---

34 Kalyan Singh (born 1932) was the U.P. Chief Minister when the demolition of the Babri Masjid happened and was in office between June, 1991 to December, 1992. The CM's Secretariat at Lucknow was headed by Nripendra Mishra (IAS, 1967), who is Principal Secretary to PM Modi.

Kalyan Singh, Chief Minister for a second time between 1997-99, was not steadfast in his loyalty to the BJP. He made a futile bid to float a new Hindutva-oriented political outfit (Jan Kranti Party) in 2010 and is the present Governor of Rajasthan.

It had been a foolhardy exercise for the first BJP government since Independence.

The Congress had no choice but to support a United Front coalition which came to power with the sole purpose of 'containing communal forces and consolidating the secular forces'. First, Deva Gowda and, then, I.K. Gujral became Prime Ministers.

Deve Gowda's tenure of less than a year was colourless except that the Ganga Waters Sharing Accord was concluded in December 1996 with Bangladesh. It owed a lot to the then Chief Minister of West Bengal, Jyoti Basu, who had come within a handshake of becoming Prime Minister when the Vajpayee government fell. At a later date, he termed it a 'historical blunder' (of the CPM's politburo) which it probably was considering that the country lost the chance of being led by a statesman of Basu's sagacity, integrity and experience. None of those who assumed the leadership hereafter could measure up to his stature.

The Gujral government (April, 1997 – March, 1998) was known for its accommodation with neighbouring countries. This policy of placating neighbours came to be known as the 'Gujral Doctrine'.

Next came two Vajpayee-led governments that lasted six years in two phases, winning an election in 1998 and the next in 1999. Both did not perform strikingly in any particular way yet the Prime Minister, given his amiable temperament, was able to keep a multi-party coalition together and afford a semblance of political stability.

Vajpayee saw it fit to virtually outsource the Government of India to his Man Friday, the supremely-powerful Brajesh Mishra, a fellow Kanyakubja Brahmin, and a long retired diplomat. Mishra is believed to have been passed over for the Secretary – level grade in the IFS when he was the Permanent Representative of India (PRI) at the United Nations in New York; it was said that the then Prime Minister had struck his name off the list.

Mishra was left with no alternative but to seek early retirement. While he had next to no exposure to the realities of administration in India, so potent (and eventually disastrous) was his influence over Vajpayee that he chose to attack the Sangh functionaries for adopting a 'frog in the well' attitude; when differences persisted, he was, apparently, instrumental in seeing the then RSS supremo, K.S. Sudarshan himself, off from New Delhi, no doubt with Vajpayee's encouraging nod.

In June 2012, Mishra told a news channel: 'First of all, we must be clear that the BJP is not going to get majority on its own. Impossible. And, therefore, he (Modi) cannot be put forward as a successor. They will have to find somebody else …'. Mishra also said that Modi continued as Chief Minister of Gujarat after the post-Godhra violence because the BJP wanted him to and Vajpayee did not overrule the party opinion. He did not live to see Modi's installation as Prime Minister in May 2014.

In the context of Mishra's role, such as it was, it should be recalled that soon after the end of the Kargil War in July 1999, the NDA government constituted a Review Committee headed by the well-known defence analyst, K. Subrahmanyam (1929–2011) to analyze the situation that had led to the government of the day being caught unawares by the Pakistani aggression. While most of the Committee's recommendations were accepted, it was the one relating to the National Security Council (set up earlier by the Vajpayee government) which did not meet with the approval of the Prime Minister. The recommendation read as follows:

> Whatever its merits, having a National Security Adviser who also happens to be Principal Secretary to the Prime Minister, can only be an interim arrangement. The Committee believes that there must be a full-time National Security Adviser and it would suggest that a second line of personnel be inducted into the system as early as possible and groomed for higher responsibility.

Lal Krishna (LK) Advani, the then Home Minister (he was designated Deputy Prime Minister in February 2002) commented as follows in his illuminating autobiography:

> Many senior ministers in the government and I felt that there was much merit in this suggestion. We repeatedly urged the Prime Minister to bifurcate the two posts held by Brajesh Mishra. Atalji, however, had a different view and did not implement this recommendation. It was, of course, the Prime Minister's prerogative to do so. In my view, the clubbing together of two critical responsibilities, each requiring focussed attention, did not contribute to harmony at the highest levels of governance[35].

Vajpayee was endowed with formidable oratorical skills and he was a shrewd political player with a strikingly high level of adaptability and sense

35 L.K. Advani: *My Country, My Life*, Rupa & Co. 2008, (p. 575).

of timing. In his own inimitable way, he tried to reinforce the notion that the BJP was a party with a difference. He had a flair for establishing friendships outside the BJP and led a non-Congress government for six years, making serious overtures to normalize relations with Pakistan; he also demonstrated a knack for survival within the Sangh Parivar.

The first big event of his premiership was the detonation of five devices (Pokharan II) in May 1998. The euphoria was short-lived since Pakistan carried out a test within a week of Pokharan-II. A controversy also erupted about the yield of the second fusion [H-bomb stage of the thermo-nuclear (TN) device] being not only far below the design prediction made by the Bhabha Atomic Research Centre (BARC) but that it had actually failed.

This contention of the then DRDO Project Director (who had been with BARC) and other experts was discussed at a meeting convened by the then NSA (Brajesh Mishra) in late 1998. Notwithstanding an extended interaction between the DRDO and BARC, both stuck to their positions on the yield of the TN device. Thereafter, the NSA took a 'voice vote' which was most unusual in a matter that was technically very complex. Even more surprisingly, the NSA held that the government would stand by the opinion of the then Chairman, Atomic Energy Commission (AEC) and, by implication, of BARC.

The contentious issue appeared to be fading away when it resurfaced some years later through the argument that the TN device had not been weaponized by BARC while the 25 kiloton fission device had been weaponized and operationally deployed on multiplate weapon platforms.

The then DRDO chief was a Bharat Ratna and the then Chairman, AEC was duly awarded the Padma Vibhushan in 1999.

In Vajpayee's day, the PMO was an extension of his household and his family which gave currency to the term PMH (Prime Minister's House). In March 2001, a senior Editor published an article in his magazine titled 'Rigging the PMO', containing verified details of certain decisions that brazenly favoured a select group of industrialists. A second article 'Vajpayee's Achilles Heel' also appeared which talked of the clout which a trio (the Principal Secretary and Secretary in the PMO and the foster son-in-law) wielded. The senior Editor was made to apologize to Vajpayee before the raids on the relevant premises by government agencies were halted by Brajesh Mishra.

This senior Editor's autobiographical memoir[36] (which appeared in 2011) contains an interesting revelation about a BJP minister in the Vajpayee

36 Vinod Mehta: *Lucknow Boy* (p. 251)

cabinet with whom a corporate lobbyist had struck up a close friendship. Many doors opened to her courtesy this link. The story of her rise and fall is generally known; her taped telephone conversations revealed her extraordinary influence in the functioning of the government, including in the allocation of ministerial portfolios. When reports began to circulate in the media that the country's aviation policy was being influenced by the minister's connection with the lobbyist, he was shifted from his position of Minister of Civil Aviation. The same BJP minister retains a Cabinet portfolio in NDA-II.

After the Kargil War, the next crisis was not long in coming. It arrived in the form of the hijacking of IC814 which was on a flight from Kathmandu to Delhi in the last week of December 1999. The episode became a classic example of ineptitude and mishandling on the part of Vajpayee's senior most advisers and the Crisis Management Group (*CMG*) headed by the then Cabinet Secretary. The only issue on which the top brass had any clarity was that there should be no casualties among the passengers. In the event, the aircraft landed at and was allowed to take off, without let or hindrance, from Amritsar, finally reaching Kandahar. The net result was that the hijackers agreed to free the hostages in lieu of the dreaded Maulana Masood Azhar, Mushtaq Ahmed Zangar and Ahmed Omar Sheikh who were lodged in the Srinagar jail.

The ignominious exchange was effected in Kandahar in the presence of Vajpayee's Foreign Minister. From the Indian side, the currently serving NSA was a principal negotiator. Far from being held accountable, the then Cabinet Secretary, a U.P. civilian, was rewarded with a governorship which he was unable to hold on to for long. But that is another story.

At a speech in Karachi in January 2000, after being released by the Vajpayee government, Masood Azhar proclaimed: 'Muslims should not rest in peace till we have destroyed India'.

Like Hafiz Muhammad Saeed now, Masood was once briefly detained, but kept out of public view till around 2009.

Is it enough for the man in the street to be informed, at this distance of time, that the ISI had a critical role to play in the hijacking? It is more important for him (or her) to appreciate that a huge sacrifice was made, in terms of the imperatives of national security, by bowing to the demands of the hijackers and their leadership across the border. There seems not much purpose to now being informed by the present NSA that 'we were getting very good intelligence about all that was happening … if these people were not getting active ISI support in Kandahar, we could have got the hijacking vacated …'.

The unavoidable conclusion is that the Indian intelligence and bureaucratic apparatus failed to respond in the whole affair. The aircraft should have been disabled at Amritsar.

Some years afterwards and, specifically, in 2015, it was being speculated that accounts of the Kandahar fiasco, including of an ex-RAW chief, had been economical with the truth. A significant factor that appears to have weighed with the decision-makers in South Block was to ensure the safety, at any cost, of one intelligence functionary, then posted with the Indian Embassy in Kathmandu, who was among the passengers and very closely connected with the high and mighty in the PMO. Here again, the truth may be expected to remain concealed in the womb of time. The Aam Aadmi who casts his vote, only once in a while, may never be enlightened, even as the fatalities continue to mount in Jammu & Kashmir.

The ultimate truth could well be that for the protection of a few, an entire nation's security was irreversibly compromised.

The military standoff between India and Pakistan following the attack on the Indian Parliament in December 2001, is not a high point of Vajpayee's prime ministership. By January, 2002, India had mobilized three armoured divisions and around 500,000 troops along the border and the Line of Control (LOC) in J&K; Pakistan also deployed some 300,000 troops in the region. Tensions ran very high before a de-escalation could be brought about.

Termed 'Operation Parakram', the eleven-month long buildup has been called a 'most punishing mistake' for the armed forces by a former Chief of Naval Staff (who was appointed by the NDA-I in a controversial decision following the dismissal of Admiral Vishnu Bhagwat by Vajpayee and George Fernandes, the then Defence Minister); he said that there was no aim or military objective for the Operation.

However, Vajpayee's high point did arrive in the summer of 2003 when he, almost single-handedly and with considerable tact and finesse, deftly wriggled out of mounting pressure from the United States to send Indian troops to Iraq. Even Advani was not entirely in the know when Vajpayee chose to exhibit his diplomatic skills to the hilt. The Indian politicians, whether of the BJP or the Congress (or others) who had advocated the despatch of Indian soldiers, should be relieved that they were outsmarted by Vajpayee.

As an upper-caste Brahmin, sensitive to considerations of creed and community, Vajpayee was circumspect enough to keep expatiating about the Dalits and the OBCs but never with the requisite conviction.

A former RAW chief (in 1999-2000, in NDA-I) who was devoted to Brajesh Mishra and a former NSA (2010-14, in UPA-II), supposedly a Mishra admirer, would have the country believe that a settlement with Pakistan, over Kashmir, was imminent when Vajpayee met with Pervez Musharraf at Agra in July 2001 and, again, during Manmohan Singh's prime ministership in UPA-II. Their fellow-Indians are none the wiser about what exactly the efforts of Vajpayee and Manmohan Singh respectively could have been expected to achieve.

To be fair to him, the former RAW chief did, later, record: 'It all centred on what Musharraf himself in 2006 called his 'four-point formula' for Kashmir. It was something that began taking shape when he met Vajpayee during the SAARC Summit in Islamabad and gradually evolved during the first few years of the Manmohan Singh era. The formula was: making borders irrelevant by allowing free movement of Kashmiris across the LOC; self-governance which meant autonomy but not independence; demilitarization and a mechanism for joint management ....'[37].

How Vajpayee, given his faith in consensual politics, hoped to move forward on this basis, on Kashmir, can only be left to one's imagination.

In late 2016, a delegation led by Yashwant Sinha, once a senior minister in the Vajpayee Cabinet, visited the Kashmir Valley and other parts of the State. Speaking only for themselves, they interacted with representatives of various shades of opinion, including the Hurriyat leadership, and, among others, a so-called firebrand Member of the Legislative Assembly, Engineer Rashid, who expressed the view that the Kashmiris have no confusion in their minds about what they want. He appears to have stressed the need for the Government of India to understand that use of force cannot be a solution to the problem, adding that Vajpayee's Kashmir policy had few takers in the Valley and that it was nothing but propaganda to claim that the people, at large, had ever been appreciative of the former Prime Minister's stand.

Had he persevered in projecting a moral base, Vajpayee might have come across as a statesman-like figure, at any rate in a South Asian context. After a few complimentary references, by Jawaharlal Nehru, no less, to his participation in Lok Sabha debates, he began to see himself, more and more, in a Nehruvian mould. In the light of his many grandiose statements on secular politics, it is even now difficult to estimate whether he followed more the line of Nehru or of Golwalkar and Deoras. He was a political actor, par excellence,

37 A.S. Dulat (with Aditya Sinha): *Kashmir, the Vajpayee Years* (Harper Collins, Publishers India, 2015), p 278.

which saw him through to occupying the prime ministerial chair.

Among the BJP slogans aimed at cashing in on Vajpayee's electoral popularity were the following:

'Drishti Atal Par, Vote Kamal Par',
and
'Abki Baari, Atal Bihari': 'The Man India Awaits'.

When the National Democratic Alliance (NDA) failed to secure a renewed mandate in the summer of 2004, the spotlight was back on the Nehru-Gandhi family immediately after Congress took charge of the nomenclature. However, since the NDA II assumed office in 2014, the focus is again on Vajpayee who incidentally, holds the distinction of having the most number of official schemes and institutions named after a leader while they are alive. He has left behind his predecessors – Jawaharlal Nehru, Indira Gandhi and Rajiv Gandhi – who were made such dedications posthumously. But the Nehru – Gandhi dynasty remains ahead of all others, including Mahatma Gandhi, when one counts the number of projects, schemes and institutions named after a leader, whether alive or deceased.

The NDA-II has recognized Vajpayee's birthday, December 25, as 'Good Governance Day'; the PM Pension Yojana is now the Atal Pension Yojana, a flagship scheme. In 2015, Prime Minister Modi launched the Atal Mission *for* Rejuvenation and Urban Transformation (AMRUT), as a replacement for the Jawaharlal Nehru National Urban Renewal Mission (JNNURM) of the UPA.

Not to be left behind, the BJP State Governments have also chipped in generously. In Rajasthan, the Rajiv Gandhi Sewa Kendras have become the Atal Sewa and Suvidha Kendras and some 9,000 Gram Panchayat Kendras have been named after Vajpayee. The Madhya Pradesh Government has established the Atal Bihari Vajpayee Institute of Good Governance and Policy Analysis at Bhopal.

Vajpayee's successor, Manmohan Singh, was an even weaker Prime Minister. On the eve of his swearing in (May 2004), an insightful pen- portrait was penned by the noted economist, I.G. Patel, who can be said to have made all this possible, in the first instance, when he wrote:

> I do not think there is much difference between Sonia Gandhi being the Prime Minister or Manmohan Singh occupying the post. Either way, Gandhi will take care of the larger political picture. It hardly makes a difference in

> terms of division of labour and nature of work. Singh's personal vibes are very soothing and he can take people together to an extent. Gandhi will, however, remain responsible to make the coalition government function smoothly. Unlike the general perception, Singh is not really a bureaucrat. My personal experience is that he is politically shrewd.
>
> However, people should not expect too much from him on the economic front. I am not very confident of Singh being able to take really bold steps, given the nature of the Congress-led coalition ... Even in 1991, Manmohan Singh could not carry reforms too far. He abolished industrial licencing and cut import duties. But these did not hurt anybody. On subsidies, though, he could not do much. He had to roll back the harsh steps he took on fertiliser subsidies. This is not Singh's weakness alone, but that of coalition politics too ... So, do not judge Singh too severely on the macro-economic front. And do not underestimate his savviness on the political front.

Having declined the Finance Ministership, I.G. Patel paved the way for Manmohan Singh's political ascent.

Manmohan Singh (in his early days in the government as an economic adviser in the 1970s) was very sympathetic to the Nehru line but found, as circumstances changed, a clever way out. He made his peace with the market but without going all-out for a free market.

Singh's triumphant moment came when, as Finance Minister, he functioned under the guidance of Prime Minister Narasimha Rao. Such would seem to have been the impact that it is now being said that Narendra Modi is a beneficiary of the forces unleashed by Narasimha Rao in 1991. At a time when the BJP appeared stifled in its economic approach by the Swadeshi Jagran Manch and the party's think-tanks, it was a Congress government that was taking the tough decisions. Slogans like 'Make in India' and 'Start up India' might never have caught on had the political discourse not been steered towards building an environment to transform India.

Presiding over big ticket corruption, Manmohan Singh has been perceived as a hapless Dhritarashtra-like figure who made no effort to rein in the avaricious ministers and top bureaucrats in his government. His first Principal Secretary, a Punjab civilian hailing from Kerala, has been alluded to as a 'notorious intriguer'[38].

38 Ramachandra Guha: Patriots & Partisans (Penguin Books, India, 2012), p.105.

The same Principal Secretary, obviously so indispensable to Manmohan Singh and his coterie that he carried on as Adviser to the Prime Minister (in the rank of Minister of State) till the end of UPA-II, was instrumental in engineering the selection of the Comptroller and Auditor General of India (C&AG) through a late-night call at the PM's House, accompanied by the influential Finance Minister. The preferred candidate, who served as the C&AG between 2008–2013, was the Secretary (Financial Services) when the Vijay Mallya matter was heating up.

The first loan was granted to Mallya in 2004 and then in February 2008. Despite the declared NPA of his companies, a loan–restructuring was, apparently, done in December 2010. The then Chairman of the State Bank of India (one of the few to have served in that position for nearly five years, that is, from June 2006 to March 2011) was very much at the centre of the Mallya affair and now heads Tata Steel. The then Joint Secretary concerned in the Department of Financial Services was repatriated to the parent IAS cadre.

Replying to a debate on the Budget on February 9, 2017, Finance Minister Arun Jaitley said that not 'a rupee benefit' was given to the businessman (Mallya) by any bank since NDA came to power and that 'most of these are loans given during 2007-08-09 period when the economy was going through a boom'.

Beneath the veneer of a humility that was almost too good to be true, Manmohan Singh was the prisoner of a level of ego not quite commensurate with his attainments, academic or otherwise. He was able to have his way in accommodating his favourites in most bureaucratic appointments, with a few exceptions, notable as these were. One was in respect of a former member of the IAS who could not make an impression on 10, Janpath and had to migrate to Patna to advise the JD(U) government; he is now with the BJP and doing extremely well with them. Another related to nomination for the top post in the Commonwealth Secretariat in London of a retiring High Commissioner (with 'family loyalist' links to the UPA supremo) who scored over an ex-Foreign Secretary considered particularly close to Manmohan Singh.

The many controversies that dogged the UPA-II were also the result of the less appetising side of the reforms process. An opening up of the economy created opportunities for large-scale profiteering through cronyism and hugely corrupt deal-making. That Manmohan Singh exercized no more than a modicum of control highlights the fact of his being a Prime Minister by proxy. If he had retired (or resigned) in 2009, by when it should have been quite clear to him that he would have to come to terms with widespread corruption in order to survive, he might be judged less harshly.

The decade and a half of the combined tenures of Vajpayee and Manmohan Singh were the wasted years of the Republic of India. A common characteristic of both regimes was the widespread corruption and nepotism that swept across the Union Government, not to mention the states, Congress and BJP alike.

To Vajpayee's credit it should be said that he lifted the BJP from being a political untouchable and brought the party into the mainstream of Indian politics.

Manmohan Singh genuinely believed that the 2009 victory owed much to his popularity and the nuclear deal. However, Sonia Gandhi had health problems in the early part of UPA-II and when the corruption scandals exploded, Singh tried to pretend that he was invisible. The Congress has been unable, to this day, to rid itself of the taint that it led a government of the corrupt.

Neither Vajpayee nor Singh were able to put in place properly organized PMOs whose composite integrity could be regarded as beyond doubt and reproach.

Manmohan Singh's PMO never seemed entirely comfortable with the setting up of the National Advisory Council (NAC) in June 2004. Singh's mentor, Sonia Gandhi, was the Chairperson for the first two years and merits full credit for bringing in the Right to Information Act during this period. The NAC-I carried on for another two years; its second avatar had a longer innings under Sonia Gandhi.

I can comment with enough knowledge on the affairs of Prasar Bharati, an autonomous entity in the Broadcasting Sector, which has seldom been allowed to function as such, and which represented, during 2008-09 (in the run-up to the Commonwealth Games), one of the worst examples of wrong-doing on the part of the political and bureaucratic bigwigs of the UPA, the then Ministers of Information and Broadcasting and the PMH included.

The findings of an Inquiry Committee headed by a former C&AG (who had to rush back home for the purpose from a sojourn abroad) led nowhere, despite Manmohan Singh's oft-declared commitment to probity, at all costs, in public life. The name of the then Delhi Chief Minister figured in the Inquiry. This was one of the real faces of UPA II.

While Jawaharlal Nehru did not experience the need of a full-fledged PMS (he did much of his writing and drafting himself), the PMS that Lal Bahadur Shastri set up (designated, later, as the PMO in the Janata Government) can still be held up as a sort of yardstick in terms of efficiency and effectiveness. Other than two of Shastri's successors – Indira Gandhi and Narasimha Rao – none of the others could operationalize a credibly functioning PMO except, perhaps, Rajiv Gandhi in a limited way.

The present Prime Minister was faced with the daunting task to revamp the administrative machinery when he took office in May 2014. That not much has so far been accomplished in the field of governance reforms should be a matter of concern for NDA-II.

Modi's initiatives in the field of foreign affairs have attracted praise and criticism alike. For all the hype of his visits abroad, the country has not yet scored a major foreign-policy win. Where it matters most, that is India's relations with her neighbours, there has been no improvement; with Pakistan and, to a certain degree, China, relations are actually worse.

In the current scenario, an area of primary anxiety for the Modi government should be the extent of joblessness in India, running at a five-year high of 5% of the 15-plus-years workforce. Over a third of the working people are employed for less than a year and about 68% of the households are earning upto only Rs.10,000/- per month, according to a Survey Report of the Labour Bureau.

Over 7.8 lakh persons in 1.6 lakh households were surveyed across the country between April – December, 2015. The findings showed that after more than a year of the government's policies being in action, the situation on the ground remained dire and, actually, the same as in the preceding UPA-II.

What does 5% unemployment and 35% under-employment mean in hard numbers? Projecting from Census 2011 figures, India had a 15 years-and-older labour force of about 45 crore, 5% of which is nearly 2.3 crore persons. In addition, there are those who work but not for the whole year, signifying hidden un-employment which works out to about 16 crore persons. Womens' employment continues to stagnate with 8.7% of women in the labour force without jobs.

In the last quarter of 2015, there was actually a decline in job creation; in the previous quarter, the figure of new jobs created stood at 1.34 lakh, in itself one of the lowest in the last six years. The total number of jobs created in 2015 stood at 1.35 lakh only, compared to 4.93 lakh in 2014 and a high of 12.56 lakh in 2009.

It has been argued that the demands for job quotas will grow with jobless growth which, in turn, relates to the nature of foreign multinational activity in India. The Patels in Gujarat, the Jats of Haryana, the Marathas in Maharashtra and the Kapus of Andhra Pradesh had launched agitations for job reservations.

The investments committed by global corporates at the last 'Make in India Week' in Mumbai may translate into not more than six million jobs because of the highly capitalistic nature of these companies.

Briefly, the impact of the government's pronouncements for job creation like Make in India, Start-up India and Digital India is yet to be seen on the ground.

India still ranks a poor 130 in the world in terms of 'Ease of Doing Business' – up by only one place from 131 in 2015, according to a World Bank Study.

A review of the commitments made by various countries in the run-up to Habitat-III revealed that India registered no improvement on its urban development indices in the last twenty years. The lately released Habitat Commitment Index (HCI) shows that India has fared worse than countries such as Nepal and Pakistan.

In November 2016, Standard and Poor (S&P), a leading credit rating agency, ruled out any upgrade in India's sovereign rating, triggering a response, in true UPA style, from the Ministry of Finance. The then Economic Affairs Secretary smugly observed 'If the rating has not been improved, it's a matter which doesn't bother us so much. It's a question which calls for introspection among those who do the rating'.

S&P's stance came despite a push by the Finance Ministry for a ratings upgrade on the ground that the fiscal deficit has been kept in check and important reforms, including the new Goods and Services Tax (GST) regime, have been cleared. However, S&P maintained the lowest investment grade rating of 'BBB –' with a stable outlook for India saying that it wished to see more efforts to lower government debt and that it did not expect revenues to rise enough to meaningfully lower the deficit over the medium term.

The Economic Affairs Secretary was, apparently, also involved in discussions in lobbying with Moody's for a ratings upgrade. It was only through a section of the media that it became known that while the government had criticized Moody's ratings methods and pushed aggressively for an upgrade, the U.S.-based agency declined to budge, citing concerns over the country's debt levels and the fragile condition of the banking system.

A better credit rating on India's sovereign debt would have been an endorsement of Prime Minister Modi's economic leadership. So far, his policies have not been rewarded with a ratings upgrade from the leading global rating agencies who feel that more needs to be done.

The Prime Minister's key advisers probably realize that they have to get their act together and that capable economists and experts require to be inducted from outside the 'organized services' of the government.

The NDA-II would do well to ponder over the well-intentioned advice that has been proffered to them from time to time, such as by Joseph Stiglitz, Nobel Laureate in Economics (2001) at Bangalore (now Bengaluru) in July 2016. Stiglitz said that India needs to be aware of its image abroad and added that '... The important thing to realize is that if India wants to grow as an open economy, you are part of an international community ... they are making judgment, whether right or wrong, and have come to a strong view about these two events (the difficulties faced by NGOs and the JNU controversy) that have had a strong effect on public opinion abroad about what has been going on in the last two years'.

He was speaking at a discussion on Global Inequality: Causes and Consequences at the Aziz Premji University and had good words for the MGNREGA (the Rural Employment Guarantee Scheme) saying: 'It is the single most innovative programme (by India) for the rest of the world'.

When the International Food Policy Research Institute (IFPRI) released its Global Hunger Index (GHI), rating 118 countries, based on four components, namely, under-nourishment, child wasting, child stunting and child mortality, India was ranked 97 on the list of 118, worse than her neighbours, Nepal, Bangladesh and Sri Lanka, and only marginally better than Pakistan. According to the Report, the levels of hunger are marked from serious to alarming; India was bracketed in the category of countries where 'hunger levels' are serious. News of deaths from malnutrition keep coming in from Maharashtra, Odisha, Madhya Pradesh and other States.

The reactions of the NDA-II to this state of affairs have been few and far between. Since India ranks high in estimates of the levels of hunger and malnutrition, the responses of the Modi government can no longer be half-hearted and faulty. It is for the youth to determine whether Narendra Modi can bring about a real change. Some of that change would have to be visible on the ground by 2018–19 when NDA-II gears up for the next verdict of the people of India.

Prime Minister Modi's PMO could usefully examine the conclusions (released in April 2009) of the Report of the National Commission for Enterprises in the Unorganized Sector which was appointed by UPA-II under the chairmanship of Dr Arjun Sengupta. The Report revealed, inter alia, that despite many years of economic growth, nearly 77% of India's population continues to live on less than Rs.120/- per day and that as much as 86% of the workforce is in the unorganized sector. The Report further revealed that the vast majority of India's 'Poor and Vulnerable' are Muslim or lower caste and, in addition to poverty, also suffer from social discrimination. According to the Report: 'These groups emerge as a sort of coalition of socially discriminated, educationally deprived and economically destitute', while less than one-fourth of the population is enjoying the fruits of economic development.

The prime ministership of Narendra Modi is a work in progress; the next few months might deliver more concrete results. At the same time, in comparison to the inertia and indecision of UPA-II, his performance will continue to shine as a star.

By the end of the 1950s, Nehru was worried enough about the growing wealth and income inequality to set up the Mahalanobis Committee; this is one page that Narendra Modi can still pull out of the Nehru narrative.

Prime Minister Nehru journeyed to Karachi in September 1960 to conclude the Indus Waters Treaty (IWT) – mediated by the World Bank – with Ayub Khan, Pakistan's first military ruler. Decades after strategic naiveté and negligence, it seems to have, lately, dawned upon the Indian establishment, at the higher levels, that this was the world's most generous (and lopsided) water-sharing pact and of indefinite duration, to boot.

The gifting away, to a perennially hostile Pakistan, of a lion's share of the waters, with India also contributing around US$ 174 million for dam and other projects, still did not mollify an implacable foe; instead, the IWT prompted armed attacks in J&K aimed at gaining control of the land through which the three largest rivers flow, although only one of them originates in J&K.

The Partition left the Indus headworks in India, arming the country with formidable water-leverage over the neighbour. India's assumption that it traded water munificence for peace in 1960 has backfired.

Had China been in India's place, it would have acted to discipline both the World Bank and Pakistan. It is inconceivable that China would have countenanced such a patently inequitable treaty. While questioning the Bank's neutrality in recent months, India has yet to demonstrate the inclination to respond through counter-measures.

Nehru would have realized, perhaps much before his 1960 visit to Karachi, that Pakistan was unlikely to be a friendly neighbour in the future. By then, only a few of his colleagues of the front rank in the Congress, like Rajendra Prasad, Rajaji, Kripalani, J.P. and Bidhan Roy remained on the scene in Independent India.

❖

The five friends who started the RSS were Dr B.S. Moonje, Dr L.V. Paranjpe, Dr Tholkar, Babarao Savarkar and Dr Hedgewar himself.

M.J. AKBAR, SENIOR JOURNALIST,
NOW A BJP MEMBER AND UNION MINISTER OF STATE.

PART III

Forces of Hindu Organization

To speak of Hindu fundamentalism is a contradiction in terms, it does not exist. Hinduism is not this kind of religion .... The older I get, the more Hindu I become.

SIR VIDIADHAR SURAJPRASAD (V.S.) NAIPAUL,
INTERNATIONALLY REPUTED NOVELIST AND ESSAYIST,
NOBEL LAUREATE IN LITERATURE, 2001

❖

INDIA WAS DECLARED TO CONSIST of two nations by Vinayak Damodar ('Veer') Savarkar in his Presidential Address at the Annual Session of the Hindu Mahasabha in 1937 – three years before the Muslim League did so and again in December 1939, three months before the Pakistan Resolution was adopted by the League at Lahore.

It was Savarkar (1883–1966) who coined the term Hindutva to represent the predominant form of Hindu nationalism in India. It has been championed by the Rashtriya Swayamsevak Sangh (RSS) and affiliated organizations like the Vishwa Hindu Parishad (VHP) of the Sangh Parivar. The French political scientist, Christophe Jaffrelot, opines that Savarkar's concept of Hindutva marked a 'qualitative change' in Hindu nationalism.

Savarkar clarified that Hindutva was a new concept:

> ... Hindutva – Hinduness – is more comprehensive than the word Hinduism. It was to draw pointed attention to this distinction that I had coined the words Hindutva, Pan Hindu and Hindudom when I framed

> the definition of the word Hindu … Hinduism concerns the religious systems of the Hindus, their theology or dogma …. This is precisely a matter which the Hindu Mahasabha leaves entirely to group conscience and faith. The Mahasabha takes its stand on no dogma, book or school of philosophy whether pantheist, monotheist or atheist ….
>
> The Mahasabha is not, in the main, a Hindu-Dharma-Sabha but is pre-eminently a Hindu-Rashtra-Sabha and is a Pan Hindu organization shaping the destiny of the Hindu Nation in all its social, political and cultural aspects. Those who commit the serious mistake of taking the Hindu Mahasabha for only a religious body would do well to keep this distinction in mind ….

In 1937, he declared that '… So far as the Hindus are concerned, there can be no distinction or conflict … between our communal and national duties as the best interests of Hindudom are simply identified with the best interests of Hindustan as a whole…'. Atal Bihari Vajpayee echoed this theme at the BJP's National Executive as late as in September 1989, saying that Hindu sentiments were synonymous with the national interest.

It should be recalled that for the previous several centuries, the different communities had lived together, in peace and amity, by and large. Undivided India had a population of 389 million (1941) comprising 255 million Hindus – including the Scheduled Castes – 92 million Muslims, 6.3 million Christians, 5.6 million Sikhs and several smaller groupings. There were Muslim majority areas (in the North-East and the North-West) and Hindu majority areas, but no part of the country was exclusively inhabited by any one community; the Hindus, Muslims and Sikhs lived as friendly neighbours. In the urban areas, there were Hindu mohallas, Muslim mohallas and Sikh mohallas but these were situated, side by side, and it could not be said of any town that it was owned by one community.

In the Punjab, Sind (now Sindh) and Bengal, the rural population was also of a mixed character. Muslim landlords had Hindu tenants and engaged Hindus as managers and accountants, while Hindu businessmen employed Muslim workers. Religion did not interfere with social relations to any great extent. Nearly 90 per cent of the Muslim and Sikh population consisted of converts from the Hindu-fold and belonged to the same stock. The converts differed, but little, in dress or appearance and behaved as members of the same society. This was especially true of the villages.

The occasional clashes between the communities were sporadic and short-lived, the direct cause more often being a political or economic issue rather than the religious factor. The Mymensingh disturbances in Bengal in May 1907 were in the nature of a rising of the Muslim peasantry against the Hindu landlords and creditors. The Bombay (now Mumbai) riots of 1929 were between the mill-workers who went on strike and the Pathan strike-breakers.

In the United Provinces and the Punjab, the relations between the Hindus and the Muslims were, generally, cordial.

In the background were the movements of national revival which materialized during the nineteenth century by way of a moral defence against British imperialism. The impact of Western thought and civilization led to an awakening of political consciousness and a sense of frustration in the face of British dominance. The Hindu mind sought solace in the hallowed memories of the Golden Age of the Vedas, in the founding of the Arya Samaj in 1875 by Swami Dayananda Saraswati (1824–1883) and in a resurrection of Chhatrapati Shivaji's cult in, primarily, present-day Maharashtra. The Hindu psyche, in trying to rehabilitate its lost pride, glorified its ancient achievements towards which, they argued, the Muslims had made no contribution.

Hindu revivalism took a religious form.

Swami Dayananda led a major Hindu reform movement of the Vedic tradition. He was the first to give the call for Swaraj as 'India for Indians' in 1876 which was taken up by Lokmanya Tilak. He worked for the revival of Vedic ideologies; among those he inspired were Swami Shraddhanand[1], Mahatma Hansraj[2], Lala Lajpat Rai and Veer Savarkar.

By a similar psychological process, the Muslims took their minds back to the glories of the Holy Prophet and the Islamic conquests of the lands around the Mediterranean. The revivalist movements gathered force and Hindus and Muslims began to assert themselves as separate entities. Hindu culture and Muslim culture were being looked upon as distinct, even irreconcilable, conceptions.

---

1 Swami Shraddhanand (1856-1926), an Arya Samaj missionary, emerged, in the 1920s, as an important force of Hindu Sanghathan.

2 Mahatma Hansraj (1864-1938) an educationist in the Arya Samaj movement and a compatriot of Lala Lajpat Rai; he started the Dayanand Anglo-Vedic Schools System (D.A.V.) in Lahore in 1886.

There gradually arose an aspiration for communal power. In 1906 (in which year the Muslim League was founded), a scheme was drafted by Lala Har Dayal and sent to Pandit Shyamji Krishna Varma in Britain for organizing a society of workers to achieve a free India which would, in effect, be a Hindu India. Har Dayal wrote:

> Many enthusiastic young men, zealous for the freedom of the Fatherland, think that the introduction of Mohammedans will bring in a jarring note. I know more than six or seven young men of the Punjab who will give up all wordly prospects for a Hindu society but not for a mixed one. I think Mr Tilak and Mr Lajpat Rai will agree in this opinion.

The Akhil Bharatiya (All India) Hindu Mahasabha was a functioning body before the Rashtriya Swayam Sewak Sangh (RSS) was founded in Nagpur in 1925. Known earlier as the All India Hindu Sabha, it amended its constitution under the presidentship of Maharaja Sir Manindra Chandra Nandy of the Cossimbazar Raj (in Bengal) to remove the clause relating to loyalty to the British Government and added a clause committing itself to a 'united and self-governing' Indian nation.

Among the prominent leaders in the Hindu Mahasabha, at one point in time, were stalwarts like Madan Mohan Malaviya and Lala Lajpat Rai. By the late 1920s, it was coming under the spell of Dr. Balakrishna Shivram (B.S.) Moonje (1872–1948) and Veer Savarkar who was a severe critic of the Congress and of the policy of enlisting Muslim support. One of the Mahasabha's influential members, Keshav Baliram (KB) Hedgewar (1889–1940) left to establish the RSS as a Hindu Volunteers Organization that abstained from active politics.

Savarkar and his older brother, Ganesh Damodar (Babarao) Savarkar had, in 1903, founded the Abhinav Bharat Society (Young India Society) as a secret society at Nasik (now Nashik) in the then Bombay Presidency. The Mitra Melas organized by the Savarkar brothers aimed at overthrowing the British rule through armed rebellion. Their revolutionary propaganda and the investigation into the assassination of A.M.T. Jackson, District Magistrate, Nasik (which revealed the existence of the Abhinav Bharat Society) led to a sentence of 'transportation for life' for Veer Savarkar and imprisonment in the Cellular Jail in the Andaman Islands in 1910.

Dr. Moonje, who was Savarkar's senior in age by some years, held a medical degree from the Grant Medical College in Bombay and was a follower of Lokmanya Tilak; their relationship was very close. Moonje introduced the Ganesh and Shivaji festivals in Central India (he was born in 1872 at Bilaspur, in the then CP and Berar, now Chhatisgarh) and mobilized funds for the Lokmanya's work. A staunch Hindu, he inspired military training programmes and set up institutions, like schools and orphanages and hostels for Dalits.

Tilak's death brought Moonje's association with the Congress to an end. He was the President of the Hindu Mahasabha from 1927 until Savarkar took over from him a decade later.

If there is a single personality who inspired the Hindutva protagonists the most before his premature demise, it was Lokmanya Tilak. Born in 1856 in the Ratnagiri District in the then Bombay Presidency, he was Gandhi's senior by thirteen years and a 'natural leader' who motivated a host of men like Moonje. Driven by realism, the triumvirate of Lal-Bal-Pal might have provided an altogether different direction to settling the Hindu-Muslim question.

The passing of Tilak in 1920 aggravated the antipathy between Gandhi and Savarkar; the latter believed that the Hindu identity was inseparable from the Indian identity. In a matter of years, the Congress eclipsed the Hindu Mahasabha. Since the narration of history belongs to the victors, the story of India's freedom movement became one of the 'cult of non-violence' espoused and advocated by Gandhi. But the opposite school of thought that Savarkar represented was not unimportant and is experiencing a revival in the NDA-II.

In a monumental work, the Indian War of Independence, 1857 which appeared in 1908, Savarkar stressed the cooperation between the Hindus and Muslims against their common adversary, the British. He depicted the revolutionary principles of Swadharma and Swaraj as being shared by Hindus and Muslims who fought the colonial rule. The text highlighted the heroic deeds of Muslims and Hindus and acknowledged the Muslims as noble sons of Mother India. About Ahmad Shah, a Muslim, who was betrayed by a Hindu Raja, Savarkar records:

> The life of the brave Mohammedan shows that a rational faith in the doctrines of Islam is in no way inconsistent with or antagonistic to a deep and all powerful love of the Indian soil, and that the true believer in Islam will feel it proud to belong to and a privilege to die for his mother-country.

The antagonism that emerged after the 1921 Moplah uprising is reflected in Savarkar's later work of 1925, *Hindu Pad-Padashahi* (Hindudom and Hindu Kingdom) where Muslims replace the British as enemies of Hindus. Here, the heroes are the Marathas who fought to avenge Hindu honour and to restore Hindu dharma to its power and glory.

Hindu Pad-Padashahi, like the Indian War of Independence, 1857, addresses the strategies whereby the Marathas created and consolidated a Hindu Empire. It emphasizes Maratha patronage of Hindu institutions and Brahmanic learning. Maratha rulers convened assemblies of scholars in Poona (now Pune) and distributed honours and prizes; under the protection of 'Maratha arms', Hindu religious teachers travelled throughout India, 'from Rameshwar to Haridwar, from Dwarka to Puri'. Through the patronage of Sanskrit scholars, the sacred language received an impetus under the Maratha rulers.

This was the backdrop in which the Hindutva network spread in Central India in the then Maratha princely states of Gwalior, Indore, Dhar, Dewas (Senior), Dewas (Junior) and others, including Rajput principalities, which merged to become Madhya Bharat, post-1947.

Savarkar prophesied the importance of the Hindu Princes to the future of the Hindu nation. He condemned Congress' attacks, from time to time, on the policies of Hindu States, extolled Mysore, Travancore and Baroda as examples of progressive administration and pronounced Hindu rulers to be capable of patriotic leadership. He also strove to unify the rulers through their support for the Hindu Mahasabha and, in 1945, presided over the All India Hindu States Conference held in Baroda (now Vadodara).

When Hindu ascetics protested the demolition of a Shiva temple in Delhi, Savarkar spoke publicly in their support. Capitalizing on the political potential of the issue, he said in his 1939 presidential address to the Hindu Mahasabha.

> The splendid and sustained struggle the Hindus have carried on at Delhi, in connection with the Shiva Mandir affair, deserves also on All-India homage. It too sounds the same warning that the Congress does not, will not and cannot defend a Hindu cause against an anti-Hindu aggression ... I already see before my mind's eye a magnificent Temple of Shiva and thousands of pilgrims crowding to worship at it before a decade passes away.

Crowds gathered at railway stations to welcome Savarkar on his arrival and Hindu organizations arranged processions, through towns and cities, to honour him and display the strength of their numbers. At the Meenakshi Temple in Madurai, the temple priests conferred on him the honours usually reserved for Maharajas and 'heads among priests' in recognition of his unceasing efforts to promote Hindu Sangathan.

In some quarters, Savarkar came to be known as '*Sangathanacharya*' (master-brain at Hindu organization) and was even described as a *Shankaracharya*, the supreme head of a new Hinduism.

During his tours, Savarkar raised funds for Hindu Sangathan projects; in 1951, he began collections to build a shrine dedicated to revolutionary martyrs. The following year, he presided over a celebration that honoured the memory of the martyrs.

Support for Savarkar's militant ideology and the Hindu Mahasabha was particularly strong among the Marathi Brahmins.

Through the 1950s and until his passing, ill health limited his public appearances. However, he maintained a devoted following which after his death, continued to propagate the ideology of Hindutva. In Pune, his supporters built a Hall which was named *Swatantryveer Savarkar Sabhagriha*.

During much of his public life, while a definite animosity characterized his relations with the Congress, a few in that party favoured an alliance and tried to induce the Hindu Mahasabha to join forces with its conservative faction. Public functions honouring Savarkar were, however, off-limits for Congress politicians; no Congress minister attended Savarkar's seventy-fifth birthday and none came to his cremation. When Lal Bahadur Shastri was the Prime Minister, a monthly honorarium was paid to him by the government.

Savarkar believed that the Hindu Mahasabha's importance would not diminish after Independence and he asked the organization to continue its mission even after Hindustan is politically free. He opposed suggestions that the Hindu Mahasabha admit non-Hindus as members, arguing that Hindu solidarity and power required an exclusively Hindu organization.

In Savarkar's view, the Mahasabha's objectives would be realized through relentless work to promote Hindu Sangathan and through involvement in electoral contests. He advised Hindu Mahasabha candidates not to be discouraged if they lost elections.

Before Independence, Savarkar counted several Hindu Congressmen as sympathetic to Hindu Sangathan, claiming they supported the Congress only because it affords them the guarantee of being elected at any polls whether to the local bodies or the legislature, or assures them of some post or profit here or there.

The Hindu Mahasabha's standing was damaged by accusations of involvement with Mahatma Gandhi's assassination. Its leaders and workers were arrested and the organization was banned. After the ban was lifted, the Mahasabha leaders disagreed over the future of the organization in

Independent India. Syama Prasad Mookerjee (1901–53), who succeeded Savarkar as the Mahasabha President, felt that it should withdraw from politics and a new political party should be formed that would be open to all religious communities, using the broadest possible definition of Hindu. Other Mahasabha leaders disagreed with Mookerjee who resigned and, later, founded a new political party, the Bharatiya Jana Sangh (BJS) in 1951.

Following Gandhi's murder, Savarkar was arrested on February 5, 1948 from his house in Shivaji Park, Bombay (now Mumbai) and kept under detention in the Arthur Road Prison. He was charged with murder, conspiracy to murder and abetment to murder. The trial of the accused persons by a Special Court comprising a member of the Judicial Branch of the ICS, Justice Atma Charan, at the Red Fort, Delhi. Savarkar was acquitted in February 1949.

In his book *The Men Who Killed Gandhi*, well-known writer Manohar Malgonkar (1913-2010)[3] mentions certain aspects about the Mahatma's murder, such as the following excerpt which relates to Savarkar's counsel at the trial, L.B. Bhopatkar:

> While in Delhi for the trial, Bhopatkar had been put up in the Hindu Mahasabha office. Bhopatkar had found it a little puzzling that while specific charges had been made against all the other accused, there was no specific charge against his client. He was pondering about his defence strategy when one morning he was told that he was wanted on the telephone, so he went up to the room in which the telephone was kept, picked up the receiver and identified himself. His caller was Dr Bhimrao Ambedkar[4], who merely said; 'Please meet me this evening at the sixth milestone on the Mathura road', but before Bhopatkar could say anything more, put down the receiver.
>
> That evening, when Bhopatkar had himself driven to the place indicated, he found Ambedkar already waiting. He motioned to Bhopatkar to get into his car which he, Ambedkar himself, was driving. A few minutes later, he stopped the car and told Bhopatkar: There is no real charge against your client; quite worthless evidence has been concocted. Several

3 Manohar Malgonkar: *The Men Who Killed Gandhi* (Roli Books, 2008) p. 284.

4 B.R. Ambedkar was the Law Minister in the Nehru Cabinet between 1947–51.

> members of the Cabinet were strongly against it, but to no avail. Even Sardar Patel could not go against these orders. But, take it from me, there just is no case. You will win.

The reference was, apparently, to the then Prime Minister.

Savarkar was taken into custody under the Preventive Detention Act, a draconian law which the Congress were no longer in a hurry to repeal after the British had left. Under its provisions, Savarkar was initially held as a 'detenu'. He remained in jail for the whole of the year which the investigation and the trial took.

A man who was in his mid-sixties and had undergone long years of imprisonment under the British was sent back to jail for another year soon after the country attained Dominion Status.

A few months after Savarkar's demise, the Government of India appointed a one-man Commission of Inquiry into the conspiracy to murder Mahatma Gandhi. Justice Jeevan Lal Kapur, a former Judge of the Supreme Court of India, completed his report in November 1969 and reached, in respect of Savarkar, a conclusion contrary to that of the Special Court which had exonerated him for want of corroborative evidence in support of the approver's confession. The Commission concluded: All these facts taken together were destructive of any theory other than the conspiracy to murder by Savarkar and his group.

Savarkar's prediction of the future success of the Sangathan movement (when the Congress would have to compete with Hindu political parties to prove their pro-Hindu credentials) now sounds uncannily apt:

> If the Hindu party persists in contesting elections, a day will come when the Congressite Hindus shall have to go to the polls with a conspicuous 'bandhan' besmeared on their foreheads and the Tulsi rosary in their hands or prove to the Hindu electorate that it was they, the Congressites, who were Hindus of a purer ray serene than the Hindu Sangathan.

Savarkar advocated a Hindu national identity based on contempt for British rule. His teachings provided an alternative for groups who considered their interests jeopardized (or constricted) by Gandhi's thinking, Nehru's secularist and socialist policies and by the Communists. He, perhaps, lacked the qualities for leading a mass movement and has been described as moody and erratic, dictatorial in conversation and unable to negotiate with other parties. Nonetheless, his powerful Hindutva polemics did lead the way for people to conceptualize and articulate their political and cultural identity in Hindu nationalist terms.

This identity presumes that Hindus are unified by their common interests. According to Savarkar, Hindutva is an inclusive term and is '… not a word but a history …. Hinduism is only … a fraction, a part of Hindutva … Hindutva embraces all the departments of thought and activity of the whole being of our Hindu race'[5]. He considered as Hindus all those who looked upon India as their Motherland or Fatherland.

Acknowledged as a leading light of the Hindu revivalist movement which was coming into its own, first under Hedgewar and then Guru Golwalkar – the founding fathers of the RSS – Savarkar is reverentially remembered for having devoted his life to the cause of Hindu Sangathan. The same could be said of Moonje and Laxman Vaman (L.V.) Paranjpe, a co-founder of the RSS and of an earlier organization, the Bharat Swayamsewak Mandal, whose volunteers were asked to wear a uniform, subsequently adopted by the RSS as its own dress code, from 1925 to 1940.

While the Congress scored impressive victories in the provincial elections of 1937, trouncing both the Muslim League and the Hindu Mahasabha, its ministers resigned two years later in protest against Viceroy Linlithgow's action – of unilaterally declaring India to be belligerent in World War II. This led to a situation in which the Hindu Mahasabha joined hands with the Muslim League (and other parties) to form coalition governments in Sindh, the NWFP and Bengal.

In Sindh, the Mahasabha members joined the Muslim League government of Sir Ghulam Hussain Hidayatullah (1879-1948).

In the NWFP, the Hindu Mahasabha joined hands with Sardar Aurangzeb Khan of the Muslim League in 1943 to run a coalition government in which Rai Bahadur Mehr Chand Khanna – much later, a member of Nehru's Council of Ministers – was the Finance Minister.

In Bengal, the Mahasabha participated in the Krishak Praja Party – led Progressive Coalition Ministry of Fazlul Haq in which Syama Prasad Mookerjee held the Finance portfolio and whose functioning drew praise from Savarkar.

These provincial coalitions ought to have been an eye-opener for the Congress, as to the possibilities of practical politics. If Maulana Azad's opinion is given due weight, a Congress-League coalition, in the U.P. alone in 1937, could have averted the Partition of India.

---

5 V.D. Savarkar: *Essentials of Hindutva* (1923).

Subhas Bose conferred with Savarkar (then heading the Hindu Mahasabha) in Bombay in 1940, their first and only interaction. The meeting was part of Bose's initiative to contact national leaders, across party lines, to build up support for a united effort against British rule. He had already quit the Congress presidency the previous year.

The Mahasabha contested the 1952, 1957 and 1962 general elections and steadily lost its electoral support. In 1952, it fielded thirty-one candidates for the Lok Sabha and four seats were won. In 1962, there were thirty-two candidates and only one seat was won. However, it remained a voice of Hindu nationalism; its political role was, in later years, much more successfully adopted by the Bharatiya Janata Party (BJP) and its religious and cultural activism by the Vishva Hindu Parishad (VHP).

Savarkar's wife died in November 1963. In early February 1966, he renounced medicines, food and water which he termed as *atmaarpan* (fast until death). He had written an article – '*Atmahatya Nahi Atmaarpan*' – in which he said that when one's life-mission is over and the ability to serve society is left no more, it is better to end the life at will rather than waiting for death.

When he passed away on February 26, 1966, an estimated 100,000 men and women came to pay their last respects and over 2,000 RSS workers lined the procession route to the cremation ground.

The Hindu Mahasabha ranks as a parent organization of Hindutva Sanghathan. It has had men like Savarkar and Syama Prasad Mookerjee at the apex; later, there was none of Mookerjee's foresight and stature to lead the Bharatiya Jana Sangh (BJS). His demise in 1953 at Srinagar, in the Kashmir Valley left a void from which the Hindutva movement took years to re-emerge as a potent political force. In 1967, Pt. Deendayal Upadhyaya, the then Jana Sangh President, himself an iconic figure, died in mysterious circumstances which have remained unexplained.

The Mahasabha's electoral importance declined, even as the organizational strength of the RSS was growing. In 1942, Syama Prasad Mookerjee took over the presidentship from Savarkar. While Mookerjee's decision to leave (after Savarkar refused to accept non-Hindus in the party) weakened the Mahasabha, other leaders were also joining the Party in the forties and fifties.

Dr. Narayan Bhaskar (N.B.) Khare (1884-1970) was an important figure to depart the Congress Party in the late thirties. He was their first Premier of the Central Provinces & Berar, an elected member of the Provincial Legislative Council since 1923 and was jailed for joining the Civil Disobedience Movement. Some months after becoming the Premier, he faced disciplinary action for removing three senior ministers, Ravi Shankar (RS) Shukla, Dwarka Prasad (DP) Mishra and D.S. Mehta from the provincial cabinet and had to resign. He squarely blamed Gandhi and Patel for this turn of events.

Khare took his degree in medicine and was, in 1913, the first M.D. of the Punjab University.

When he was in the Viceroy's Executive Council (1943–46), the other Indians were mostly non-officials (that is, prominent politicians) and some of them had been ministers in the provincial governments but not one of them was representative of either the Congress or the Muslim League. The sympathies of a few like the Kanpur – based industrialist, Sir J.P. Srivastava, lay with the Hindu Mahasabha.

Khare was the Member for Commonwealth Relations in the Executive Council and, later, Prime Minister of the Alwar State (1947–48) when he was placed under house arrest in Delhi in connection with the Mahatma's murder. On the subject of Gandhi's health, he seems to have told Viceroy Wavell on May 16, 1944 that 'he (Gandhi) was duping us, or the doctors were, and that he would recover...'.

Khare joined the Hindu Mahasabha in 1949. He wrote his autobiography in 1959 in which he claimed that he had prevented the Maharaja of Alwar from joining Pakistan.

The RSS was born on the day of Vijayadashmi in 1925 and Dr Hedgewar insisted on the term 'rashtriya' for his Hindu organization; this is confirmed by the 'prarthana' (prayer) sung at the end of every shakha meeting, along with the slogans of Bharat Mata Ki Jai.

Laxman Vaman (LV) Paranjpe was a co-founder of the RSS, In the 1920 session of the Indian National Congress held in Nagpur, a volunteer organization called the Bharat Swayamsewak Mandal was formed by Paranjpe and Hedgewar, which was a precursor to the RSS. All the volunteers were asked to wear a uniform which was later adopted by the RSS as its own official uniform from 1925 to 1940. Paranjpe also served as the Sarsanghchalak (1930-31) when Hedgewar went to jail during the Forest Satyagraha.

In the twenties and thirties, many of the public figures patronizing the RSS were connected to the Hindu Mahasabha. In addition to Malaviya and Moonje, the RSS enjoyed the support of Padam Raj Jain of Calcutta who had been impressed by the Nagpur Shakha which he visited after the Mahasabha's session in Pune in 1935. He told Hedgewar how much he appreciated his 'silent but highly important work'.

As General Secretary of the Hindu Mahasabha, Jain helped Vasant Rao Oak establish the Delhi Shakha in the central office of the Mahasabha. From the 1940s, the Delhi branch of the RSS benefitted from the patronage of a leading businessman, Hans Raj Gupta, an Arya Samajist, while, in the United Provinces, Moonje's influence contributed to the RSS' growth.

Having assisted the Sangh's expansion, the Hindu Mahasabha would have felt entitled to ask for the support of the RSS swayamsevaks. The Nagpur leadership, however, demurred and was not willing to divert the organization from its long-term objective of a Hindu Rashtra.

An examination of the trajectory of the Hindu Mahasabha under Savarkar and of the way in which the RSS unfolded itself during those days makes it clear that there were basic differences in priorities between the two organizations. Savarkar's emphasis was on turning the Mahasabha into a political party in opposition to the Congress whereas neither Hedgewar nor Golwalkar wished to be associated with confrontational activities directed against the Congress. By the early 1950s, the Mahasabha and the Jana Sangh were in contest for the same political space in an environment that was not conducive for either of them. The RSS and the Jana Sangh were, by now, maintaining a distance from Savarkar.

The lack of interest shown by the RSS in political activity reflected the conviction that this would distract its rank and file from the main goal. When Hedgewar took part in the Civil Disobedience Movement, he made clear that he was doing so strictly as an individual and entrusted his colleagues with the task of running the RSS. It was only his old connections with Moonje and Savarkar that persuaded him to associate with the Mahasabha. The situation changed after Guru Golwalkar took over the RSS organization; in 1940, the Mahasabha developed its own paramilitary group, the *Ram Sena*.

A similar process occurred in North India where the RSS freed itself of any subordinate position that may have been envisaged for it by the Mahasabha. New patrons also appeared on the horizon, including the Hindu princes, who were anxious to find a counterweight to the Muslim groups that were emerging in their States, such as in Alwar (then Rajputana) where the RSS maintained its training camps.

The RSS membership increased from around 76,000 in 1943 to about 600,000 in early 1948. In the late forties, the fortunes of the RSS were inevitably linked to the events surrounding the Partition. It speaks volumes of the sincerity and unremitting toil of the RSS cadre who helped the lakhs of Hindu refugees fleeing the western Punjab, thereby adding much to the organization's prestige. A Hindu Sahayata Samiti was set up in which the discipline of the swayamsevaks proved to be a great asset and which, in turn, contributed to the RSS' evolution towards social and cultural unity.

Ideologically akin to the Hindu Mahasabha, the RSS expanded rapidly with Hedgewar as the founding *Sarsanghchalak* and was soon to be seen as a competitor for the core constituency of the Mahasabha. Its main focus was on Hindu organization and on ways and means to strengthen it, giving the call: 'Hindi, Hindu, Hindustan'

Hedgewar was influenced by the writings of Lokmanya Tilak and Veer Savarkar (both Chitpavan Brahmins, like the famed revolutionary, Wasudeo Balwant Phadke), whereas he himself was born in a Marathi Deshastha Brahmin family in Nagpur. His early followers included Prabhakar Balwant (Bhaiyyaji) Dani, Babasaheb Apte and Balasaheb Deoras, as also Madhukar Rao Bhagwat whose son, Mohan Madhukar Bhagwat, is the present Sarsanghchalak.

In school in Nagpur, Hedgewar was rusticated for singing 'Vande Mataram' in contravention of a circular issued by the British authorities. He was sent to Calcutta (now Kolkata) by Moonje to pursue medical studies and was, for a while, connected with Congress activities. He was disillusioned after Hindu-Muslim riots broke out which drew his mind towards an alternate model of nation-building.

One of the first public tasks assigned to the RSS volunteers by Dr Hedgewar included a religious element, that is, to protect pilgrims against the rapacity of faqirs and priests at the festival of Ramanavami held at Ramtek, near Nagpur. In the past, Muslims had stopped the Ganesh procession, when it passed before a mosque, with music. In 1927, Hedgewar came in front of the procession and 'because of him all the others also came along beating the drums'.

The RSS founder set up a Womens' Wing in 1936.

With Hedgewar at the helm, the RSS declared that the Hindu religious and cultural heritage should be the basis of Indian nationhood. The organization was kept away from the political arena. At the annual Sangh Shiksha Varg in 1940, Hedgewar gave his last message to the Swayamsewaks, saying: 'I see before my eyes today a miniature Hindu Rashtra'.

Dogged by failing health, he had started delegating his responsibilities to Madhav Sadashiv (M.S.) Golwalkar (1906–73) who was declared as the *Sarkaryavah* (the second-most important position in the RSS) at a gurudakshina festival in 1939 and became the Sarsanghchalak the following year. He was widely known as Guruji.

Bhaiyyaji Dani was among the first pracharaks (full-time propagators) to be involved in spreading the RSS ideology through personal contact, meetings and public lectures and he played a crucial role in expanding its network in the erstwhile Madhya Bharat where, during 1940-46, his first team of pracharaks included Manohar Rao Moghe who went to Ujjain, Kushabhau Thakre (1922–2003), a later-day BJP President, who went to Mandsaur-Ratlam and Haribhau Wakankar who went to Kukshi.

Earlier, Hedgewar had sent Dani as a pracharak to the Banaras Hindu University (BHU) with the approval of the University's founder, Madan Mohan Malaviya, and with the instruction to intermix with the students. Among those recruited by him at the BHU was a young lecturer, M.S. Golwalkar.

The RSS was banned once during the British rule and thrice, post-1947 – first, following the assassination of Mahatma Gandhi in 1948, second, during the Emergency (1975-77) and for a third time after the demolition of the Babri Masjid in 1992.

When the Sangh was banned in 1948, in the aftermath of Mahatma Gandhi's assassination, Golwalkar was imprisoned and nearly 2,000 swayamsewaks were arrested in the satyagraha launched to protest the ban, a large number being from Madhya Bharat. It was the strong foundation established by Dani and his team that led to the rise of the BJS in Central India in later years.

Dani was appointed as the General Secretary (Sarkaryavaha) of the RSS in 1946, a position in which he served till 1956 and, again, from 1962 to 1965 when he passed away. Following the ban on the RSS and the mass arrests, Eknath Ranade, Balasaheb Deoras and he negotiated with Sardar Patel the issue of lifting of the ban. The three of them wrote a constitution for the RSS, which was a pre-condition to lifting the ban. In practice, however, the democratic measures put into the written constitution had little effect since an exact number of candidates was nominated for all posts without the need for any elections.

Among the first pracharaks to take initiation from Dr Hedgewar was Umakant Keshav (Babasaheb) Apte (1903-71) who was born in a Chitpavan Brahmin family in Vidarbha. He formed a Vidyarthi Mandal for discussing revolutionary ideas; a visit by Hedgewar provided sufficient inspiration for Apte to merge his fledging organization with the RSS.

In the early 1930s, Apte was active in spreading the network of RSS shakhas in the Marathi-speaking areas. He toured the Punjab in 1935 and established contacts with the Arya Samaj to prepare the ground for the RSS in that province.

The RSS honoured him as a Karmayogi. To commemorate his special interest in rewriting Indian history in the mould of Hindutva and popularizing Sanskrit, the Babasaheb Apte Smarak Samiti was set up in 1973 for commissioning and publishing books on these subjects.

The memory of Eknath Ranade (1914-82), another leading figure of the RSS, was honoured at an event organized in connection with his Centenary Celebrations in November 2014. Prime Minister Modi described him as 'a perfectionist that others found difficult to match'. He succeeded Bhaiyyaji Dani as the Sarkaryavaha.

Having long been under the influence of Swami Vivekananda's teachings, Ranade published a tribute Rousing Call to Hindu Nation and took up, with the wholehearted support of Guru Golwalkar, the project of building the Vivekananda Rock Memorial near Kanyakumari where the Swami had meditated in 1892. He later founded the Vivekananda Kendra as a Hindu spiritual organization, based on the principles of Renunciation and Service. There are now around 640 Vivekananda Kendras across India. Ranade also started an Order of non-Sanyasis (whom he called *Jeevan-Vratis*) dedicated to the ideals of Swami Vivekananda.

Bhaiyyaji Dani, Babasaheb Apte and Eknath Ranade are among the men of rare integrity who, led by Dr Hedgewar, put the RSS on a firm footing and whose pioneering zeal accounts for its growing strength on the ground.

Hedgewar's choice of Golwalkar as his successor came as a surprise, since senior activists were passed over. One factor that, apparently, weighed with Hedgewar was Golwalkar's educational credentials, his unshakeable determination and his organizational skills. It was also thought that he would maintain the independence of the RSS, otherwise liable to be regarded as a youth front of the Hindu Mahasabha.

Guru Golwalkar had come under the spell of Swami Akhandananda (1864-1937), a direct disciple, like Swami Vivekananda, of Sri Ramakrishna Paramahamsa. He received his 'diksha' in January 1937 but travelled to Nagpur in a state of depression after his guru's death. It was Hegdewar who convinced him that his obligation to society could best be fulfilled by working in the RSS.

A record of a conversation[6] between Mahatma Gandhi and Dr Hedgewar at Wardha in 1934 runs as follows:

Gandhiji:	Doctor Saheb, what made you start an independent organization like the Rashtriya Swayamsevak Sangh? You were in Congress and surely you could have built up such a voluntary body in the Congress itself. Did you feel the dearth of funds in the Congress?
Dr Hedgewar:	No, not at all. Fact is, that creation of the kind of Swayamsevaks I had in mind, was simply not possible through the Congress.
Gandhiji:	Why so?
Dr Hedgewar:	Because the Congress, after all, is a political party and its volunteers are just boys of errands, arranging chairs and tables, saluting and cheering the leaders, looking to their arrangements and such other sundry jobs, whereas my concept of a Swayamsevak is altogether different.
Gandhiji:	What is your concept, Doctor Saheb?
Hedgewar:	One who offers himself voluntarily in the cause of national upliftment in a spirit of total selflessness – such a person alone is a Swayamsevak. I also believe that it is only on the strength of such Swayamsevaks that our nation can ultimately rise to its full glory.

In the annals of the RSS, Guru Golwalkar occupies a very special position. In 1938, he translated Babarao Savarkar's Rashtra Mimansa (Nationalism) from Marathi to Hindi and English which was published as We, or our Nationhood Defined and is regarded as a treatise for the RSS cadres.

In his early years as the Sarsangchalak, the RSS footprint spread to the then Jammu and Kashmir State when Balraj Madhok, later President of the BJS, was sent as a pracharak to Jammu and a shakha was opened in Srinagar four years later.

In the pre-Independence years, Guru Golwalkar took care not to give the British authorities an excuse to take action against the RSS. On their part, the colonial government acknowledged that the RSS organization 'scrupulously kept itself within the law and refrained from taking part in the disturbances that broke out in August 1942'.

---

6 Guru Golwalkar: *Bunch of Thoughts*, Jagarana Prakashan, Bangalore (1966).

His primary aim was to defend Hindu religion and culture. On more than one occasion, he praised Savarkar's Essentials of Hindutva and in May 1963 acknowledged his debt to Hindutva philosophy.

In the preceding decades, a confluence had been emerging of intellectual and historical currents that had remained under the surface, so much so that the people of a vast sub-continent were bereft of an answer for their subjugation by a foreign power. One popular explanation was that a steep decline from a glorious Hindu past had occurred and that, having lost touch with this past, the Hindus were vanquished by the invaders, whether Muslim or British.

Most of those who subscribed to this history believed that the decline could be corrected by reviving the ancient past. The Indian Muslims had also put forward their version of the same argument, maintaining that the decay of their rule was a result of deviation from the fundamentals of Islam. But while the fundamentals could be traced back to a text, the Quran, the re-creation of a great Hindu past rested on an invention of that past.

It was Savarkar's book *Hindutva: Who is a Hindu?* that effectively addressed this question and became the ideological basis for subsequent attempts at Hindu consolidation. Marked by logic and clarity, his exposition of the concept of Hindutva inspired Dr Hedgewar who had (on returning to Nagpur from Calcutta) become a member of both the Congress and the Hindu Mahasabha. This co-existence grew less comfortable as Gandhi began exercising a hold on the Congress. Hedgewar was disillusioned when Gandhi made overtures to the Muslims during the Khilafat Movement that called for the restoration of a caliphate across several countries, which many Hindu leaders criticized, arguing that its adherents in India showed more loyalty to their religion than to their homeland.

After taking over as head of the RSS in 1940, Guru Golwalkar continued the organizational expansion that Dr Hedgewar had overseen – particularly in the Vidarbha region and the Central Provinces. He had no direct exposure to political work. When the Congress – led by Gandhi – announced the Quit India movement in 1942, Golwalkar said: 'Right from the beginning, the Sangh has decided to observe certain constraints in some matters'. He argued that 'the Congress leaders did not make adequate preparations ... On careful thought, I have realized that we cannot reach our goal even if we took part in it with all our might ... In such a situation, I think the Sangh's participation in the movement would serve no purpose'.

Balraj Madhok, who had played a key role in setting up the ABVP, wrote in 2008 that, after quitting the Nehru cabinet, Mookerjee appealed to all sections of Hindu society, particularly those connected with the Arya Samaj and the RSS, to extend support to his new party. According to Madhok, while the attitude of the Arya Samaj was encouraging, no response came from the RSS. However, Golwalkar remained in discussion with Mookerjee. The RSS leadership indicated preference for a *Kesari* (saffron) flag and a Hindi name for the party, such as Bharatiya Lok Sangh or Bharatiya Jana Sangh. Mookerjee chose the latter. Eventually, Golwalkar and Mookerjee agreed that for the newly-established party to enlist the cooperation of the Sangh Swayamsevaks, it should have the same ideal as the Sangh.

Guru Golwalkar's last major institutional endeavour was the founding of the Vishva Hindu Parishad (VHP) in 1966, by when the RSS labour wing, the Bharatiya Mazdoor Sangh (BMS), had already been formed.

The creation of the VHP as an entity that could directly intervene in Hindu religious causes was particularly important for Golwalkar. A senior RSS functionary, Shivram Shankar Apte, was selected as the first general secretary of the VHP and RSS workers were instrumental in establishing its organizational network.

After the RSS provided help to the civil administration in the Sino-Indian hostilities in 1962, even Nehru seems to have given up his antipathy and a Sangh contingent participated in the 1963 Republic Day Parade.

By the time of the Guruji's passing in 1973, the Sangh Parivar, as we know it today, was essentially in place. The organizations of the Sangh could grow more quickly by drawing from the pool of people in the Shakhas. The organizational principles and the discipline of the RSS transferred to these bodies, as did the Sangh's ideology which had its roots in Savarkar's work. But it was Golwalkar who developed the principles more fully and infused the RSS with them.

Dr. K.M. Munshi, a veteran freedom-fighter and an adherent of Sardar Patel, set up the Bharatiya Vidya Bhawan as an institution to popularize Hindu cultural nationalism. He joined the Swatantra Party established by Rajaji and was also a VHP founder.

In 2008, after his second Assembly Election win in 2007 in Gujarat. Narendra Modi authored *Jyotipunj* ('beams of light') in which he recounted the stories of the lives of the extraordinary men who have inspired him. The longest biography is of the RSS' second Sarsanghchalak, Guru Golwalkar, who historically expanded the organization after he was given its charge by the founder.

The reverence with which Modi writes about Guru Golwalkar in the essay titled '*Pujniya Shri Guruji*' suggests that the Guruji was an extremely important influence in his life.

Narendra Modi says that while Guru Golwalkar was spiritually inclined, he was later convinced that he could best contribute to the task of nation-building (in line with Swami Vivekananda's message) through the Sangh. He never wavered in his faith and in his devotion to Dr Hegdewar, saying: 'Doctorji's speeches didn't really enter my mind. Over time, they seeped into my being. He seized all of me. Whenever I am in difficulty, his life inspires me and a road opens up.' He always asked swayamsevaks to study Dr Hegdewar's work.

Not many might be aware of the role played by Guru Golwalkar in persuading Maharaja Hari Singh of Jammu and Kashmir to accede to India. The State Sanghachalak of the RSS, Pt. Prem Nath Dogra, had been petitioning the Maharaja in this behalf but to little avail. On October 17, 1947, at Sardar Patel's instance, Guru Golwalkar flew to Srinagar to explain to the Maharaja the futility of entertaining ideas about Kashmir's independence. The Maharaja expressed willingness to sign the Instrument of Accession in favour of the Dominion of India, which was reported to Sardar Patel. However, the invasion of the State by tribesmen from the Pakistan side in the next few days altered the situation completely.

The country is still paying the price for the issue having been left unresolved at that time.

Hindu leaders, including Savarkar, supported the State of Israel at its formation and Golwalkar praised the Jews for preserving their 'religion, culture and language'.

A leader of true RSS extraction, Narendra Modi has become the first Indian PM to visit Israel, with which this country established diplomatic ties in 1992 during the tenure of Narasimha Rao. In his foreign policy, Rao was imaginative enough to digress from the Nehruvian trajectory and it was his foresight, as a Congress PM, that strengthened the foundation of an Indo-Israeli partnership. The Congress Party has done nothing to stake claim on Rao's initiative which Modi has now taken several steps forward. The Congress' decline in all directions is due also to the party's unwillingness to acknowledge the contribution of its many leaders who were from outside the Nehru family.

Vasant Rao Oak, a Chitpavan Brahmin of Nagpur, who joined the RSS in 1927 is remembered for his devotion to Hindutva, as also Nanaji Deshmukh (1916-2010) who joined the RSS in 1929 in Akola and became a leading figure in the Jana Sangh, the Janata Party and, then, the BJP.

Oak was among the earliest to join the RSS after the first Sangh Shakha was founded at Mohitewada in Nagpur, the RSS headquarters; Mohitewada was a prime centre of the old Nagpur city and Dr Hedgewar's residence was about half a mile away on the other side in the ltwari locality where Balasaheb Deoras' father lived.

Madhukar Dattatraya (Balasaheb) Deoras became a Swayamsevak in 1926 when he was about eleven years of age; he rose in the Sangh, from a Swayamsevak to a Mukhya Sikshak, a Shakha Karyavah, a Varga Sikshak, Sarkaryavah and, then, the third Sarsanghchalak.

Balasaheb Deoras (1915–1996) met Dr Hedgewar regularly at the shakha. Years later, he recalled that Hedgewar displayed rare qualities of leadership; he himself cleaned the *Sanghasthan* (the site where a shakha is held), sprinkled water that was brought from a nearby well and participated in all the physical activities, along with other swayamsevaks.

He was quick to imbibe these qualities; his working pattern was like that of Dr Hedgewar and he did not impose decisions on the swayamsevaks. During the first ban on the RSS in 1948, Guru Golwalkar and Balasaheb together came to Delhi after their release from Nagpur. It was planned to launch a countrywide satyagraha against the ban, but Guru Golwalkar was again arrested in Delhi. The next day a note was received from him from the jail in which he directed that the plans to launch the satyagraha should go ahead.

This responsibility was entrusted to Balasaheb who felt that the call of starting satyagraha should be taken by the swayamsevaks. He suggested that a meeting of all the Prant Pramukhs (provincial heads) should be called; in that meeting, the Prant Pramukhs were of opinion that the proposed satyagraha must be launched. Bhaiyyaji Dani was to come to Delhi on December 12, 1949, at the Old Delhi Railway Station and was to be received by a group of swayamsevaks and taken in a procession to *Phowara* (Fountain) in Chandni Chowk. He was, however, arrested at the Railway Station itself.

Addressing a meeting in Pune as the Sarsanghchalak, Guru Golwalkar had said, 'if you want to know what Dr Hedgewar was, know Balasaheb Deoras! He is the real image of Dr Hedgewar.'

During the ban on the RSS in 1975 Balasaheb Deoras was the Sarsanghchalak and other organizations, apart from RSS, were also banned. Balasaheb was detained in Pune Jail.

As the Sarsanghchalak, he was invited to deliver a lecture when he quoted Abraham Lincoln 'if slavery is not wrong, there is nothing wrong in this world' and added 'if untouchability is not wrong, there is nothing wrong in this country …'.

During his term as the Prime Minister, between 1977-79, Morarji Desai approved the setting up of a Minorities Commission. Balasaheb opposed the decision and argued that a Human Rights Commission should have been formed in its place. He pitched for Indianisation, saying 'if a person is reluctant to call himself Hindu, he must, at least, identify himself as a Bharatiya, irrespective of his form of worship …'.

Balasaheb echoed Savarkar in stating 'We do believe in the one-culture and one-nation Hindu Rashtra. But our definition of Hindu is not limited to any particular kind of faith. Our definition of Hindu includes those who believe in the one-culture and one-nation theory of this country. They can all form part of the Hindu Rashtra. So by Hindu we do not mean any particular type of faith. We use the word Hindu in a broader sense …'. The Swadeshi Jagaran Manch founded in 1993 was his brainchild and was conceived as a protectionist bulwark against economic liberalization.

He was more involved with political work than his two predecessors. As the Sarsanghachalak, he strengthened the RSS' links with the BJS whose annual meeting he had addressed and he got the RSS to support the J.P. movement against the Indira Gandhi government.

Assam's governor, Banwari Lal Purohit, who was duly rewarded by the BJP in 2016, has been a politician of standing from Vidarbha (Maharashtra) and has thrice been a Lok Sabha member – twice from the Congress and once from the BJP. In 2007, he controversially disclosed that he had arranged an hour-long meeting between the then RSS chief Balasaheb Deoras and the then Prime Minister Rajiv Gandhi in 1989. Purohit's claim was that Rajiv Gandhi had forged a secret pact with the RSS to permit Shilanyas and construction of Ram Temple at Ayodhya in exchange for RSS support to the Congress in the 1989 elections.

In 1991, when still a Congress Member of Parliament, Purohit took part in kar seva in Ayodhya leading to his expulsion. He is not alone among those, with roots in the Congress, who have maintained links with the RSS so as to secure its support in pursuing political careers.

For reasons of poor health, Balasaheb Deoras stepped down in 1994 paving the way for Professor Rajendra Singh (Rajju Bhaiya) to replace him. He survived just long enough to witness, in May 1996, the installation of a 13-day government headed by Vajpayee, the first politician of RSS affiliation, to become Prime Minister.

Rajju Bhaiya (1922-2003) had been active in the Quit India Movement in 1942 and it was, at this time, that he was first in contact with the RSS. His father had risen to the position of Chief Engineer in the then United Provinces. A Professor of Physics at the Allahabad University (where Murli Manohar Joshi was an outstanding student), it was the mission of the Sangh that really dominated his life and he quit his post in 1966 to devote himself, full-time, to the RSS. He was the first non-Brahmin and the first non-Maharashtrian to head the RSS.

Rajju Bhaiya was among the first to authoritatively announce that Vajpayee was the BJP's prime ministerial face, ostensibly to secure the support of the so-called 'secular' parties. He is also thought to have interceded with Vajpayee, after a lapse of time, for designating Advani as Deputy Prime Minister, a move that Vajpayee is said to have been not overly anxious to make.

Of the same age as Rajju Bhaiya but from the pre-partition Punjab was Bhai Mahavir (1922-2016), son of Bhai Parmanand[7]. The two were as senior as Vajpayee in the RSS organization but Rajju Bhaiya chose not to, because of an innate decency, exercise that depth of influence which Guru Golwalkar or Balasaheb Deoras would (if alive) have exerted over the NDA-I.

Rajju Bhaiya's generation in the RSS also had men like H.V. Sheshadri (1926-2005) who were selflessly dedicated to the Hindu cause. Inspired by the principles of the RSS since childhood, Seshadriji played a pivotal role in the growth of the Sangh in what is present–day Karnataka. He was the Sarkaryavaha in 1987 and retired in 2000 for health reasons; thereafter, he was the organization's Akhil Bharatiya Pracharak Pramukh until his death.

K.S. Sudarshan, popularly known in the Sangh circles as Sudarshanji (1931-2012), assumed the reins from Rajju Bhaiya on the latter's retirement, because of declining health, in March 2000. In his acceptance speech, he recalled how he was hand-picked to head the Madhya Bharat region and that he had been hesitant to take up the responsibility. He said that it was the then Sarsanghchalak, Guru Golwalkar, who helped him to make up his mind, adding that 'I was able to discharge my duties because people senior to me cooperated fully...'

He was born in Raipur in the then CP& Berar (now in Chhattisgarh) in a Sanketi Brahmin family, was an unsparing votary of Swadeshi and was

---

7 Bhai Parmanand (1876-1947) belonged to an Arya Samaj family of Jhelum district, West Punjab. He went on a hunger-strike in the Andaman Islands to protest against the harsh treatment of political prisoners.

seen as one of the hardliners in the RSS who often criticized the NDA-I government, in general, and the BJP, in particular, for its economic policies. After the BJP-led coalition had been voted out, he expressed, in 2005, that both Vajpayee and Advani should make way for a younger leadership to take charge of the BJP; his statements created a stir in the Sangh Parivar.

Sudarshanji's standing stood compromised in the Vajpayee-led NDA-I which, from the Hindutva point of view, was a big disappointment. Vajpayee took down Advani with him, seeking shelter behind the compulsions of 'coalition' dharma.

Party Presidents like Kushabhau Thakre (1922-2003) and Jana Krishnamurthi (1928-2007) were studiously ignored. During a period of six years (1998-2004), the foster family, the PMO and a since deceased Central Minister hailing from Maharashtra (who coined the slogan India Shining) were literally calling the shots across the Government of India, barring Advani's domain of the Home and Personnel Ministries.

The waywardness of the Vajpayee government continued, unchecked.

Sudarshanji stepped down as the Sarsanghchalak in March 2009 and was succeeded by Mohan Madhukar Bhagwat (born in 1950 in Chandrapur, Maharashtra) signifying a generational change in the RSS.

In the Bharatiya Jana Sangh (BJS) and the BJP, two individuals, Dr Syama Prasad Mookerjee (1901-53) and Pandit Deendayal Upadhyaya (1916-68), stand out. Mookerjee, a remarkable figure in Indian public life in the forties and early fifties and a fearless nationalist, is admired for his lofty idealism and impeccable character. An educationist at an early age, he became the youngest Vice-Chancellor of the Calcutta University.

His father, the esteemed Sir Ashutosh Mookerji (1864-1924) had been the second Indian Vice-Chancellor of the University and is credited with having recognized the talent of S. Radhakrishnan and C.V. Raman. He made his mark as a political leader when he outmanoeuvred the British and the Muslim League to install a Fazlul Huq-led Coalition Ministry in Bengal.

In April, 1950, Mookerjee, along with K.C. Neogy[8], resigned from the Union Cabinet following disagreement over the Pact concluded between Prime Ministers Nehru and Liaquat Ali Khan, the provisions of which, he thought, left the Hindus in East Bengal at the mercy of Pakistan. He was also

---

8 Kshitish Chandra (K.C.) Neogy was a member of the Constituent Assembly. He was Minister of Rehabilitation in the first Nehru cabinet and took charge, after the resignation of R.K. Shanmukham Chetty, as the second Finance Minister in 1950. However, he held office for only 35 days since he resigned alongwith Syama Prasad Mookerjee.

opposed to Article 370 whose abrogation became an article of faith with the newly-formed BJS. The Jammu and Kashmir State was allowed its own Flag, with Sheikh Abdullah becoming the first Prime Minister, to which Mookerjee responded: '*Ek Desh mein do Vidhan, do Pradhan aur do Nishan, nahi chalenge*'. (One country can't have two Vidhans, two Vidhans and two symbols).

Speaking in July, 2017 at the release of a book entitled *Syama Prasad Mookerji: His Vision of Education*, the incumbent BJP Chief, Amit Shah, said that 'If Jammu and Kashmir is our part today, the maximum contribution is of Mookerjee's ... his sacrifice ensured that we Indians do not need a permit to visit Kashmir'. Amit Shah attributed the BJP's presence across the country to Mookerjee's 'farsightedness' in forming the BJS, the parent party, adding that Mookerjee knew that the country needed different policies.

Syama Prasad Mookerji and Deendayal Upadhyaya did not live long enough to fulfil the multi-dimensional impact that they had the potential to achieve; they are the two pillars on which the future of the BJP will rest in the years ahead. Around the time of founding the BJS in 1951, Mookerji was so impressed with Upadhyaya's dedication that he said: 'Give me two Deendayals and I will completely change the face of the nation'.

It is for his enunciation of a philosophy of integral humanism that Upadhyaya is particularly remembered. Even though certain similarities are discernible with Mahatma Gandhi's views on the rural economy, Upadhyaya's thought is essentially grounded in Hindu spirituality.

Unlike some others who rose phenomenally in the BJP, Upadhyaya was extremely simple in his habits, abjuring personal comforts. He did not subscribe either to the strident march of capitalism or to the commonly understood elements of socialism, emphasizing that the quest for greater wealth had not made the West any the happier nor had socialism been able to ensure human dignity.

A moving tribute to Deendayal Upadhyaya was offered by Barrister N.C. Chatterjee[9], a leading parliamentarian and a former President of the Hindu Mahasabha who had presided over its Gwalior session in 1947:

> I was struck by Shri Upadhyaya's wonderful organizing effort and his quiet and unostentatious manner of working; he was a synthesizing force and

9 Nirmal Chandra Chatterjee (1895-1971) was thrice elected to the Lok Sabha; his son, Somnath Chatterjee, associated with the Communist Party (Marxist was Speaker of the Lok Sabha between 2004-09).

> he did admirable work ... I had the privilege of being arrested, alongwith Dr Syama Prasad Mookerji, in the Kashmir movement ... Dr Mookerji used to tell me that he had great admiration for Shri Deendayal Upadhyaya. Jana Sangh is particularly unfortunate in having had a triple tragedy in losing three distinguished Presidents – Dr Syama Prasad Mookerji in very tragic circumstances in Srinagar in the Kashmir movement, Dr Raghu Vira and now this young man when he was at the height of his glory and power.

Prime Minister Modi has long regarded Upadhyaya as an outstanding intellectual and organizational genius of the BJP. A year-long programme to commemorate the Birth Centenary of this outstanding ideologue, who led them between 1953–68, has been launched by the Party.

In the first general elections of 1952, the BJS won three Lok Sabha seats, including Mookerji who was elected from West Bengal. The Hindu Mahasabha (four seats) and the Ram Rajya Parishad (three seats) were the other like-minded parties that formed a block in Parliament led by Mookerjee.

The Akhil Bharatiya Ram Rajya Parishad (RRP), a right-wing Hindu body, was founded by Swami Karpatri[10] around 1948. In addition to a few seats in the Lok Sabha between 1952-62, the RRP won seats in the Vidhan Sabhas of the Hindi belt and, like the other Hindutva-based formations, supported the implementation of a Uniform Civil Code. Being purely Dharmic, it commanded loyalty in the core Hindu orthodoxy and eventually merged with the Jana Sangh.

The year 1963 is of significance in Indian politics because to that period can be traced the incipient idea of alignments between the Jana Sangh and the Socialists. In three Lok Sabha by-elections that year, the Congress was defeated by Acharya Kripalani in Amroha (U.P.), Ram Manohar Lohia in Farrukhabad (U.P.) and Minoo Masani in Rajkot (Gujarat) as a result of joint campaigning by the two formations from the same platform. Each of the three victors was seen as leading an anti-Nehru voice; in these by-elections, held shortly after India had lost the War to China, they were together able to amplify the sense of political uncertainty in the country.

Heading the Jana Sangh in 1963 was Professor Raghu Vira, a distinguished linguist and scholar, who had been a Member of the Constituent Assembly

10 Swami Karpatri (1907-82) hailed from Pratapgarh (U.P.) and was a monk in the Hindu dashanami monastic tradition. He was a disciple of the Shankaracharya of Jyotir Math, Swami Brahmananda Saraswati, who passed away in 1953.

and had left the Congress in 1961 over differences with Nehru on the China policy. Jayaprakash Narayan and Lohia – socialists to the core – held Raghu Vira in high esteem and spoke of him in affectionate terms on his death in a car accident when travelling to canvas for Lohia. Surprisingly, many in the top echelons of the BJP today are unaware of his noteworthy contributions.

It was in 1967 that a more decisive blow was delivered to the Congress as it lost power in Tamil Nadu and West Bengal and Samyukta Vidhayak Dal (SVD) coalition governments were formed in states like Madhya Pradesh where a Congress ministry headed by D.P. Mishra was 'toppled' through the strenuous efforts of the Rajmata Vijaya Raje Scindia of Gwalior. The defections from the Congress resulted in a political coup which became the first occasion for the Jana Sangh to be in a power-sharing arrangement.

While much has changed since 1967, the SVD experiment offers insights to the present and the future. What is especially striking is that politics then was the obverse of what it is today. The Jana Sangh, struggling on the margins, prised open the doors of power with alliances. The Congress, then the pre-eminent force, now stands at about the same electoral level as the Jana Sangh then and is seen to be displaying the same anxiety to make friends and contest polls as a front.

A major beneficiary of the Emergency (1975-77) was the Hindu Right. The participation of the RSS in the JP movement as well as the civil disobedience against the government gave it a new legitimacy. The active involvement of the RSS cadres during this period also provided the template for the Hindutva mobilizations of the late eighties and early nineties. The Jana Sangh got its first taste of power at the national level following Indira Gandhi's ouster in 1977. When she returned as prime minister three years later, she began appropriating elements of Hindu majoritarian politics.

In the immediate post-Emergency phase, Janata Party governments came into being in which the (former) Jana Sangh was a key constituent. Later, BJP governments took office in 1990 in Madhya Pradesh, Rajasthan and Himachal Pradesh with party stalwarts – Sundarlal Patwa, Bhairon Singh Shekhawat and Shanta Kumar – as the respective Chief Ministers.

After Upadhyaya's demise, Vajpayee found himself catapulted to the leadership, with seniors like Balraj Madhok (1920-2016) being sidelined; Madhok, who was instrumental in establishing the Student Wing – the Akhil Bharatiya Vidyarthi Parishad (ABVP) – was even expelled from the Party.

The contribution of the Rajmata of Gwalior (1919-2001) to the BJS and, subsequently, the BJP, over several decades, were invaluable. After leaving the Congress, she remained steadfast in her commitment to Hindutva; Vajpayee's own political career might never have got so far as it did but for her unflinching support.

On a broader Hindu nationalist plank, the BJS found a powerful ally in the Shiv Sena (SS) – founded in June 1966 – which follows an aggressively pro-Marathi ideology. The BJP-SS alliance has had its ups and downs coming close to termination in the wake of the last municipal polls in Maharashtra but then managing to stay afloat after the BJP conceded the position of the Mumbai Mayor to the Shiv Sena.

Generally speaking, the BJP-Sena ties have plummetted under the NDA-II.

At a poll rally in September 2014 (days after the BJP-SS alliance had, apparently collapsed in the backdrop of the Maharashtra Assembly elections), Uddhav Thackeray, the SS head, claimed that it was his father, Bal Thackeray, the party patriarch, who had stood up to protect Narendra Modi amid the clamour for his removal as Chief Minister, Gujarat. Uddhav Thackeray said that Balasaheb had categorically advised L.K. Advani that if Modi were to be replaced, the BJP would lose Gujarat forever.

Had the Hindu Mahasabha and the RSS agreed upon a common set of objectives, pre-1947, both could, have opposed the Partition more vigorously. The two approaches tried out by Mahatma Gandhi and the Mahasabha could not bridge the gap. Gandhi endeavoured to placate the Muslims and the Mahasabha stretched the issue of separateness, resulting in the failure of both the approaches.

The expression of political views by the RSS commenced after the ban on it was lifted; Guru Golwalkar at a Press Conference on August 14, 1949 in Delhi termed Pakistan an 'uncertain State', observing that 'as far as possible, we must continue our efforts to unite these two divided States .... Nobody is happy with Partition'.

The RSS put across their concept of an Akhand Bharat, based on Hindu cultural similarities. Even today, a select few hope that, some day, the territories which separated 70 years ago will again, through popular goodwill, come together and an Akhand Bharat would be formed.

In the early 1960s, a meeting was arranged between Dr Ram Manohar Lohia and Pt. Deendayal Upadhyaya – reportedly by L.K. Advani, then a journalist with the RSS weekly, *Organizer* – which turned out to be an intensive discussion on relations between India and Pakistan and between Hindus and Muslims. Lohia seems to have told Upadhyaya that the concept of Akhand Bharat had become a hurdle in trying to normalize India-Pakistan ties. He (Lohia) said that 'many Pakistanis believe that if the Jana Sangh came to power in New Delhi, it would forcibly reunify Pakistan with India', to which Upadhyaya replied: 'We have no such intentions. We are willing to put to rest all the concerns on this score'.

In a rare demonstration of consensus-building among leaders of diametrically opposed ideologies, Lohia and Upadhyaya issued a joint statement on April 12, 1964 appealing for equal protection for Hindus and Muslims in the sub-continent and urged both sides to hold comprehensive (not 'piecemeal' talks) so as to make a 'beginning towards the formation of some sort of India – Pakistan Confederation'.

On March 23, 2017 at Lucknow, the incumbent U.P. Chief Minister, Mahant Yogi Adityanath (born June, 1972) paid glowing tributes to Dr Lohia on his death anniversary, which was being interpreted as a gesture to all-inclusive politics. The Samajwadis have refrained from acknowledging Deendayal Upadhayay; by recalling Lohia's achievements, the Chief Minister was subtly conveying that thinkers (like Lohia) cannot be the property of any one individual or political party.

Mahant Yogi Adityanath belongs to a tradition of Hindutva politics in Uttar Pradesh that is traced back to Mahant Digvijay Nath, who led the Babri Masjid agitation in Ayodhya in December 1949. Both Mahant Digvijay Nath (1894-1969) and his successor, Mahant Avaidyanath (1921-2014), were aligned to the Hindu Mahasabha and were elected to the Lok Sabha on that Party's ticket. The BJP and the Sangh Parivar joined the Ayodhya movement and Mahant Avaidyanath switched to the BJP in 1991.

Mahant Digvijay Nath was initially in the Congress and was arrested for taking part in the protests in Chauri Chaura in 1922. He entered the Hindu Mahasabha in 1937 (when Savarkar was its President), became the head of the U.P. unit and was imprisoned for nine months in 1948 for, allegedly, inflaming passions. After release, he spearheaded the Ram Janmabhoomi movement of 1949, and organized a recitation of the Ramcharit Manas, at the end of which the idols of Rama and Sita were placed inside the Babri Masjid which was locked down as a result. This led to Mahant Digvijay Nath's rise in the Hindu Mahasabha.

Under Mahant Avaidyanath, the Gorakhnath Mutt moved closer to the Sangh Parivar. This was a time when several monastic orders located in U.P. became politicized through their involvement in the Ram Janmabhoomi movement.

After Mahant Avaidyanath, the next spiritual successor, Yogi Adityanath became the Mahant (Peethadhishwar) of the Mutt. He was elected to the Lok Sabha in 1998 on BJP ticket. Once regarded as a leader of eastern U.P. – or Gorakhpur, to be precise – his profile has shot up dramatically following his ascension as the state Chief Minister. After Narendra Modi, he is now the most sought-after BJP leader in the campaigning for elections.

The Hindu organizations attracted, over the years, a growing band of sincere and dedicated workers, be it the Mahasabha or the RSS or the BJS and its reincarnation, the BJP. While the inter-relationships tended to be of a complementary nature, they seldom pulled their weight together at a given point in time, the exception being the strong ideological and organizational links that developed between the RSS, the BJS and, later, the BJP. This combination of forces contributed importantly to enlarging the spheres of influence of both bodies, as also the electoral successes of the BJP.

Some years back, a nephew of Veer Savarkar referred to what he called the hypocrisy underlying the attempts of the Sangh Parivar to become the real heirs to his legacy, especially when it was well-known that they were not in tune with his thinking and approach. At present, when the Hindu Mahasabha stands relegated, more or less, to the political sidelines, acrimonious exchanges have sometimes erupted, such as when a senior functionary of the Mahasabha expressed an opinion in November 2015 that 'the BJP and the RSS have … hijacked issues started by the Hindu Mahasabha. For instance, it was the Hindu Mahasabha that put Lord Rama's idol in the Babri mosque in December 1949. Even in police reports, the Hindu Mahasabha has been indicted for doing the same. Where was the BJP, Jana Sangh or RSS at that time?'.

In February 2017, Prime Minister Modi saluted Savarkar's memory on his death anniversary: 'Remembering Veer Savarkar on his *punya tithi*. He was a true patriot who envisioned a strong and developed India'.

He was criticized for calling Savarkar a 'patriot'.

Whatever the dynamics in play, the fact remains that Savarkar was a very influential figure and a pioneering theoretician of the idea of Hindu Rashtra. Syama Prasad Mookerjee and he are the only two Hindutva personalities whose portraits adorn the Central Hall of Parliament. Mookerjee's portrait – donated by the BJP – was unveiled by President R. Venkataraman in May 1991. A bust-size portrait of Swatantryaveer Vinayak Damodar Savarkar was unveiled by President A.P.J. Abdul Kalam in February, 2003 during Vajpayee's prime ministership.

It was as late as in January 1978 that Subhas Bose's portrait found a place in this Gallery of Fame.

Vajpayee was no archetypal Hindu nationalist leader. Given his long connection with the RSS, his ideological and cultural roots in the organization should have, with the passage of years, grown stronger rather than weaker. Future verdicts of history may not be very kind to him, as could also be the outcome for Manmohan Singh but for not the same reasons.

During the six years that he was in office, Vajpayee with his flexible outlook, winning ways and affable temperament, succeeded in conveying that the BJP was no longer an 'untouchable' in electoral politics and was on the path to becoming a major player. He can be said to have, unwittingly, pushed back the rise of an Hindutva that should, in a modern setting, not be inimical to the minorities' rights and interests and can purposively drive the processes of growth, with equity, in the country.

The RSS and the BJP can consider themselves lucky that the setback was short-lived; with Narendra Modi's ascension to the national leadership, the forces of Hindu Organization are here to stay in Indian politics.

At the Jaipur Literature Festival (JLF) held in January 2017, a controversy arose following the decision of the organizers to invite RSS functionaries. For some, this was unusual and unexpected, for others, it was undesirable; it showed that the exclusion of the RSS from intellectual discourse was considered legitimate by the Nehruvian and Marxist class of intellectuals, for the reason that it represents majoritarianism and the only discussion that is called for is on how to fight it.

Efforts to suppress intellectual streams have, usually, not worked in India. There is no political force – Right or Left – that has not allied with the RSS, via the BJS or the BJP, in the past. In 1967, the CPI justified its alliance with the BJS as being based on concrete programmes; it was attacked by the CPM which itself colluded with the RSS during the Emergency and then, in 1999, to install V.P. Singh as Prime Minister. The Socialists have also cohabited with the BJP.

In the early decades of Independence, the Nehruvian-Left propagated one of its primary tasks as being that of combating the RSS. The Right intellectuals, fewer in number, grew in a milieu of countering Left domination.

The country – once known for its independent and critical spirit – is witnessing its decline. Consequently, intellectuals have faced the indifference of society which was in evidence as far back as in the early thirties when Bipin Chandra Pal[11] passed away. The nationalist papers paid high tribute, describing

11 Bipin Chandra Pal (1858 – 1932) was of the triumvirate of Lal Bal Pal (Lala Lajpat Rai, Bal Gangadhar Tilak and he himself). He was born in Habiganj in pre-partition Bengal.

him as one of the luminaries who gave a voice to India's aspirations. Even as his services were recognized in death, in life he had, to struggle hard for the help he received from those who now acclaimed his greatness.

Pal was opposed to the Congress taking up Khilafat. In his *Memories of my Life and Times*, he wrote how he dreaded the virus of Pan-Islamism among the Indian Muslims. He had warned Gandhi: 'You want to do magic, while I try to give you logic'. He understood, like his comrade, Lajpat Rai, the depth of the Muslim question; it was under his influential leadership that the Bengal partition of 1905 was defeated.

The post-Independence polity has seen intellectuals playing second fiddle in statecraft, compounded by the imposition of sectarianism on academic activity. In the late seventies, it was left to a CPM member-Zahoor Siddiqui – to say that 'it was not the RSS which imposed the Emergency ... There was no Golwalkar at Turkman Gate, Muzaffarnagar or Pipli'.

The anti-RSS propaganda has been led by individuals and groups whose academic embellishments appear grand but who have actually promoted segregation. Polemics cannot be a permanent feature of thinking societies, which is why the alternative narratives of the RSS on nationalism and culture present complex dilemmas to those who regard intellectualism as a monopoly of a particular stream and are unable to countenance the demolition of monolithic debate.

The BJP's sway over power since 2014 has fuelled a shift towards right-wing nationalist studies in several campuses. A Professor of Political Science at the BHU asserts that '... this is the time for Indian researchers to move beyond Karl Marx and Vladimir Lenin and assess Indian personalities and polity, Indian culture and consciousness...'.

A Professor at the Chaudhary Charan Singh University, Meerut is known to have told his post-graduate students to do research on topics which have remained untouched, such as the Bharatiya Jana Sangh leaders – Syama Prasad Mookerjee and Deendayal Upadhyaya – and the RSS and its social service. Among others, scholars at the Maharaja Ganga Singh University in Bikaner (Rajasthan) are writing on 'Sarsanghchalaks of the RSS' and 'The Cultural Outlook of the RSS'.

Academics, with Sangh affiliations, have been appointed to head major institutions like the ICHR, the BHU and Nalanda University.

The family of the present Sarsanghchalak, Mohan Bhagwat, has been associated with the RSS for three generations. Both Narendra Modi and he were born in September 1950 and he is believed to have pushed for Modi as the BJP's prime ministerial candidate, his reasoning being that the old order had to change. His preference for younger leaders was clear when he ensured that, at 52 years, Nitin Gadkari became the youngest-ever BJP chief in December, 2009.

He is a man of action and a strict disciplinarian. His success in mobilizing the RSS cadres ahead of the 2014 elections has added to his stature. Under his guidance, the RSS strategists and key BJP leaders analysed the data and found that the BJP had won at least once from around 278 seats across the country and that there were 70-75 seats where the party was second. The RSS chalked out a strategy to focus on these 350-odd seats. The results were unprecedented.

As the term of President Pranab Mukherjee approached completion in July 2017, speculation had been rife about the possible successors. Quite out of the blue, the BJP's old ally, the Shiv Sena, suggested that Mohan Bhagwat would make an ideal candidate for the august position. In a response that speaks volumes of his commitment and self-effacement, Bhagwat said:

> On entering the RSS, I closed all other doors. Even if my name is recommended, I will not accept ... Every swayamsevak knows that I can never be a presidential candidate ... I am a swayamsevak first and I have responsibilities in the Sangh ... The speculative reports in the media ... should be seen only as entertainment.

Mohan Bhagwat and Modi would turn 75 when the RSS celebrates its Centenary in the year 2025. Were they to step down then, they would set an example in regard to the policy of a retirement age for leaders of the Sangh Parivar.

What can be said, with certainty, is that the upcoming state polls and the Lok Sabha elections of 2019, and thereafter, will be of crucial importance for the votaries of Hindutva who have secured access to the 'commanding heights', as it were.

❖

'Partition, in a way, was the gift the Congress gave to the Hindu Right which, in the fullness of time, is today's Hindutva … even for Nehru, like all the other leaders, including the Mahatma, the secular project was negotiable'.

SAEED NAQVI
NOTED INDIAN JOURNALIST AND MEDIA PERSONALITY

Lord Mountbatten, Viceroy-designate and Lady Mountbatten leaving for India, February, 1947

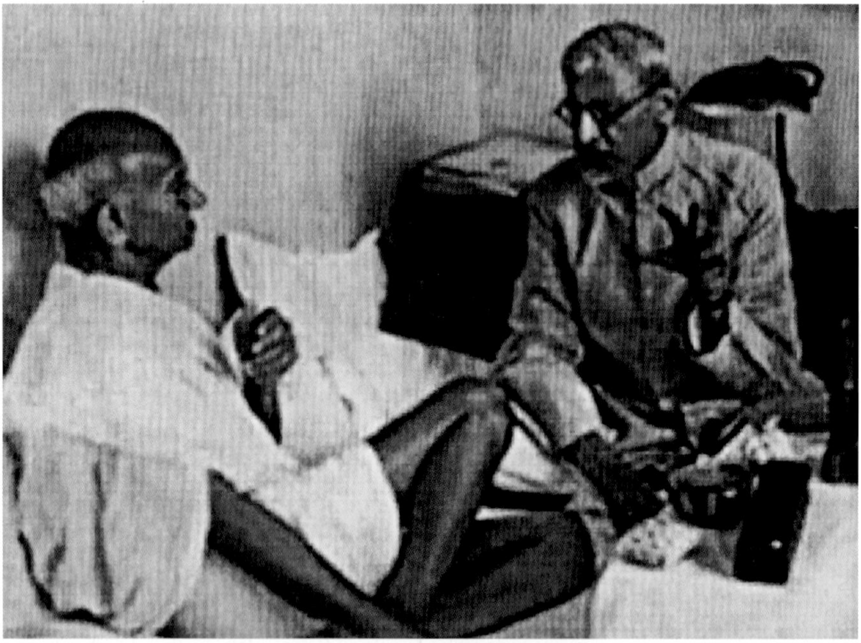

Above: Mahatma Gandhi in converstaion with Maulana Sayyid Abul Kalam Ghulam Muhiyuddin Azad who was the Congress President (1940–46)

Below: Jinnah and Subhas Bose: a common aversion to Gandhi

Above: Prime Minister Indira Gandhi and P.N. Haksar, Deputy Chairman at a meeting of the Full Planning Commission after the latter had moved out of the PMO; Union Ministers C. Subramaniam, Y.B. Chavan and Kamalapati Tripathi also seen here

Below: Ambedkar and Periyar, 1954

Above: Prime Minister Zhou Enlai greets Prime Minister Mohammad Ali Bogra; Nehru (partly) and Indira Gandhi, as also U Nu of Burma are seen (Bandung Conference, 1955)

Below: Lal Bahadur Shastri becomes Prime Minister, June 9, 1964

Sheikh Mujibur Rahman (1920–75) with his mentor, H.S. Suhrawardy and the Chinese Prime Minister, Zhou Enlai in Dacca (in the then East Pakistan), 1957

Clockwise from top (left): Dr Hedgewar believed that the cultural and religious heritage of the Hindu should be the basis of Indian nationhood. He founded the RSS in 1925 at Nagpur – an organization that has grown from strength to strength

Sir Muhammad Iqbal with his son, Javid (1924–2015), who was a Judge of the Supreme Court of Pakistan between 1986–89

R.G. Casey at Government House. Calcutta during World War II. He was made a life peer of the British House of Lords in 1960. It was by then becoming an anomaly that an Australian should be appointed to another country's Parliament

Clockwise from top (left): Nehru with Sir Girija Shankar Bajpai whom he appointed as the first Secretary General of the Ministry of External Affairs in 1947

Field Marshal Lord Wavell (1883–1950), the penultimate Viceroy, tried hard to keep a United India, as was conveyed to him by C. Rajagopalachari: '...you wanted a settlement honourable to all. And you worked for it with great ability'.

Prof. Rajendra Singh (Rajju Bhaiya, the first non-Brahmin, non-Maharashtrian RSS chief), incognito, in 1976 during the Emergency – the moustache is missing and the attire is different

Above: Pt. Deendayal Upadhyaya conceived the political philosophy of Integral Humanism which has guided the BJP. He was the President of its forerunner, the Bharatiya Jana Sangh, at the time of his premature death, still shrouded in mystery, in 1968. It was a severe blow to Hindutva.

Below: Prime Minister Modi plays a traditional instrument during his visit to Mongolia in May, 2015

PART IV

Problems and Prospects

If Hindu Raj does become a fact, it will … be the greatest calamity for this country … Hindu Raj must be prevented at any cost.

DR B.R. AMBEDKAR
(PAKISTAN OR THE PARTITION OF INDIA, 1946)

❖

WRITING ABOUT JINNAH IN THE EIGHTIES, one of his biographers, Stanley Wolpert[1], had this to say:

> 'Few individuals significantly alter the course of history. Fewer still modify the map of the world. Hardly anyone can be credited with creating a nation-state. Muhammad Ali Jinnah did all three'.

Jinnah's achievement assures him a place in world history. It is possible that Ambedkar might have somewhat modified the views expressed by him on Hindu Raj when Pakistan was on the verge of becoming a reality.

He would, of course, have realized that the Partition of India was bound to set both the successor-states to the British Raj back by a long period of time.

One is tempted to look back to the dangers that Babasaheb, one of Prime Minister Modi's role models, foresaw in his last speech to the Constituent

1 Stanley Wolpert (born 1927), an American academic, has authored the political and intellectual history of modern India and Pakistan. His well-known works include *Jinnah of Pakistan* (1982) and *Shameful Flight: The Last Years of the British Empire in India* (2006).

Assembly. One such was Ambedkar's opinion that the measures Mahatma Gandhi had adopted to resist British rule were liable to be misused – he said that, in a democracy, methods like civil disobedience, non-cooperation and the like were the 'grammar of anarchy'.

By disobeying the rules of procedure and behaving like rival mobs of unruly protestors, the parliamentarians of today, the very people who should be upholding the dignity of the legislatures, have turned parliamentary language into the grammar of anarchy. No political party can absolve itself of blame for establishing this anarchic tradition.

Ambedkar also warned that the Bhakti tradition made India vulnerable to hero worship, which can lead to parties and, indeed, nations being dominated by one person and democracy being derailed. He told the Constituent Assembly: 'Bhakti in religion may be a road to the salvation of the soul. But in politics Bhakti, or hero worship, is a sure road to degradation and to eventual dictatorship.'

In a broadcast over All India Radio (AIR) on the evening of June 3, 1947, Viceroy Mountbatten gave an account of his discussions with the leaders of the political parties, saying it had been his firm opinion that, with a reasonable degree of goodwill between the communities, a unified India would be, by far, the best solution. However, the Muslim League had demanded Partition and the Congress had used the same argument for demanding, in that event, the Partition of certain provinces.

As regards the position of the Sikhs, the Viceroy said they were so distributed that any Partition of the Punjab would inevitably divide them – it was sad the Partition could not avoid splitting them.

Simultaneously, an examination had begun of the steps that would be necessary to effect an early Partition. A note was prepared by Walter John Christie, ICS, Joint Private Secretary to the Viceroy, that dealt with matters like the division of staff organizations, records, services and institutions, assets and liabilities, and future economic relations. It suggested, in particular, the setting up of a Partition Council and of Expert Committees to address various issues.

This note, which took the shape of a thirty-three page document entitled The Administrative Consequences of Partition, was presented by Lord Mountbatten to the party leaders at the end of the meeting at which the Partition Plan had been accepted. The effect[2] it made on those present was indicated by the complete silence which followed. The political leadership

2 V.P. Menon: *The Transfer of Power in India* (Orient Longman, 1957).

had, for the first time, been made to realize the magnitude and complexity of the task that confronted them.

Jinnah questioned the authority of the Government of India to make arrangements for the Partition – a responsibility which, he felt, was entirely that of His Majesty's Government. Lord Mountbatten was able to persuade him to agree to the setting up of a Partition Committee which was, later, replaced by a Partition Council when the provinces had decided on Partition.

In South Asia, beginning with India, measures to abolish the feudal and semi-feudal tenures were initiated as a first step in land reforms. India's was a pioneering start in this direction and laws were expeditiously enacted by the Congress Party led by Nehru, such as the U.P. Zamindari Abolition and Land Reforms Act, 1950.

In East Bengal (later East Pakistan), more than ninety per cent of the land was held in Zamindari tenure whose abolition was enforced in the early fifties. A majority of the Rajbari families and the bigger zamindars in East Bengal were of the Hindu fold and many of them migrated to India, in due course. The Muslim Nawabs (like those of Dhaka and Bogra) remained prominent in public life.

While the West Pakistan Land Reforms also abolished jagirs and similar intermediaries, the feudal elements were influential there for much longer and are very much a force to reckon with in Pakistan politics.

Under Congress rule, the Indian government's socio-economic policies had a distinct socialistic slant. In the early years, a good deal of energy and resources were expended on tackling the problems arising out of Partition, not least the Relief and Rehabilitation measures that had to be operationalized.

The available administrative structure did not ensure that the benefits intended for the poverty-stricken did, indeed, reach them. Today, there are unmistakable signs of the rich getting richer and the poor even poorer.

A study carried out by OXFAM[3] shows that 57 billionaires in India now have the same wealth (US$ 216 billion) as the bottom 70 per cent population of the country. In a report titled An Economy for the 99%, OXFAM says that there are 84 billionaires in India with a collective wealth of US$ 248 billion; the country's total wealth is estimated at US$ 3.1 trillion.

Indian women form 60 per cent of the lowest paid wage labour and only 15 per cent of the highest wage earners which means that they are not only

3 OXFAM, an international federation of charitable organizations, focusses on the alleviation of global poverty.

poorly represented in the top bracket of wage earners but also experience wide gender pay gap at the bottom.

The departure of Raghuram Rajan from the Reserve Bank of India in September 2016 was a setback; the signal that went out was that there is no place in the country for professionals with domain knowledge and who are not dependent on the ruling elite.

Rajan's frankly expressed views on the economy contradicted important functionaries in the government. He was thought to be questioning the rationale underlying the slogan 'Make in India' by pointing out that it seemed too late for India to be a global hub and that the effort should instead be to 'Make for India' since the domestic market itself was so large.

The comment that turned out to be the most controversial was his remark that the Indian economy was a one-eyed King in the land of the blind. Rajan was, in fact, trying to moderate the euphoria generated of a high growth rate by clarifying that virtually all major economies were in a near-recessionary situation. He had also said that the 'flattering' comparison of our superior growth rate with that of China was misleading because the size of the Chinese economy was much larger than that of ours.

All this could hardly have gone down well with the arrogance that is often obtained at the top and would have bruised the ego of a few senior ministers. Consequently, Rajan was not adequately defended by those in authority and an 'honourable' exit was for him the better option.

Rajan guarded the Central Bank's autonomy. He had expressed reservations about hasty demonetisation; had he been in charge, he would have urged proper planning and careful implementation.

The question is also about how the Aam Aadmi in India is being compelled to believe that he or she is living in a soft state where the rule of law is routinely sent for a toss. Should this perception be allowed to persist, business leaders might refrain from investing in a country that is unable to uphold the law. The aspirations to become a leading player on the global scene would have vanished in smoke.

The economy continues to face legacy problems, even after a lapse of around three years since the present government came in. Demand, especially investment demand, has not quite picked up. As is well known, if demand is sluggish, fresh capacity is not created and new investment does not take place. Existing industries are not doing too well either. In July and August 2016, the index of industrial production registered negative growth and in September the growth was a meagre 0.7 percent.

These legacy problems from the last dispensation may take some more time to resolve. Nevertheless, there is much that is going right for the government; its ratings are high and the recent electoral successes have provided a huge boost. More needs to be done for the infrastructure, housing and real estate, small and medium industries and self-employment sectors in order to create more employment opportunities which is the most critical issue in the economy. The policies are in place and vigorous implementation is now required.

Earlier this year, Nobel laureate David Jonathan Gross, winner of the 2004 Prize for Physics, expressed the view in Kolkata that while India has taken huge strides in the field of science and technology and has the potential to be a global leader, what holds back the country is its bureaucracy. He said:

> Most educational and scientific institutes are still governed by civil servants .... Everything is so centralized and inflexible. Also, there is political influence over science ... bureaucracy in India has not changed in all these years. Otherwise, the country can easily surpass China in the field of science in a decade or so. Unlike in China, India has a culture of science education ...

Professor Gross also spoke at Ahmedabad and observed:

> India has to go beyond being a minor collaborator in big science research projects and take the lead, but there are inexcusable political and legal delays .... China is fast seizing these opportunities .... I don't see India's hurdles as environmental ... they stem from lack of strong political will ....

A quantum leap in the quality of scientific research and its application to the needs of the common man as also in the organization of science and technology in India is overdue. It will call for, to begin with, the sustained interest and involvement of the Prime Minister himself and regular interaction with scientists and technocrats, much beyond the deliberations at the Indian Science Congress in the first week of January every year or at other fora. Premier bodies like the Atomic Energy Commission and the Space Commission are over-bureaucratized, affording as much representation for retired and serving civil servants (and diplomats) as for active members of the scientific community who can also be drawn from the universities and independent research institutes. For things to get re-energized on this front, fairly wide-ranging changes will need to be introduced.

Sections of the press have carried reports, from time to time, about the atrocities being perpetrated against Dalits in different states. One such stated that Pintooben, Sarpanch of Rahemalpur village in Gujarat – who contributed from personal savings to the construction of a new shrine dedicated to Lord Shiva – is not allowed to enter the sanctum of the Hindu temple because of her Dalit identity. She said that she spent Rs.10 lakh: 'its my money, not from the panchayat'. When asked: 'You are spending so much, wouldn't you like to step into the temple?', she replied: 'I'd like to but there's opposition. There can be a ruckus …'.

Pintooben summed up the fears of the Dalit community; four lower-caste men were stripped, humiliated and beaten with sticks and rods for skinning a dead cow. At a Rama temple at Sadra in Mehsana, the priest was said to display upper-caste supremacy over faith, saying that he is well within his right to deny entry to Dalits.

The appointments of Dalits and members of the backward classes to top positions, including constitutional posts, cannot become a subterfuge to paper over government inaction on caste-based atrocities.

Almost every other month, the Prime Minister holds a review meeting of the Rural Development sector and it was at one such discussion that the question was posed: 'How can we ensure that the money being spent is going to the right person.'

That question sparked off a serious exercise in the bureaucracy to shake up the system, as it were, coinciding with the government's renewed thrust on rural areas which was largely missing in Modi's first year in power. The government has revamped the existing schemes but a new approach for village-centred programmes is still lacking. The real problem is the growing aspirations of rural youth which, in turn, reflects a basic difference between how the UPA and the NDA look at poverty eradication. The former believed in directly addressing the issue whereas the Modi administration seems to believe that the effects of economic growth will gradually trickle down.

As things stand, the spectre of large-scale job losses haunts India's IT industry; this will require to be introspected quickly, with the guidance and assistance of the government, if a way out is to be found.

The Prime Minister has shown that he is a capable administrator of the economic machinery bequeathed by the UPA-II. However, he was also foreseen as a reformer promising minimum government, maximum governance. Hopes were raised in regard to a comprehensive re-energization of the socio-economic imperatives, a stronger push towards liberalization and wider and better provision of the basic services. Some three and a half years down the line, these hopes are fading.

Modi thinks his personal role is immensely important. But sweeping reform is not his forte. Instead, his government has proved adept at dealing with the consequences of faulty policy rather than recasting policy itself. The numerous government schemes launched in the first half of the NDA-II, each accompanied by a public-relations blitz, have generally been aimed at introducing a quick-fix to a symptom of economic malaise, unaccompanied by any attempt to tackle the underlying cause.

There are those who, having served in top positions in the country's security set-up in the past, express the view that the Maoist insurgency is a consequence of socio-economic conflict, that it has only been looked at from a law and order angle and since no government has effectively protected the rights of tribals, the Maoists have organized them to fight the authorities. Some are worried about the constant chest-thumping and jingoism of the ruling party, ignoring the real concerns of internal security. The ambush and killing of Central Reserve Police Force (CRPF) personnel in Bastar's Sukma in April 2017, reminiscent of the 2010 attack, has strengthened the impression that the Maoist violence is among the problems 'worst handled' by the government.

More daunting than the domestic challenges are those that face the NDA-II in the area of foreign policy, with reference, in particular, to China and Pakistan – often described as iron friends – who are united in a common objective of containing India.

On separate occasions in the past, China's President, Xi Jinping, announced a new 'Silk Road Economic Belt' and a 'Maritime Silk Road' which together have become known as 'One Belt, One Road' (OBOR). China invited other countries to be partners in this venture, which would be mainly financed from its own considerable resources. Although not previously consulted, over fifty countries have endorsed the OBOR, accepting the Chinese assurance that 'we are not imperialists and we do not want to colonize the world'. India has not joined that number, even as the OBOR's connectivity and integration could provide the stimuli required for improving Indian manufacturing and competitiveness.

India's position on OBOR was indicated by Prime Minister Modi when he referred to 'the compelling logic of regional connectivity' and added that connectivity could not 'override or undermine the sovereignty of other nations'. India has described the OBOR as a unilateral Chinese initiative with only a limited role for participating countries and has objected to the route of the China-Pakistan corridor that passes through Gilgit-Baltistan in the Pakistan-occupied Kashmir (PoK) en route to Gwadar in Balochistan.

Enhancing the suspicions on the Indian side are signals that the early strains between the Trump White House and Beijing may be dissipating and may lead to a revival of the four-nation group (the USA, Pakistan, China and Afghanistan) to mediate between Kabul and the Taliban. This could result in diminishing India's role in the region, as also its preferential status with Washington – which seems, at times, to be no more than wishful thinking on India's part, more specifically the PMO and the Ministry of External Affairs.

After the Trump-Modi discussions in Washington D.C., the U.S.-India Joint Statement sent a message to Pakistan that the White House views the issue of cross-border terrorism seriously; there was not much, beyond that. The Statement underlined that military ties and defence cooperation will probably grow in the coming years and that the two countries can find common ground to counter Chinese infrastructure and maritime plans. President Trump indicated that U.S. exports would expand, suggesting thereby that a US$ 31 billion trade deficit should be bridged through greater market access.

Significantly, the Statement was silent on the H-1B visa question. The best that India could do is to more effectively engage with various stakeholders to resolve misgivings about job losses in the USA. On Climate Change, the inference can be drawn that New Delhi will need to pursue efforts to get Washington D.C. to keep its commitment to India's renewable power programme.

Characteristically, the Indian Foreign Office played down the reference to 'Indian-administered Jammu and Kashmir', even as this was being questioned by P. Chidambaram of the Congress.

While the Indian case on the China-Pakistan corridor may rest on solid grounds, it is seldom wise to stand alone as the sole dissenter. In any case, a careful reassessment is called for; the long-term consequences of the OBOR project for India can be significant, especially if it ends up enabling China to consolidate its presence in the Indian Ocean. In the circumstances, any hurried appraisal to either support the Chinese initiative or to junk it should be avoided for the present.

In July 2016, the Chinese media flashed pictures of Pakistani and Chinese troops teaming up for their first 'joint patrol' of the Pakistan – China border. For anyone familiar with the geography, Pakistan has no boundary with China except in the PoK, (bordering Xinjiang) which India claims as its own.

China has weighed in on the spate of violence in J&K and is taking a more pro-Pakistan line. A Chinese Foreign Ministry spokesperson had observed: '... The Kashmir issue is left over from history. China holds a consistent stance and hopes relevant parties will address the issue peacefully through dialogue.'

In seeking to accord de facto legitimacy to Pakistan's illegal occupation of PoK, China is dispelling decades of ambiguity, to side with Pakistan on Kashmir. Her increasing investments in PoK under the CPEC have the potential to legitimize any future involvement for Beijing in the Kashmir imbroglio.

While officially maintaining that the Kashmir issue is for India and Pakistan to address bilaterally, there are signs from the Chinese side that they perceive this to be one of their toughest challenges in dealing with regional affairs to safeguard overseas commitments. A comparison is being drawn with mediation between Myanmar and Bangladesh by China over the Rohingya problem which is projected as 'the increased ability of Beijing in resolving conflicts beyond its borders to maintain stability'.

Beijing's intention to mediate on Kashmir has been discreetly hinted at, the argument being that China is entitled to play the mediator because of the interests of Chinese firms investing in PoK.

China and Pakistan are closer today than ever before. Because of the China Pakistan Economic Corridor (CPEC), Pakistan gets higher-level political attention from China, according to the author of The China-Pakistan Axis, Andrew Small, who writes: 'On the Pakistani side, the CPEC makes China a far more important patron than it was when the two sides were purely security partners.' Pakistan and Russia are lining up with China on the South China Sea issue.

More recently, the reports that President Xi Jinping had snubbed the then Pakistan Prime Minister, Nawaz Sharif, by not meeting him at the Shanghai Cooperation Organization (SCO) Summit in June 2017 were rejected as nonsense by the Chinese Foreign Ministry spokesman who said that China and Pakistan share an all-weather strategic partnership.

Apprehensions continue to be raised that the Belt and Road Initiative could cost Pakistan its financial independence. Be that as it may, this is a wake up call for India. Alongside engaging in patient dialogue with China, New Delhi needs to articulate a political framework for commercial and economic cooperation across the contested frontiers of Jammu and Kashmir.

Early in 2017, the docking of a Chinese submarine at a port in Malaysia underlined deeper military ties between the two countries who are already partners in the development of the Beijing-led Maritime Silk Road. Submarine port visits happen when mutual trust between two navies has reached new heights, since submarine operations are very secretive and sensitive. This was the second confirmed port visit by a Chinese submarine, after a visit to Sri Lanka in 2014.

There is already an air of inevitability about a future Sino-centric Asia.

In regard to the latest visit of the Dalai Lama to Arunachal Pradesh – a territory claimed by China – reservations were expressed, in strong language, by the Chinese authorities. One such statement said:

> China and India are two major developing countries and we are close neighbours. It is very important for the two peoples to maintain sound and steady China – India relations. But such a relationship has to be built on certain foundations ... It will come down to India to make a choice ... India should be very clear with the true nature of the Dalai-clique. But despite this India still invited the Dalai Lama to visit the region. ... We urge India to stick to its political statements, respect the consensus and avoid doing anything that might further complicate the matter.

A South Asia expert at an influential Chinese institute said:

> Your (India's) Minister of State for Internal Affairs will accompany him (Dalai Lama) … so it couldn't be totally religious. Dalai Lama's activities cannot only be understood in a religious way. And, we know that the visit to the 'disputed' area itself is a very politically sensitive issue in China. So, it adds another dimension to bilateral relations ….

The Dalai Lama went to the area and to the Tawang Monastery amid reports that 'Beijing may suspend ties with New Delhi'.

The tone of the Chinese officials was unusually sharp when a protest was lodged by summoning the Indian Ambassador to the Ministry of Foreign Affairs in Beijing. An indication was given by the Ministry's spokesperson that the Dalai Lama's visit had severely damaged Sino-Indian ties and 'will escalate the dispute in border areas'.

While India stood firm and did not yield to pressure over the Dalai Lama's visit, China has got used to riding roughshod over Indian concerns. As expected, the Chinese media pulled no punches; one tabloid threatened that Beijing could interfere in turbulent Kashmir in retaliation. The more sober

China Daily said in an editorial that '... Beijing should not hesitate to answer blows with blows', an observation open to various and not necessarily pacific interpretations.

The Dalai Lama was in Arunachal Pradesh six times between 1983–2009; he was received in Tawang in November 2009 by the late Chief Minister (and father of the present Chief Minister), Dorjee Khandu. Each time the Chinese protested but not as vociferously as now.

China considers the Dalai Lama episode a 'sting' in its ties with India, which causes pain to Beijing after the bite, as expressed by a senior Chinese official, after it became clear as to why Foreign Minister, Wang Yi, cancelled a visit to New Delhi in April 2017 for the Russia-India-China (RIC) trilateral meeting. The official said that Beijing 'did not expect the Modi government to give the Dalai Lama clearance to visit Arunachal Pradesh and to facilitate his visit, accompanied by an Indian minister, adding that, for the Chinese people he (Dalai Lama) is a bad guy and his visit has created mistrust'.

On the other hand, the BJP's ideological parent, the RSS, is unhappy over China stalling India's move to impose a U.N. ban on the Pakistan-based Masood Azhar (who was let off in Kandahar in December 1999 during the NDA-I) and are also critical of Beijing consistently blocking India's bid to join the Nuclear Suppliers Group (NSG), suggesting that 'there is a need to overhaul our China policy...'.

Years of steady economic growth have propelled China to a leading position in the world. The presidential change in the White House has ended the linear predictability and the policy parameters of the Obama era, which facilitated Russia and China to expand their spheres of influence. However, in the absence, so far, of any coherent foreign policy vision from the Trump administration, there is uncertainty about Washington's future role in the world order.

For India, the change has brought major foreign policy dilemmas. The advent of the Modi government had witnessed a deepening of the relationship with the USA and the elevation of India as a significant defence partner with greater access to advanced technologies. This was accompanied by a more self-assured stance towards China in seeking a reciprocal recognition of each other's security concerns.

The proximity to the USA and the strengthening of defence infrastructure along the India-China border, particularly around the areas that China claims as its own, have caused annoyance in Beijing. The degree of mutual trust between India and China has plunged. Apart from the growing military and strategic ties with Pakistan (India being the target), China has significantly expanded its footprint in India's neighbourhood through infrastructure projects and increased defence cooperation with countries in the region. The harsh reality is that there remain few areas of strategic convergence – and many of conflict – in an uneasy relationship.

With an unfriendly China at its doorstep and the USA reluctant to take on global leadership. India's options are not unlimited and must centre around building its own strength and asserting the same through effective diplomacy.

The West Asia policy of 'engaging all' has meant inviting the Presidents of both Cyprus and Turkey – arch rivals – to New Delhi in April 2017 but when Prime Minister Modi headed to Israel in July 2017 he did not to visit Palestine. Further, after making the NSG membership an overriding priority the whole of last year, the South Block now seems inclined – in a reversal of strategy – to wait until China is convinced.

This is a time of flux in the world when the Indian government needs to be more sure-footed in order to demonstrate better clarity on its principles of engagement. Its position cannot only be guided by the Prime Minister's next overseas destination.

The 'neighbourhood first' policy is in shambles; it could, perhaps, be retrieved partially by the Prime Minister. There are other countries like Uzbekistan which Modi visited in July 2015. He gifted a reproduction of the *Khamsa-e-Khusru* (written in Persian by none other than Amir Khusrau[4]) to the Uzbek President, Islam Karimov. However, when Karimov passed away in September 2016, not much was in evidence in New Delhi to mourn his death, other than a signing of the Condolence Book at the Uzbek embassy by a Minister of State for External Affairs. The Chinese President sent a vice-premier as his special emissary to Karimov's funeral in Samarkand – a strategic move of the kind Modi can emulate. The larger question is whether India's hesitation to follow through well-conceived initiatives is becoming a serious handicap.

Nehru's government sent no one to Riyadh to condole the death of the first King and founder of Saudi Arabia, Abdul Aziz Ibn Saud, in 1953 –the Saudis refused to forget that omission. The Uzbeks may not forget either.

By the same token, Indo-Russian ties are unlikely to be revitalized only through high-level visits or by the naming of a road in the national capital

4 Ab'ul Hasan Yamin ud-Din Khusrau is an iconic figure in the cultural history of the sub-continent. He was a spiritual disciple of Hazrat Nizamuddin Auliya of Delhi and a renowned Sufi musician, poet and scholar.

after the late Alexander M Kadakin, a long-serving Ambassador to India. A decisive thrust in this field will need to be viewed as credible, for the longer term, by President Putin and his advisers.

The bleak external environment calls for reflection on India's foreign policy track record. The erratic posturings, based on unreal assumptions, have often led to the under-estimation of adversaries who have outmanoeuvred us from time to time. Having contributed to the creation of Bangladesh, the then Foreign Office mandarins botched up the 1972 Simla Agreement and have achieved little in countering the China-Pakistan axis.

Doing the same thing, over and over again, but expecting different results, is not smart – the failure to resolve endemic problems, since 1947 should, under Narendra Modi, cause a re-think in the highest political circles.

Ayesha Siddiqa[5] of Pakistan feels that: 'From economy to social cohesion, India ... does not present a very stable image.'

India's attempts to counter the growing Chinese influence have not succeeded in Sri Lanka, where China is believed to possess some 80 percent equity in the Hambantota Port. With bases coming up in Djibouti and Gwadar, the Chinese string of pearls is becoming a reality; the forays into Bangladesh, Myanmar and Nepal would further complete the circle.

The figures of the Nepalese government show that China accounts for as much as 68 percent of the FDI pledged to Nepal for the current fiscal by various countries.

That Nepal and China have moved much closer than Indian foreign policy analysts will accept is borne out by an announcement of Nepal's Deputy Prime Minister that the rail network project connecting Kathmandu to Kerung, a border town in China, will be finalized soon. Coming close on the heels of a joint Sino-Nepalese military exercise carried out in April 2017, these developments are of significance in India's immediate neighbourhood.

The Nepalese have been candid in justifying their decision to join the OBOR project; they acknowledge that Nepal cannot ignore China, an economic powerhouse and a neighbour. They also say that 'Nepal will never give India grief but it cannot remain indifferent to a big economic power like China as it seeks more foreign investment and development'.

Calling India's US$ 1 billion aid to Mongolia a 'bribe', the Chinese official media had said that 'there would be endless trouble in Sino-India ties if New Delhi viewed China's cargo service with land-locked Nepal as a threat

5 Ayesha Siddiqa (born 1966) is a Pakistani political commentator and author.

to the sale of Indian goods .... China will not be overly sensitive about India's cooperation with Mongolia whose economy is highly dependent on China ... As such, China's influence on Mongolia's economy cannot be replaced by India in the short run ...'.

Experts predict that the country's 'economic gap' with China will continue to widen over the next ten years or so.

In the clouded China-India relations, there has been a silver lining that relates to the exemplary work done in the late 1930s by a Medical Team from India which laboured in China for four years to provide relief during the second Sino-Japanese conflict. Dr Dwarkanath Kotnis, who died in China in December 1942, was a member of the Team. Deeply touched by Kotnis' contribution, the future Chairman, Mao Zedong, a calligraphist himself, sent a moving tribute and condolence message to his family in Solapur where the doctor was born. In 1940, he wrote: 'The army has lost a helping hand, the nation has lost a friend. Let us always bear in mind his internationalist spirit.'

The three-foot long letter was written on traditional rice paper using charcoal black ink. In due course, it was given to the Kotnis Museum run by the municipal corporation. In December 2016, two Chinese experts came to Solapur to restore the letter. They combined their collective experience, employing specialized tools from China, and followed scientific methods to restore the letter.

President Xi Jinping met Dr. Kotnis' sister in September 2014. If there is one Indian hero whose memory is cherished in China, it is Dr. Kotnis.

Prime Minister Modi's decision to 'skip' the 17th summit of the Non-Aligned Movement (NAM) in Venezuela in September 2016 pointed to the drastic reordering of his government's priorities in the field of external relations, not just a break with the joint legacy built by Nehru, Nasser, Nkrumah, Sukarno and Tito in the early sixties. Under Modi, India is seeking a change of perception that portrays her as a country in transition which is shifting its strategy from that of a 'balancing power' to one of a 'leading power'.

As of now, every African country, other than South Sudan, is a NAM member, the total membership being around 120. Nelson Mandela led the Movement in 1998–99. The September summit, originally slated for July 2015, was rescheduled to suit Modi's convenience; subsequently, Venezeula ruled out another postponement, having by now received a signal about a founding member – India's – altered approach. This was not the only sign that countries associated with the NAM had been reading; they would also have recalled that at the third (and largest) India-Africa Forum Summit held in

New Delhi in October 2015, Prime Minister Modi did not once refer to the NAM, even though the organization was, traditionally, a key bond between the African continent and India.

At a time when ties with China and Pakistan are worsening and the neighbourhood is not bending over backwards to accommodate India's concerns, one wonders whether the drift away from the NAM was such a good idea after all and whether the mandarins of South Block had evaluated all the likely consequences.

A potentially serious matter concerns the attacks on African students and citizens in India, prompting senior African diplomats to issue a joint statement which noted that effective and deterring measures had to be taken by the Indian authorities. The African Heads of Missions said that strong condemnation was expected from the highest political levels, failing which they may be left with no option but to ask for the intervention of Human Rights Organizations. In an uncharacteristic reaction, External Affairs Minister, Sushma Swaraj, chose to criticize the joint statement, as being based on wrong information. A probe was ordered by the government.

During a visit to China in August 2016, Aung San Suu Kyi, Myanmar's State Counsellor and Foreign Minister was given a red carpet welcome. She was virtually treated as the Prime Minister and held discussions with President Xi Jinping and the Chinese elite, a clear indication that China saw her as the leader. The two sides had begun fashioning a basis for mutual cooperation.

In later discussions, an exercise was conducted to craft a mutually beneficial 'give and take'. More specifically, China conveyed an assurance of support for Myanmar's economic development and national reconciliation. Myanmar has welcomed China's One Belt, One Road Initiative and also the proposed economic corridor connecting Bangladesh, China, India and Myanmar (BCIM) – about which India is not excited – and has refrained from expressing a view on the contentious South China Sea issue.

The opportunity may yet be within India's grasp to reinforce relations with a resurgent Myanmar led by Aung San Suu Kyi who fought relentlessly for the restoration of democracy. In fact, a sustained 'mending' of the relationship is called for. The Indian government and civil society have to work harder on deepening the multi-dimensional ties.

Myanmar is crucial to India's Act East policy, particularly as India tries to balance out China's massive presence in the country. Having missed several deadlines, India has to try hard to speed up its infrastructure commitments in

Myanmar; tardiness in project implementation has marred India's reputation. The Beijing-Yangon relations have improved under Aung San Suu Kyi's watch, probably more than with India.

Prime Minister Modi recognizes the urgency of preventing India's graph from dipping further among her immediate neighbours. In a master-stroke, he departed from protocol to receive the Bangladesh Prime Minister, Sheikh Hasina, at the airport on April 7, 2017, signalling the importance of the visit. It was the first time Modi made the exception for the head of government of a neighbouring country, having done so, earlier, only for the then U.S. President Barack Obama and the Crown Prince of Abu Dhabi.

Sheikh Hasina's India connect has often been criticized in Bangladesh and this could intensify without a deal on Teesta water sharing. But she put up a brave face, saying the ties between the two South Asian neighbours will undergo 'another transformation' with the water agreement coming through at a later date.

In the decades that have flown by since Independence and Partition, there have been numerous changes, not all for the better, that have occurred in India; Jammu and Kashmir, a Muslim-majority province, the North East and the Naxal-affected areas in several States are prime examples.

Through the tortuous history of this hostile relationship, beginning with the Partition of India, there may seldom have been a more outrageously provocative statement than the one made by the Pakistan High Commissioner, Abdul Basit, in New Delhi on August 14, 2016 when he said:

> As far as Jammu and Kashmir is concerned, we are dedicating this year's Independence Day to the freedom of Kashmir. And we firmly believe that the sacrifices made by the people of Jammu and Kashmir will not go in vain. .... Pakistan will continue to extend its full diplomatic, political and moral support to the valiant people of Jammu and Kashmir till they get their right to self-determination. [He repeated the performance on Pakistan's National Day in March 2017].

In a timely move, Prime Minister Modi placed the contentious issues between the two neighbours on a wider canvas, making no bones about India's support to the protests which have broken out in the POK, Gilgit and Baltistan, as also in Balochistan, against the Islamabad authorities.

However, it is also pertinent to look beyond Pakistan which has long been fishing in troubled waters and to acknowledge that it has taken something more than its meddling for the situation to deteriorate so alarmingly in the Valley. It would be nearer the truth to recognize the anger on the ground, that the anger had been growing stronger for quite some time and has now erupted and that it is imperative to tackle the root cause of this anger. The perceived inability to address the political nature of the problem is what is keeping the anger alive.

It is also instructive to delve into the past. After the Instrument of Accession to the Dominion of India was virtually forced out from Maharaja Hari Singh (who had left Srinagar for Jammu in the wake of the invasion of tribesmen), Jawaharlal Nehru's trusted ally, Sheikh Abdullah, was installed as the first Prime Minister – the then nomenclature of the head of government – and Nehru had declared at Srinagar's Lal Chowk on November 2, 1947.

> The fate of Kashmir will ultimately be decided by the people … It is not only a pledge to the people of Kashmir but to the world. We … cannot back out of it.

The Kashmir question was internationalized when Nehru made that speech.

A further step towards complicating the matter was taken when Sheikh Abdullah was removed as the Premier and placed under arrest. New Delhi's interventions contributed to the State elections becoming a farce in which corruption was rampant. Nonetheless, the common Kashmiri did precious little to encourage the Pakistan Army's intrusion in the Akhnoor sector in 1965. In early August that year, groups of irregulars had also begun crossing the ceasefire line, blowing up bridges and attacking government installations. The intention was to create confusion and spark unrest. The Pakistan media announced that a popular uprising had erupted in the Valley. In fact, the local people were mostly apathetic – some intruders were even handed over to the police. This was an important reason for the comprehensive failure of Pakistan's 1965 misadventure.

Notwithstanding Sheikh Abdullah's return to national politics in 1975 (or rather because of it), the political temperature in the Valley continued to simmer. The unceremonious dismissal of Farooq Abdullah in 1984 marked the dawn of another era of turmoil; the episode almost cost Governor B.K. Nehru his gubernatorial position because he opposed the move. Being a Nehru, he still got away lightly, with a transfer to the Gujarat Raj Bhavan.

While the scene today may appear similar to the summers of 2008 and 2010, there are perceptible differences.

In those years, the dead were being counted. The 2010 protests (largely restricted to Srinagar, Baramulla, Sopore and Anantnag) were the outcome of 17 year old Tufail Mattoo being shot in police firing, leaving about 120 people dead; in 2008, a campaign against the transfer of land to the Amarnath Shrine Board snowballed into violence causing nearly 70 deaths.

This time, in 2016-17, the hundreds of injured men, women and children in the hospitals – maimed, crippled, blinded for life – will long be a reminder of what has gone so seriously wrong. The crux of the unrest lies in the rural areas and the trigger was the widespread public sympathy for the slain, Burhan Wani, whose funeral was attended by thousands. The year 2016 went down as one of the bloodiest in the state's history.

More than one Srinagar-based journalist is of opinion that if the previous generation was anti-India, the present generation hates India. More Kashmiri Muslims now subscribe to the view that Sheikh Abdullah made the wrong choice in 1947 when he chose a self-declared secular India over a theocratic Pakistan.

In 2016, for the first time in 26 years since the onset of the militancy, no Eid congregations were held at the Idgah and Hazratbal shrines in the Valley.

In May–June 2017, during the holy Ramzan, there was an alarming increase in incidents of stone-pelting, compared to 2016. The steep rise followed the killing of Hizb Commander, Sabzar Ahmad Bhat, and shows the growing tendency to obstruct the anti-terror operations of the armed forces. Considering the religious sanctity attached to the Ramzan period, the levels of violence generally see a downward trend.

An opportunity to assuage the anger was regrettably missed when the 2014 floods were causing extreme distress and devastation. A special effort, at a very early stage, on the part of the PMO and the State Governor to reach succour and relief to the people who had suffered (and to create gainful employment) might have gone some way in building emotional bridges.

The National Conference (NC) was not invited to the All Party deliberations convened in New Delhi in August 2016. There can be no credible explanation for this omission, except that the NC would have raised difficult questions and, perhaps, queered the pitch of the discussions, apparently a concern more central to the powers that be than getting to the root of the matter and breaking the deadlock in the Valley.

The NC would have better served the cause of the Kashmiri people by extending issue-based support to a PDP government, without preconditions. Unlike the BJP and the Congress, the People's Democratic Party (PDP) and the NC are Kashmir-centric parties whose special responsibility it should be to promote the well-being of the State. Both have non-Muslims, including Pandits, in their ranks and should, looking beyond their narrow interests, join hands to pursue a liberal and egalitarian approach in all parts of the State.

The NC and the PDP are dynasty-led parties of the Abdullah and Mufti families respectively. By sinking differences in the best interests of J&K, they could still show that politics is the art of the possible.

Generally reliable reports suggest that the killings of terrorists and civilians have become a catalyst for the Hizbul Mujahideen to recruit heavily in the Valley, particularly in the southern districts of Anantnag, Kulgam, Pulwama and Shopian. The youth are turning to the gun in larger numbers and the home-grown militants already in the Hizb and the Lashkar-e-Taiba have been roaming the villages, delivering fiery speeches and are being welcomed by the local people.

That the Hizb and other outfits are seizing the rage to their advantage is a crucial factor which the previous Northern Army Commander would have taken into account when he said:

> We all have to sit down, put our heads together and see if we can find an end to this. I know it is not easy. The situation is difficult. Everybody who is in any way involved in J&K needs to introspect. No one person or one organization could solve the crisis in the Valley. This is not a political statement. It is a statement of facts because everybody is involved, whether it is security forces, separatists, governments, student leaders, so my appeal is to everyone. I think we need to find some way forward in this.

This was the first time that the Army, as an institution, was recognizing a role for the separatist leadership in restoring peace in the Valley, at variance with the view that there can be no talks with the Hurriyat. Among the first to react, Mirwaiz Umar Farooq said that this was a message from the Army Commander to the country's political leadership and that 'it reflects an urgency and inevitability of finding a political resolution …'

Arun Jaitley (who has Jammu connections but no direct responsibility for Kashmir Affairs) and other central ministers have called the stone-pelters 'stooges of Pakistan' and stone-pelting as a 'new form of attack by Pakistan on India's unity and integrity'. On the other side, there is the comment of Muzaffar Wani, Burhan's father (a school headmaster, who has lost two sons to the strife in the Valley) to the effect that:

> Islam says that God, Quran and Prophet are bigger than anything, even bigger and more important than our sons .... Our God should be happy with us even if my son's or my sacrifice is needed for that .... Our generation feared guns. This generation doesn't. Give them a gun and they'll disappear into the mountains and train as militants like my son did....
>
> [Uska (Burhan's) raasta theek tha .... He was a mujahid, not a terrorist. He hit out through social media ... the (ruling) PDP had said they would remove the army after coming to power, but the government is bringing in additional companies, she is running a 'kathputli sarkar' .... Mehbooba should leave her chair now. She is in power because of us, but her voters are the ones being wounded and killed. She is not even sticking to the agenda of alliance ....]

As the protests continued and the 'pellet guns' were being employed, Mehbooba Mufti's 'shallow' assurances carried little meaning. Those willing to speak are emphatic that the current phase of unrest is very different: 'The youth are fearless; they are not scared of coming right upto the gates of our fortified camps to protest.'

In a blatant attempt to pass the buck and absolve the PDP-BJP alliance of blame for its extremely disappointing performance, Ms Mehbooba Mufti (speaking at the inauguration of a flyover in Jammu in May, 2017) observed:

> ... I say today with authority and I know I will be criticized for it ... if anyone can find a solution for the Jammu and Kashmir problem, it is PM Narendra Modi. He has a strong mandate, whatever decision he takes, the country will support him .... If anyone can pull us out of the sticky situation we are in, it is Prime Minister Modi.

Brave words indeed, but without an iota of credibility to reinforce them and with no relation to the ground realities. Mufti went on to say that '...Before Modi, a Prime Minister had also desired to go to Pakistan for over 10 years. He wanted to see his home there. He could have tried to end the confrontation between the two countries and bring J&K out of this unfortunate situation, but he had no courage to do that'. She lauded Modi's visit to Lahore on December 25, 2015 and said that it was 'a sign of strength'.

Mehbooba extended credit to former PM Vajpayee and her father, former CM Mufti Sayeed, for initiating the dialogue for peace in 2002, adding that:

> they tried their best … the NDA government opened the roads between the two countries via LoC ... these were not small developments. But unfortunately Mufti was out of the government and Vajpayeeji left and the process came to a grinding halt.

In a typical example of refusing to recognize the true picture, she blamed the then UPA government at the Centre and the earlier state government, pointing out that '… there was pent-up lava and it started to come out during the street protests in 2006, 2009 and 2010. That lava has now spread in the Valley and we are facing it'.

She might have paused to reflect upon whether the PDP-BJP alliance crafted between the most unlikely bedfellows was also not one of the root-causes of the escalating insurgency. Did her own family-led party actually believe that the Kashmiri Muslims would ever countenance a power-sharing arrangement with the BJP?

A senior PDP minister, Nayeem Akhtar, was frank in airing his views:

> This alliance is the last possible credible democratic experiment for many, many years. If it fails, nothing else is likely to succeed in the present scenario. And if it collapses, it would be a problem not only for PDP or Kashmir; its failure is going to be a huge setback for the country in finding a solution to its most intractable challenge. … Though we believe in India and have reposed our trust in its democratic institutions, the challenge is that more and more people in J&K don't share that feeling. Mehbooba can't do much in dealing with this. Only the national leadership can do this.

Way back in 1987, Syed Salahudeen, head of the militant organization, Hizb-ul-Mujahideen (who now lives in Pakistan), contested the J&K assembly election on the ticket of the Muslim United Front (MUF), a coalition of political parties, in Srinagar's Amirakadal constituency. He came second after Ghulam Mohiuddin Shah of the NC who won the seat in what was widely perceived to be a 'rigged' election. Salahudeen was arrested for his violent agitations and joined the Hizb in 1989.

He was in his early forties when forced out of mainstream politics.

In December 2013, Professor Bhim Singh[6] of the Jammu and Kashmir

6 Professor Bhim Singh (born August 1941) was a member of the Youth Congress. He was also an AICC General Secretary before breaking away to form the JKNPP in 1982.

National Panthers Party (JKNPP) said that Syed Ali Shah Geelani[7] was right in describing the 1987 Assembly Elections as rigged and coercive, opining that Dr Farooq Abdullah of the National Conference played a major role in the rigging and that at least twenty-two candidates of the MUF were forced to accept defeat at the behest of the National Conference.

One is reminded of what Farooq Abdullah had told Vajpayee in the year 2000 – after the State Assembly had passed the Autonomy Resolution and sent it to New Delhi for adoption – that were the moment to be lost, a time could come when the Centre might offer autonomy and be rejected by J&K.

The elements inimical to the accession of Kashmir imagine that the ongoing disturbances can yield a fruit well beyond autonomy.

The game plan of the groups perpetrating violence in J&K is to terrorize the locals into submission to their reprehensible programme of creating a Wahabi society with Kashmiriyat, Jamhooriyat and Insaaniyat, all vanishing into thin air.

The current crisis in the Valley has a long history. In the 1970s, in the only Muslim majority province in India, where Muslims co-existed peacefully with Hindus, a Wahabi project was initiated to radicalize the State which the Government of India did little to counter in good time.

During Bakshi Ghulam Mohammed's regime (1953-64), it was routine practice for New Delhi to transfer slush funds to Srinagar to keep him and his henchmen in a happy frame of mind. Two ICS officers borne on the U.P. cadre – Vishnu Sahay and Shanker Prasada – served, successively, as Secretary, Kashmir Affairs, in the Nehru dispensation. Making the monthly cash transfer was one of their less desirable duties.

The Congress governments at the Centre effectively tried to bribe the Kashmiri leadership on the one hand and impose the iron hand of the security agencies on the other. The common Kashmiri people neither received any of the slush funds nor could they escape the ham-handed behaviour of the armed forces.

A Jihadi movement has gathered strength in Kashmir due to the sheer incompetence and cynical corruption of the ruling elite, regardless of party affiliation. A very good chance did come the way of Omar Abdullah to reverse this cycle, but he blew it away. His family (and he) have contributed to the de-legitimization of the State; his father, a former CM, cannot evade responsibility for the governance-deficit. He now calls for third-party assistance, such as from the U.S. or China, to settle the Kashmir question.

---

7 Geelani (born September 1929), a Kashmiri separatist Hurriyat leader, was previously with the Jamaat-e-Islami and later founded his own party, the Tehreek-e-Hurriyat. He was thrice an MLA from the Sopore constituency.

The people, who have nowhere to go, fall easy prey to the Jihadis.

The violence, the continuing loss of lives and the appallingly low turnout of voters that the Valley witnessed in a recent parliamentary by-election tell their own story. Among those killed were teenagers, one a class VI student.

The Kashmiris feel disillusioned about their place and future in the Indian State which, they feel, is responsible for most of the problems that have arisen.

The revolt against the by-election process gave another horrific glimpse of how far removed the intelligence agencies and the political class are from the ground reality. The unrest is moving towards the villages, making southern Kashmir the new centre of militancy. The rallying of neighbourhoods to defend militants has become a common occurrence.

For some time, it had seemed that the findings of the Yashwant Sinha-led Team that visited the State could help in resolving the impasse and re-open channels of communication. The Team came back with the distinct impression that the anger in the rural areas is palpably greater than in Srinagar, that a persistent sense of discrimination pervades the minds of vocal sections of the people, that there is near-complete lack of faith in the Government of India's promises because of a long chain of broken commitments and that further despair is bound to set in if the Kashmiri youth see no future for themselves.

Pakistan has been trying to push the prominent faces of the Hurriyat, Syed Ali Shah Geelani, Mirwaiz Umar and Yasin Malik, onto a common platform. Together, the threesome have presented an image of a united movement. They are no longer fully in charge and have ceded space to the ultra-extremists and to the joint functioning of militant groups.

Once a cradle of communal harmony in the truest sense that was a 'model' for all of India (which I experienced for myself during the seventies and the eighties), the Valley has, for months, been ravaged by indiscriminate violence and the pallor of death.

The prevailing conditions bring to mind a stanza of the poetry of one who needs no introduction in the sub-continent, Faiz Ahmed Faiz:

> '*Kab nazar mein ayegi bedaag sabze ki bahaar,*
> *Khoon ke dhabbe dhulein ge kitni barsaaton ke baad*'

> [When will a vision of pristine greenery appear, Many a monsoon it may take to wash away the stains of blood]

So much is at stake here for India and Indians.

The portents are ominous. Media reports suggest that while a shrine in Shareefabad (Tral) in the Valley to the revered Sufi saint, Mir Syed Ali Hamdani, has long drawn devotees from the neighbouring villages, it is a grave a few blocks away that has been attracting larger numbers over the past year. This is Burhan Wani's grave. There is hardly a day when crowds do not visit the grave which seems no less than a shrine; if it has not become one it is because shrines are forbidden under the puritanical tenets of Islam being followed, of late, by many in Kashmir.

The ISIS black flags having already appeared in the Valley, Al-Qaida announced a new Kashmir-based terror group to be led by a former Hizb commander, an engineering college dropout and one of Burhan Wani's successors, Zakir Musa. This is a new threat that should be nipped in the bud and without any one in the security forces being carried away by such opinions as that of a senior police officer: 'Burhan was an icon and Musa is a slogan. He has to fight many wars to establish his credibility, but he has no damaging capability as of now'.

As things stand, the strategy of containment, by force, has failed in the Valley; a muscular approach has not worked. An all-out drive by the security forces against terrorism and terrorists that is reported to be in hard might show better results. The disquieting thing is that no one – in Srinagar or New Delhi – is inclined to face the truth squarely.

Should the international environment turn against India, China will get more aggressive. Our alignment with the United States may not yield dividends on Pakistan whose strategic space has increased. China's interference in Kashmir will be on the rise as a result of the economic corridor through the Pakistan – held PoK where the Chinese military presence is growing, even near the ceasefire line. India now faces Chinese troops on both flanks of its position in J&K.

The number of Indian security personnel killed in gun-battles with terrorists in J&K in 2016 was the highest in years.

The government's reluctance to back up its words with action was conspicuous when a Private Member's Bill to declare Pakistan as a state sponsor of terrorism was withdrawn in the Rajya Sabha. If India as the principal target of Pakistani terrorism is hesitant to take definite steps, can it realistically expect the United States to take the lead on this issue?

After months of terrorist attacks, mutilations of soldiers' bodies and so on, the ball is back in the Indian Prime Minister's court. He had approved the surgical strike route after the killing of 19 army men in Uri but, with little follow up, the move largely stayed in the realm of the tactical.

Back-channel negotiators, such as businessman Sajjan Jindal, should not be expected to deliver much.

The fact is that India lacks a coherent and consistent policy vis-à-vis Pakistan and the Pakistan Army continues to take advantage of the situation, with not much regard for that country's civilian leadership.

An ancient military strategist Chinese and philosopher, Sun Tzu, who is credited as the author of the treatise, *Art of War*, put it aptly by saying: 'Strategy without tactics is the slowest route to victory. Tactics without strategy is the noise before defeat.'

The confused Pakistan policy predates Narendra Modi. Successive Indian governments have failed to formulate a consistent, long-term approach. Consequently, waging an unconventional war against India remains an effective, lost-cost option for Pakistan.

A major plank on which Narendra Modi won the 2014 general election was the promise to defeat Pakistan's proxy war. A blow-hot-blow-cold approach suggests that a coherent strategy has yet to be put in place.

It is not too late to develop a set of policies that impose punitive costs on Pakistan, in diplomatic, political and economic terms. If Pakistan can wage an unconventional war with a nuclear shield, a similarly armed India can respond by taking the unconventional war to the enemy's own land and exploiting its ethnic and sectarian faultlines.

No bigger challenge confronts the Indian State than to restore normalcy in Jammu and Kashmir. With discernible signals, lately, of external interest in mediating between the two neighbours, the sooner this is brought about the better. It is also likely to be one of the parameters on which the Modi government would be assessed in the run-up to the 2019 elections.

The measures that can be attempted to address the issues in Kashmir need to be based on a flexible approach which is acceptable to various segments of the Kashmiri community (including the Pandits and the Ladakhi Buddhists) and is accompanied by major job creation for the youth.

A grand gesture could be a good start: a Speech of the Prime Minister in Srinagar, even a Mann ki Baat with the Kashmiri youth. Most importantly, the governance-deficit, already out of hand, will have to be progressively bridged.

Beyond the borders, there is the overhanging threat of Islamic fundamentalism, on a larger scale, for which the Valley affords, at present, a hospitable terrain.

The so-called Islamic State (IS), also known as the Islamic State of Iraq and Syria (ISIS), has been in the news in India. The number of Indians linked to IS has steadily grown. From only one confirmed individual in 2013, the numbers reportedly increased to six in 2014, 35 in 2015 and 75 in 2016. The IS challenge is a serious one and attempts could be made to incite Muslims in other areas of the country.

While there are several cases of self-radicalization, IS is known to also graft onto pre-existing organizations like the Indian Mujahideen (IM), the Students Islamic Movement of India (SIMI) or the IS-inspired groups, such as Junood ul Khalifa Fil Hind (JKH). The IS radicalization spreads through family, school or neighbourhood ties, of which the Ansarul Khilafa Kerala is an example. When IS is defeated as a State (a self-proclaimed Caliphate with defined territory and a military), it could morph into a global network, akin to al-Qaida, which would present a new kind of challenge for India.

India has drifted away from the NAM and no longer seeks entry to another body, the Organization of Islamic Cooperation (OIC) which has 57 members, 56 being also member-states of the United Nations. Some, especially in West Africa, have large Muslim populations but are not necessarily Muslim majority countries. A few with significant Muslim populations, including Russia, sit as Observer States.

India, which has the world's second largest Muslim population, after Indonesia, had shown interest in joining the OIC at the time of its formation in 1969 and was opposed by Pakistan. No formal application to enter the OIC, as a Member-State or as an Observer, has been made by India whose potential candidacy (though, initially, supported by a few members) was blocked by Pakistan on the ground that an aspirant State should not be involved in an ongoing conflict with a member State (in this case, Kashmir).

The OIC always backs Pakistan on the Kashmir issue which has been a top item on its agenda.

The Turkish President, Recep Tayyip Erdogan, who was in India some months back, has been a vocal supporter of the OIC's position on Kashmir. At home, Erdogan has been trying to employ Islamism to shore up his credibility. His visit to New Delhi was also informed by this larger agenda. Ahead of his arrival, he suggested a 'multilateral dialogue' on Kashmir, even offering to mediate between India and Pakistan to 'seek ways to settle the issue once and for all'. If his intent was to improve Indo-Turkish ties, then this was clearly an injudicious start.

Iran's supreme leader, Ayatollah Ali Khamenei, thought it fit to use a Ramzan message in late June, 2017 to urge Muslims around the world to support Kashmiris against 'oppressors and tyrants', signalling fresh tensions with India.

The message is known to have come amid concerns in Iran that India has slowed down its implementation of the Chabahar port project on the Gulf of Oman following apprehensions that the Trump-led administration might withdraw from an Agreement over Tehran's nuclear programme; that Agreement had led to a thaw in U.S.-Iran relations which allowed India to engage with Tehran. Some years back, when New Delhi was progressively reducing oil imports from Iran under U.S. pressure, Tehran repeatedly referred to Kashmir over a period of a few months.

Narendra Modi has energetically sustained a series of bilateral initiatives since 2014. For this process to go forward to achieve results for India, internationally, his many visits abroad and the wide-ranging military purchases being made (or contemplated) cannot alone suffice. Neither will the rhetoric that is periodically resorted to.

He has had the benefit of advice from two Foreign Secretaries, neither of them strong enough in matters concerning Pakistan. The top intelligence establishment has gained in stature and importance, more by making the political bosses vulnerable than through any special expertise on China or Pakistan, which also happened with Rajiv Gandhi, another outsider to the system.

It is for the Prime Minister to consider taking a call on whether bringing in 'a new eye and a new hand' would be of help with the China-Pakistan policy and in addressing the situation in J&K.

What is more obvious is the importance of a political appointment to the Governor's position, which would mean sending out someone whose sincerity, integrity and capacity are unchallengeable and who, preferably, has previous ministerial experience. The present Governor has been on the scene for about nine years and has become a part of the problem. The inability to find a replacement is proof of inherent indecisiveness.

The Modi-led administration seems to face constraints in identifying, in actual terms, a viable number of serving bureaucrats who are able, as a cohesive group, to measure up to the task of working towards the changed goal-post of ushering in a New India over the next five years. This cannot be another face of the Achhe Din promise which, Nitin Gadkari acknowledged, had become a mill-stone around the NDA-II's neck.

The moment of reckoning and of having to answer for performance can be expected to arrive not long after the year 2020, the rhetoric and bombast notwithstanding.

Being much more heavily dependent on the bureaucratic structure than his predecessors like Narasimha Rao and very little on political colleagues, the

Prime Minister, presumably, feels that he has the requisite talent and capability in the Civil Services at his command to achieve the delivery of results by 2022. Even so, one of the first actions of NDA-II in May 2014 was to promulgate an Ordinance to overcome a legal infirmity that had, belatedly, come to light in making a very senior appointment. Ironically enough, before then, the BJP had spared no opportunity to attack the Congress for following the Ordinance route, through the ten years of UPA rule.

The National Security Advisers, past and present, have been handpicked out of retirement, wielding more authority and influence than most cabinet ministers. But the scope and nature of the accountability of the incumbents remains hazy and ill-defined. In a properly established system and hierarchy, such accountability should necessarily be to Parliament and enforced through the Prime Minister and the Council of Ministers.

Buoyed by its electoral successes, its organizational strength, the labours of the RSS cadres and its unwavering determination to win the future polls, the BJP is already being seen as the winners of 2019. Some of the regional parties may, for reasons of political survival, be able to forge a National Alliance to take on the BJP. A section of the UPA leadership avers that if the Left could join hands with the BJP to oust the Rajiv Gandhi government in 1989, why couldn't the Left now team up with Trinamool to tackle, as they see it, the communal threat looming large over the country. However, it is the young voters who will matter most of all in the electoral outcomes and they may not think that an unwieldly grouping of parties would hold out much hope of improved governance and real reform.

The Congress finds itself at a critical juncture. It is ruling-either directly or through alliances – in only a few states while the BJP (and its allies) have a much higher number to their name. This has led to senior leaders prescribing radical surgery for the party structure. But change has to begin at the top. The leadership of Sonia Gandhi and Rahul Gandhi is no longer helping the party. If the argument that Congress needs the Gandhis to serve as a glue is valid, then Sonia and Rahul should seriously consider quitting their posts and work in an Advisory Council to guide the party and bring in young leaders and fresh blood at all levels in the Congress.

So far, there is little to suggest that the Congress is earnest about reappraising its core ideological principles. The long-touted secularism has come to be identified as playing the minority card – allowing the BJP to take away the majority votes; the plank of social justice has been reduced to a scramble for quotas. These are games that other caste-based outfits, have also been playing.

The All India Majlis-e-Ittehadul Muslimeen (headed by Asaduddin Owaisi of Hyderabad) and, to some extent, the All India Muslim Majlis (founded by Dr A.J. Faridi of Lucknow in 1968) would, possibly, be in contention as options for the Muslim vote. The prospects for the Congress to hold on to this vote, which they had substantially secured for themselves, post-Partition, in northern India, diminished after V.P. Singh took over as Prime Minister in December 1989.

The Congress was afforded a chance to consolidate its minorities' base (including the Christians) in the preceding tenures of Indira Gandhi and her son. It failed to do so.

The regional parties, of socialist orientation, which came to power in U.P. and Bihar caused further damage. Had the Gandhis then been alive to the need to encourage and facilitate the growth of a younger and committed Muslim leadership from within the community and gone ahead with implementable schemes for the economic upliftment of the Muslim masses, rather than follow the easy option of selecting Muslims, with no popular support to adorn ceremonial positions, the possibilities for the party might have been quite different.

It is probably fair to say that there is a crisis of confidence in the Congress whose credibility has been grievously eroded.

The hopelessness of the political Opposition is alarming. The collapse of the Congress will mean that the BJP is the only national party that has to battle the regional entities who have their narrow agendas. As such, the BJP will not be called upon to challenge an alternative vision for the New India that it has projected – not necessarily a positive for the country since ideas and policies, unless contested, are liable to turn static.

Rahul Gandhi was right, for once, when he demanded at an election rally in Imphal (Manipur) on February 28, 2017 that the contents of the Naga Accord signed by the Prime Minister be made public and asked as to why the people of Manipur were being kept in the dark on this matter, saying also that baseless allegations of corruption had been levelled against the Ibobi Singh government.

Some years back, in the UPA-II era, he visited Bhopal on party work for the Congress. He did not take a commercial flight; he came by a special aircraft and, for his personal protection, a bulletproof armoured vehicle was sent in advance from New Delhi by train. Rahul Gandhi was accompanied by his Special Protection Group (SPG) escort and more than a thousand policemen were deployed for his protection and the general bandobast. He travelled in a convoy of several cars, piloted and escorted by the police and barricades were erected for crowd control.

The different political dynasties, with the Gandhis at the apex, maintain a lifestyle which must cost a great deal of money, certainly much more than can be afforded by the emoluments earned by Members of Parliament. The question which the people of India must ask is, 'Where is all this money coming from?'

Considering the opulent levels of living of India's politicians, regardless of party affiliation, the cost of their travel and the huge amounts spent during elections (all at the taxpayers' cost), it is clear that parties and party leaders are accepting money from business houses, whereas their followers are extorting money from smaller businessmen. Why should a business house give money to any politician unless he (or she) is convinced that this is a form of investment which can be encashed at huge profit, to the advantage of the politicians and also for overlooking malpractices of the business houses?

Party funds have been largely dependent on contributions from business houses and from people indulging in illegal business. This is a root cause of corruption and, surely, the question should be raised: 'Why are parties and politicians sourcing funds from businessmen and why are businessmen doling out such huge amounts?'

Corrupt conduct is the handle with which the government of the day extorts money, but nothing happens in terms of legal retribution. The final question which people must ask is, 'When will the law prevail and the guilty brought to book?'

At a time when the Anna Hazare movement – India Against Corruption – was in full flow in 2011-12, a no-holds barred criticism was directed at the Congress for the delay in enacting the Lokpal. The BJP leader, Sushma Swaraj, spoke eloquently about 'an old man who keeps fasting to fight corruption ....' and Arun Jaitley, a BJP luminary, said: 'We are ready to pass it (Lokpal Bill) without a debate'.

However, when the Bill was before Parliament, the BJP opposed it. It was passed in both the Houses at the end of 2012 and, after the Presidential Assent, was brought into force in January 2014. More than three years down the line, there is no sign from a Modi-led government that the appointment of Lokpal is likely to materialize any time soon. This from a party which has derived much pride in projecting itself as a party with a difference.

One tangible outcome of Anna Hazare's campaign is that some of his erstwhile lieutenants are, currently, in the enjoyment of political office, whether in the BJP or the AAP.

Before very long, India would be entering the last phase in the run-up to the Lok Sabha elections of 2019. However, the time is long overdue for the political leadership – cutting across the barriers of parties – to accept responsibility and play a pro-active role in promoting productive governance, curbing the divisiveness along religious and caste lines that is straining community relations and eradicating corruption and maladministration. The most daunting challenge is to visibly reduce economic and social inequalities. If the chance is lost, these inequalities could unleash conflicts and confrontations, leading to chaos and disorder in various parts of the country. For this reason alone, it is imperative to ensure that the administrative system functions in a manner that progressively eliminates injustice and the lack of fair play, particularly to the oppressed sections.

Indira Gandhi could not seize the opportunity when re-elected to office through a convincing victory in the 1971 (Garibi Hatao) Lok Sabha elections. Narendra Modi, likewise, would have been better placed in his first year as Prime Minister than he may now be to tackle the major challenges in the domestic sector, namely, corruption and the Kashmir issue, as also in the external sector, namely, the China-Pakistan axis and expanding cooperation and trust with the neighbouring countries. He could have a second go at it when – as is becoming more and more evident – the NDA is returned to power in 2019.

Modi is astute enough to realize that he needs only to bide his time until he secures a second term in May, 2019. Other than Amit Shah and the tight group around him, very few in the government really know what he has in mind.

One of the alternatives projected was not of the Gandhi-Nehru family; Nitish Kumar would not have been leading an Opposition Alliance or Mahagathbandhan. He switched sides. The power equations having changed, he may ultimately have to remain satisfied with retaining the Bihar chief ministership in 2020.

The dominant narrative in 2019 would likely be a repeat of 2014; in other words, that India is being held back by corrupt leaders who have allowed the country to be grievously harmed because they are only interested in themselves and in enriching their families. And rightly so, Tamil Nadu and Bihar being the latest examples.

The fate of the Raebareli and Amethi parliamentary constituencies in U.P. in the 2019 elections will be interesting to watch.

While the internal difficulties could await resolution, those that have arisen beyond the borders carry greater urgency. A perception has been gaining ground that China's animus for India stems from its annoyance with an assertive Modi-led government. If so, there could be more than one reason for this, apart from the Dalai Lama's last visit to Arunachal Pradesh. China's anger has to do with India building alliances with its adversaries in Asia, and the United States.

The latest standoff at the trijunction of China, India and Bhutan has occurred some time after the expression of differing views on India's China policy, one being that since Rajiv Gandhi's rule, successive governments have taken away border management from the generals and entrusted it to the diplomats. The latter created a fiction about the stability of the border and negotiated agreements that tied the hands of the army in an attempt to secure an uneasy truce along the de facto boundary.

More worrisome is the contention that the country's political leaders – in conjunction with the diplomats – have been selling falsehoods to the Indian people on the border issue. It is argued that the claims of Indian troops intruding into Chinese territory are patently wrong and that all such intrusions have been one-sided.

A Chinese expert has stated that his country's troops would be entitled to enter the Indian side of Kashmir by extending the logic that has allowed Indian soldiers to enter an area disputed by China and Bhutan. He writes that

> ... Even if India were requested to defend Bhutan's territory, this could only be limited to its established territory, not the disputed area ... otherwise, under India's logic, if the Pakistan government requests, a third country's army can enter the area disputed by India and Pakistan, including India – controlled Kashmir. China can internationalize the Doklam controversy without worrying about the Western countries because the West has a lot of business to do with China.

Not long after India's Foreign Secretary was rebuffed by Beijing for suggesting that India and China could resolve their differences over Doklam as they had handled similar incidents in the past, the Communist Party-run *Global Times* accused External Affairs Minister, Sushma Swaraj[8], of lying in her statements on the standoff. This was another provocative move expressed through a scathing editorial which said that the military deployments and drills of the People's Liberation Army (PLA) in the area were 'not for show' and that

---

8 Swaraj (born 1952) has been the Minister of External Affairs since May 2014 and was lucky to escape cutting a '*sorry figure*' in respect of the 2014 abduction of Indian nationals in *Iraq* who are untraced and whose families are clamouring to be told the truth.

Beijing would not call back troops unless they recover the Chinese territory. While refusing to recognize the Bhutanese authority and India's locus standi, the editorial said: 'Not one inch of Chinese land can be lost.' Another issue touched upon was the maritime tensions between the two countries.

Post-1962, Chinese bellicosity has seldom reached the level that it did during the Doklam standoff, with the *Global Times* saying that NSA Doval '… is believed to be one of the main schemers behind the current border standoff' and that 'Doval will inevitably be disappointed if he attempts to bargain with Beijing over border disputes'.

Hopes were being raised in sections of the media about a positive outcome during Doval's discussions with Chinese State Councillor, Yang Jiechi. Since there was no comment or read-out from the Indian side after this meeting, all one had to go by was the version of China's Ministry of Foreign Affairs that 'major problems' and 'regional issues' were discussed, Yang also exchanged views with the other senior representatives of the BRICS grouping who together called on the Chinese President on June 28, 2017; Doval was not single in receiving an audience.

Doklam was not good news for the third country, Bhutan. It may also have sent a signal to other smaller countries that potentially the costs of siding with India can be high.

New Delhi's special treaty relationship with Thimphu has yet to induce Bhutan to openly back India's position on the Doklam issue. Should Bhutan fail to go beyond passive resistance, this stance might prove catastrophic for India. When Sushma Swaraj – who now confines herself to Bhasha Sayyam (Restraint in Language) in relation to China – met her Bhutanese counterpart, Damcho Dorji, in Kathmandu, the latter said 'we hope the situation in Doklam will be resolved peacefully and amicably'. In other words, does Bhutan wish to remain neutral in the standoff?

In the past, there have been murmurs among the elite in Bhutan about India's predominant position, its even being suggested that, by being close to India, Bhutan could incur China's wrath. The former King of Bhutan dealt with such criticism through flexibility on the foreign policy front without diluting the security arrangement with India.

Bhutan has been deepening its own channels of communication with China. The frequency of meetings at senior diplomatic levels has increased after certain areas of disagreement have surfaced between Thimphu and New Delhi. The feeling in Bhutan that India is not always sensitive to its concerns has grown after the hits taken because of India's demonetisation, as also the

GST and the hydropower policies. According to Bhutan's Central Bank, the country held about Rs.3000 crore worth of the banned currency which has yet to be exchanged by the Reserve Bank of India.

While it may be safe to assume that China does not seek an escalation or a wider conflict, the fact is that it holds more cards than India; our ability to stand upto China has increased but India is still much more vulnerable than her powerful neighbour.

The Chinese have refused to budge from their position. As a face-saving mechanism and to defuse the tension, the Bhutanese could consider making a joint appeal to India and China to restore the status quo ante, before trilateral negotiations are initiated. The Chinese may have cause to feel content inasmuch as Bhutan would be perceived to have found its own voice.

The critical challenges will lie in the playing out of Sino-Indian rivalry in Nepal, Sri Lanka and the Maldives and whether India would be in a position to counter the penetration of Chinese influence in the neighbourhood. The response to the situation in the Maldives amounted to poor geo-strategic management of a crucial island chain that provides forward maritime defence to India.

The lesson that China is seeking to teach India is that the cosy relationship it has with Bhutan will not last and that the Chinese will complete the string of pearls to encircle India and establish their supremacy in the entire region.

The long-term strategy or goals that the Chinese wish to advance by taking an uncompromising position are to restrict India's influence globally and to curb its emergence as a pre-eminent power in South Asia. The stakes are very high for India. Chinese control over this territory would not only nullify the one place over the LOC where India has a significant tactical advantage, it would also position Chinese forces near the vulnerable Chicken's Neck.

As of now, the net result is that the India-China relationship, carefully constructed, despite the odds, in the last three decades is disintegrating and this too in a very short period of time.

The removal of Nawaz Sharif, an elected prime minister, by the Pakistan Supreme Court may redefine politics in that country for years to come. What took place marked a total erosion of civilian authority and a forceful assertion of the army's dominating role. Imran Khan, an early political beneficiary, was quoted as saying that '... with this investigation, it is quite clear that we have the capability to put a check on corruption ...Everyone will be held accountable now. This is the beginning.'

A celebrity in his own right, Khan may well have moved one step closer to the prime ministership.

The developments can be expected to go against India's interests. Long regarded as a 'dove' by the Islamist hardliners and the Rawalpindi generals, Sharif had tried, in his own way, to improve ties with India and expand trade relations. The Dawn Leaks did not help and the generals struck to wrest back their control.

The manner of his dethronement is likely to discourage successive governments to essay serious talks with India and even encourage the possibility of heightened adventurism by the military.

And so, the sub-continent reaches the 70th Anniversary of Independence and Partition in 2017.

Always intolerant of the idea of Independence for India, Winston Churchill (1874–1965) spoke deprecatingly of the politicians who had fought the British Raj in a parliamentary debate on March 6, 1947 when he was in the Opposition:

> Let the House remember this. The Indian political parties and political classes do not represent the Indian masses. It is a delusion to believe that they do. I wish they did. They are not as representative of them as the movements in Britain represent the surges and impulses of the British nation. This has been proved in the war, and I can show the House how it was proved. The Congress Party declared non-cooperation with Great Britain and the Allies. The other great political party, to whom all main power is to be given, the Muslim League, sought to make a bargain about it, but no bargain was made. So both great political parties in India, the only forces that have been dealt with so far, stood aside. Nevertheless, the only great volunteer army in the world that fought on either side in that struggle was formed in India. More than three and a half million men came forward to support the King-Emperor and the cause of Britain; they came forward not by conscription or compulsion, but out of their loyalty to Britain and to all that Britain stood for in their lives. In handing over the Government of India to these so-called political classes, we are handing over to men of straw, of whom, in a few years, no trace will remain.
>
> This Government, by their latest action, this 14 months limitation – which is what I am coming to – cripple the new Viceroy and destroy the prospect of even going through the business on the agenda which has to be settled. This can only be explained as the complete adoption of one of Mr. Gandhi's most scatterbrained observations, which I will read

> to the House. It was made on 24th May, 1942, after the [Cripps] Mission. He said: 'Leave India in God's hands, in modern parlance, to anarchy; and that anarchy may lead to internecine warfare for a time, or to unrestricted dacoities. From these a true India will arise in place of the false one we see.' There, as far as I can see, is a statement indistinguishable from the policy His Majesty's Government are determined to pursue.

Haven't the governing elite in India, across party lines, and the civil services, worked incredibly hard, in recent times, to show themselves as 'men of straw' and to prove Churchill right?

Churchill was not only against Independence, he favoured the formation of Pakistan. Historians have been aware of the connection between Churchill and Jinnah, as revealed in certain confidential letters that have surfaced and which betray Churchill's bias against Hindus. In a letter to Jinnah of August 3, 1946 Churchill wrote, 'I am very much opposed to the handing over of India to Hindu caste rule, as seems very largely to be intended ....'

The controversies enveloping the Partition, the appallingly unfortunate episode itself, are unlikely to find closure till such time as, by an Act of Providence (or through sheer miracle), the India-Pakistan relations progress towards a degree of normalization. The advent of new generations in Pakistan has not subsumed the animosities, even though the terrible memories have tended to subside on the Indian side.

In October 2016, a Partition Museum dedicated to the memory of one of the most painful upheavals of human history and presenting first-hand accounts of its devastating impact became functional at Amritsar. Among the objects on display are two that belonged to a betrothed Sikh couple who were separated in the mayhem, namely, a phulkari coat belonging to Pritam Kaur of Gujranwala and a leather brief case of Bhagwan Singh Maini of Mianwali. Both cities went to Pakistan. The couple found their way to a refugee camp in Amritsar and spotted each other while standing in a long, winding queue for food. They married in 1948.

This Museum, which receives visitors, including partition survivors, also offers a ray of hope; one of its sections depicts inspiring stories of bravery and struggles for success in new homelands.

The Partition is history, tragic history, but history.

Epilogue

There cannot be any democracy … without politics. The only true antidote to the perversions of politics is more politics and better politics …. My interest is not in the capture of power, but in the control of power by the people.

JAYAPRAKASH NARAYAN

❖

THE SEVENTIETH ANNIVERSARY of Independence and Partition revealed a disturbing feature: the tragedy of Partition is set to displace the idea of Freedom and to dominate the national discourse on the events of August, 1947.

The trend can be viewed in the light of what some of the surviving freedom fighters – octogenarians, nonagenarians and centenarians (there are only about twenty-nine in Delhi/NCR) have had to say: 'this is not the India we struggled for' and that 'the country we dreamed of did not become a reality'.

Among them, there might still be a few who remember:

Goron apne gharon ko lauto,
Ab yeh desh hamara hai,
ab yeh raaj hamara hai
and
'Balle balle Jawaharlal, apne kar diya kamaal,
Dharti phaad Punjab ki, hamein de diyaa ek rumaal ki aankhen poncho'

[What a feat, Jawaharlal, tearing asunder the soil of Punjab, you give a handkerchief for us to wipe our tears].

The Gorakhpur child deaths on the eve of the Seventieth Anniversary left the nation shocked, the common people much more than the government agencies whose initial response was 'buck passing', followed by removal of doctors and the institution of fact-finding enquiries; it was the usual sequence of events all over again.

While callous corruption and rank dereliction of duty seem the immediate cause in this particular case, who is to be held responsible for the pattern of the deaths in Gorakhpur, in U.P. and in the country which has been the world's largest contributor to all levels of child deaths since 1953 – the first year for which Indian data is available?

Gorakhpur was but an acute manifestation of the chronic malady that ails our healthcare administration whose systemic failures will have to be fixed. Lip service alone will not do.

In the U.K. media, while it is standard practice, more or less, on an independence anniversary to remember the 'jewel in the crown', the empire and pass judgement on how the sub-continent has fared, post-1947, this time around there was a marked focus on Partition, with little mention of Britain's role and the colonial power's responsibility in what was one of the worst tragedies of the twentieth century.

The Indian Independence Bill, 1947 was drafted on the premise that the Dominion of India would continue India's international personality, as was apparent from the statement of the then (and last) Secretary of State for India, Lord Listowel, at a press conference in London on July 4, 1947. The representatives of Pakistan raised objections in the United Nations, arguing that on August 15, 1947, two independent Dominions of equal international status were to come into being as successors to the existing Government of India which would disappear altogether as an entity. The view that ultimately prevailed was that Pakistan would be regarded as having broken off and become a new State; as a new non-member State, it was required to seek admission to the United Nations pursuant to the provisions of Article 4 of the Charter. Thus, India stood as the successor-state and was advised, as per the previous diplomatic practice, to furnish her representatives with new credentials issued by the appropriate authorities of the Dominion of India.

The anticipation in Pakistan, based on a generic animosity, of India disintegrating, over a period of time, has not subsided. In the event, it was Pakistan that faced dismemberment through the emergence of Bangladesh. But separatist agitations and insurgencies have yet to find closure on the Indian side.

This year on August 14, Pakistan's Independence Day, the usual spewing of venom at the High Commission in New Delhi was missing. Days earlier, however, the outgoing High Commissioner, Abdul Basit, said: 'Meetings between leaders are very important ... Prime Ministers Narendra Modi and Nawaz Sharif had a good personal equation but that did not help India and Pakistan to move beyond "optics".... We appreciate gestures and overtures but it did not lead to anything concrete....'

It is the China-Pakistan ties that have kept moving forward. The Chinese Vice-Premier, Wang Yang, was in Islamabad in August, 2017 to take part in the Independence Day celebrations, as a special gesture on the directions of President Xi Jinping; the Pakistan Foreign Office stated that 'his visit on this important milestone for Pakistan is a reflection of the all-weather strategic cooperative partnership....'

Wang Yang later headed to Nepal.

India's relations with China are unlikely to be at any satisfactory level after the standoff at Doklam, whatever way the situation unfolds. India's strategic advantage in Doklam cannot rule out skirmishes in other parts of the LOAC – from Ladakh to Arunachal Pradesh. What is particularly intriguing is that the mindset in the government, whether the UPA or the NDA, still does not recognize the possibility of a serious confrontation with China in the future. Had the government, as also public opinion, been more supportive of the military's concerns, the infrastructure on the northern borders would not have remained weak and insufficient.

So far, only twenty-seven 'strategic roads' of the seventy-three identified for construction along with LOAC over fifteen years ago have been completed. There has been scant progress on the 'strategic railway lines' for the western and eastern fronts.

The endorsement of the Indian position at Doklam by Japan is a positive development. However, Russia has taken a neutral stand, saying that the next round of Russia-India military drills does not target China. Responding to a question at her weekly media briefing, the Russian Foreign Ministry spokesperson reportedly observed that '... Russia has brilliant relations with China ... attempts to distort the situation can only be viewed as a provocation.'

After Defence Minister Jaitley had boasted of an India that is different from 1962 and the Army Chief had claimed capability to fight on two-and-a-half fronts, it is believed that most of the Indian troops have been withdrawn from Doklam. The white flag has been also raised at the political level by Sushma Swaraj. With the Chinese repeatedly saying that they have come to stay, it is open to question whether a deal has been struck between Bhutan and China behind India's back.

The perception that Doklam was at best a losing draw is bound to sink in over time.

The days of India viewing Bhutan as a 'protectorate' are over. India's Big-Brother demeanour has not helped, either with Bhutan or with Nepal, or elsewhere.

China's growing influence in South Asia amounts to creating a web of strategic alliances with India's neighbours, eclipsing her influence in the region. There can be no underestimation of the Chinese threat.

On India's Independence Day, Chinese military officers did not show up for the ceremonial border personnel meetings.

In the years ahead, India's international status is likely to be determined by its competition with China. With some confusion still prevailing as regards the strategic focus of the United States and uncertainty over its rebalance to Asia, ASEAN countries could eventually look in the direction of Japan and India to provide a counterweight to China. For this to happen, India will have to enhance its credibility. The India-Myanmar-Thailand Trilateral Highway (conceived in 2002) has missed its scheduled date and is now expected to be commissioned around 2020. Such delays do not inspire confidence in India's capacity to deliver.

The Prime Minister's schedule of foreign visits has been impressive and he has succeeded in injecting a degree of dynamism into the functioning of the South Block mandarins. That said, the question may be asked as to why New Delhi's concerns are accorded, less and less, the attention of which there used to be ample proof in the past. Among the neighbours, with Nepal drifting away, Bhutan may now be the lone exception to such indifference.

Under Modi, while the diplomatic styles have changed, the substance appears to have hardly altered. The recent visit to Israel was a big success, but then Israel was already one of the handful of countries to have shown in-depth understanding of India's defence and security requirements. The diplomatic establishment needs to find a way to steer through the difficult environment of an increasingly aggressive China, a perennially hostile Pakistan, an uncertain South Asian and West Asian neighbourhood and an unstable global scenario.

On the domestic front has come the mid-year *Economic Survey* released in August, 2017 which accepts that the Indian economy is unlikely to achieve the upper end of its projected growth of 6.75 percent to 7.50 percent this fiscal year.

Growth slowed to 6.1 percent in the fourth quarter ending March, 2017 after the demonetization drive wiped out over 80 percent of the cash in circulation to crack down on tax defaulters. The CPM General Secretary, a particularly vocal critic of the NDA-II, was prompted to say: 'From slowdown, India has slid into a contraction – greater unemployment, more misery for the common Indian. The government has only spin to offer.'

The top official advisers may have erred by holding on to high interest rates, thereby attracting capital inflows into the country, as evidenced by the large foreign exchange reserves. This is probably causing the rupee to be stronger than it should be and, in turn, stunting exports and also growth.

Amid the loud talk for more than three years of meritocracy and of exemplary performance being recognized, the NDA-II have actually shown themselves quite good at depleting their small pool of talent. After Raghuram Rajan's exit came the departure of Arvind Panagariya, one of the very few in the government who was doing serious, long-term economic thinking.

The introduction of bullet trains, such as between Mumbai and Ahmedabad, should be accompanied by a drastic correction in the falling standards of safety and passenger services on the Indian Railway. Elsewhere in the world, technology has enabled fatality-free rail travel. Japan's Shinkansen bullet trains have been operating without fatality for over fifty years.

Even as Modi (and Amit Shah) seem poised to sail through in 2019, a governance-deficit that undoubtedly exists will need to be progressively bridged, in the longer-term. This would call for a re-think of the centralized approach that obtains at present in respect of all significant issues and to address the urgent and formidable domestic agenda, ahead of ambitions for a global role. A second Green Revolution must be ushered in. The Prime Minister may also have to re-think the excessive reliance on former and serving bureaucrats. The administrative apparatus being in an advanced state of decay and collapse, it is imperative to tone up and tighten the government machinery and enforce accountability in the higher civil services. Nor can the country achieve its development goals if it is trapped in the morass of communal conflicts and ethnic strife.

A crucial electoral test will come in the Gujarat polls later this year. The prospects seem somewhat less buoyant when one ponders over Yashwant Sinha's statement that 'demonetisation has proved to be an unmitigated economic disaster, a badly conceived and poorly implemented GST has played havoc ...'

Had the government been less nervous, it could have argued that the return of 99 percent of the demonetised currency notes is an indication of the success and not the failure of demonetisation showing, as it does, that large numbers of tax evaders have preferred to deposit their money in banks and pay the penalty, rather than lose the money altogether. It could have been asserted that the true measure of success is not the currency that did not return but the sudden increase of money in peoples' bank accounts that has since taken place.

However, the biggest cause of worry should be that the Government continues to be in denial mode of the actual state of the economy and often opts for diversionary action such as the setting up of yet another Economic Advisory Council. This denial is extremely dangerous since the first step to resolving a problem is to acknowledge that it exists. No less disturbing is Sinha's comment that many in the BJP are afraid to speak up openly.

In the fourth year of its term, the NDA-II faces a major crisis which has emerged not from issues like Pakistan and terrorism that dominate the headlines, but from the vital issue of the middle class' standards of living and its expectations. Global fuel prices are much lower than they were during the UPA, but the benefit of the drop in prices has not been passed on to the consumer. The situation is critical enough to force the preparation of a stimulus package, even at the risk of increasing the fiscal deficit.

Narendra Modi is arguably India's most influential Prime Minister after Independence – Indira Gandhi included – with the exception only of Jawaharlal Nehru in the early fifties. He stands on the threshold of securing his place in history. His priorities should include concrete measures for women and child welfare, time-bound projects for flood control and revitalizing the bureaucracy.

If the Congress is further decimated (or improves its tally just marginally) in 2019, the stage would have been reached to contemplate the last rites. One option could be to hand over the Grand Old Party, lock, stock and barrel, to a regional leader who is irrevocably opposed to the BJP and commands popular support. The West Bengal chief minister – if she undertakes to effect a merger of the TMC – would be an obvious candidate. However, no such possibility might ever be explored as it would mark the 'formal' demise of a long-lasting political dynasty that simply refuses to let go.

The combined Opposition that is in place to take on the BJP-led alliance in less than two years' time ought to direct its energies to attacking and exposing the government's performance and the results achieved on the ground instead of engaging in an unending secularism versus communalism debate.

A one-time minister in the UPA who chose to quit his professional field of foreign affairs in order to serve Rajiv Gandhi (and his successors) full-time was unabashed enough to opine that if the Opposition nominees had been elected as President and Vice President on the last occasion '… the India of our dreams would have been realized….' His friend, the outgoing Vice President, preferred to end his ten-year term in a blaze of controversy and critical comment.

The situation in J&K remains ever so revealing of the attitude of the politicians of the Valley. The Abdullahs and the Muftis have exploited its resources and political potential and should have come together to restore peace and tranquillity rather than to only project a common approach on constitutional issues. Chief Minister Mehbooba Mufti went so far as to say that if 'Article 35A is tinkered with, there would be no one in Kashmir to hold the Indian tricolour'.

Does more need to be said about the depth of allegiance to the Indian Union?

It has been enlightening for me to go through the many writings and observe the debates on Partition. I have not found a more truthful and poignant depiction of the pain and pathos, the communal tension and mindless violence of the last weeks of the undivided Punjab as in Tamas, a 1988 television film, based on the Hindi novel of the same name by the late Bhisham Sahni[1]. The novel had earlier won the Sahitya Akademi Award and the story-line still carries, I believe, a message of realism and hope for the younger generations in the sub-continent.

❖

1 Bhisham Sahni (1915-2003), an acclaimed Hindi writer, was born in Rawalpindi and is best remembered for his novel and television screenplay, Tamas (Darkness), a passionate account of the Partition of India.

Index

Pre-Partition India (August, 1947)

.- Muslim Demands for Pakistan

- Princely States

- British India